READER'S DIGEST

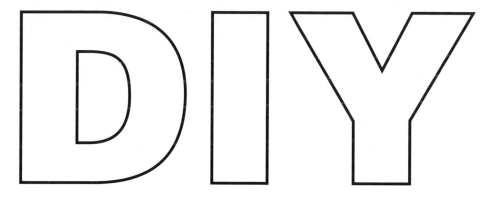

DIY

HANDBOOK

PUBLISHED BY THE
READER'S DIGEST ASSOCIATION LIMITED
LONDON • NEW YORK • SYDNEY
CAPE TOWN • MONTREAL

Reader's Digest DIY Handbook
was edited and designed by
The Reader's Digest Association Limited, London

First edition copyright © 1995
This edition copyright © 1996
The Reader's Digest Association Limited
Berkeley Square House, Berkeley Square,
London W1X 6AB

Copyright © 1996 Reader's Digest Association Far East Limited
Philippines copyright © 1996 Reader's Digest Association Far East Limited

ISBN 0 276 42232 5

Previously published as the *Shredded Wheat Reader's Digest DIY Handbook.*
The information in this book is based on *Reader's Digest Complete DIY Manual,*
first published in 1994.

The typeface used for the main text of this book
is 8½ point Helvetica light

Printed in Italy

Contents

Introduction *5*

Doors *6-11*

Fitting latches and locks *6-7*
Fitting door furniture *7*
Choosing handles, knobs, letterplates
    and other door furniture *8*
Curing faults in doors *9-11*

Windows *12-13*

Replacing a broken window pane *12*
Replacing double-glazed panes *13*

Walls, Ceilings and Fireplaces *14-24*

Patching damaged plaster *14-15*
Filling holes in lath and plaster *15*
Repairing and reinforcing corners *16*
Repairing holes in plasterboard *16-17*
Filling plasterboard joints *18*
Fitting a plasterboard ceiling *19*
Repairing ceilings and cornices *19*
Choosing a lining for a wall or ceiling *20*
Moving switches, sockets and ceiling
    lights *21*
Locating joists in a floor or ceiling *21*
Removing and refitting skirting
    boards *22-23*
Removing an old fireplace *23-24*

Draughtproofing and Insulation *25-32*

Draughtproofing and ventilation *25*
Draughtproofing a window *25*
Draughtproofing a door *26*
Draughtproofing a timber floor *27*
Choosing insulation material for a
    loft *28*

Insulating a loft *29*
Insulating hot and cold water pipes *30*
Lagging a cold-water cistern *30-31*
Insulating a roof *31-32*
Insulating the walls of a house *32*

Floors and Staircases *33-53*

Lifting and replacing a floorboard *33*
Repairing a damaged floor *34*
Replacing a floor with chipboard
    34-35
Preparing a wooden floor to lay a
    covering *35-36*
Preparing a solid floor to lay a
    covering *36*
Choosing floorings for different parts
    of the house *37*
Sanding and varnishing a wooden
    floor *38*
Laying vinyl or cork tiles *39-41*
Laying ceramic tiles *41-42*
Laying carpet tiles *42*
Laying sheet vinyl in strips *43-44*
Covering a small area with sheet
    vinyl *44*
Fitting sheet vinyl without a seam *45*
Laying foam-backed carpets *46-47*
Laying carpet with separate underlay
    47-49
Patching a damaged carpet *49*
Fitting a stair carpet *50-51*
Dealing with landings *51*
Moving stair carpet to avoid wear *52*
Removing stains from carpets *52-53*

Plumbing *54-79*

Plumbing emergencies: What to do *54*
How water is supplied to the home *55*

What type of water system do you
   have? 55
The tools for the job 56-57
Cutting off the water supply 58
Choosing a tap 59
Repairing a dripping tap 60-61
Curing a leak from a spindle or
   spout 61-62
Dealing with an airlock 63
Different ways of joining pipes 63-65
Bending copper piping 65
Repairing a burst pipe 65-66
Installing an outside tap 66-67
Renovating and repainting a bath 68
Removing an old cast-iron bath 68
Installing a new bath 69
Choosing a shower 70
Planning a shower 71
Installing a shower 72
Repairing a faulty lavatory system 73
Dealing with a faulty lavatory pan 74
Replacing a lavatory pan 74-75
How a ball-valve works 76
Repairing a faulty ball-valve 76-77
Fitting a new ball-valve 78
Adjusting the cistern water level 78
Plumbing-in a washing machine or
   dish washer 79

Central Heating 80-82

Radiators that do not heat up 80
Leaks in a central heating system 80
Draining down the system 81
Preventing a freeze-up during a
   winter holiday 81
Protecting a system with corrosion
   proofer 81
Replacing a radiator 82
Changing a central heating pump 82

Home Electrics 83-87

Electrical emergencies: What to do 83
Home electrics: Tools for the job 84
Reconnecting a flex to a lampholder 85
Connecting a light flex to a ceiling
   rose 85-86
Rewiring a table lamp or standard
   lamp 86
Choosing flexes for appliances and
   lights 87

Home Security 88-96

Ten easy ways to avoid a burglary 88
Checking the security of your house
   doors 89
Additional devices for door security 90
Fitting a new mechanism to a lock 90
Replacing a mortise lock 91
Adding security bolts to doors 91
Protecting outbuildings 92
Fitting a lock to a casement window 92
Choosing security locks for your
   windows 93
Fitting a lock to a metal frame 94
Fitting a dual screw to a sash
   window 94
Installing a small home safe 94
Choosing a burglar alarm to protect
   your house 95
Choosing time controls for security
   and convenience 96

Making Home Maintenance Easier

As millions of people across the length and breadth of the land have found over the years, do-it-yourself home maintenance need not be a chore. In fact, it can be downright enjoyable, provided you bear in mind a few simple rules. These, like the information in the rest of this book, will make tackling any job easier.

First and foremost, any DIY task benefits from a little advance thought and planning. Have you got all the tools you need, for instance, and are there any special ones you might require? It's certainly a good idea to invest in a basic DIY tool kit – and to keep the tools in it well maintained as well. Equally, though, you may well find it cheaper and more convenient to hire certain specialised tools as and when you need them, rather than to buy them outright. Let your fingers do the walking and consult your local *Yellow Pages* or trade directory; it will save you time for only a little extra expense. If you are thinking of having some doors stripped, for instance, it is far quicker and more convenient to find a firm that strips doors in a bath of hot caustic soda. This saves a lot of time and a lot of hard work. It also means that you avoid the risk of scorching a door with a blow torch, the obvious alternative.

When undertaking any DIY job, safety should be your first priority. Accidents can happen even to the most experienced and proficient do-it-yourselfer, so, together with your basic tool kit, you should keep an adequately stocked first-aid kit to hand in the bathroom or your workroom. In addition to plasters, bandages, antiseptics and so on, you should make two special purchases. Whenever you undertake a task in which there is a risk of a flying chip or fragment getting into unprotected eyes, you should always wear an effective eye shield. Similarly, if you are working in dusty conditions or in a room where, say, paint fumes are affecting you, even with the best possible ventilation, then you should wear a protective face mask. The type worn by cyclists is perfectly adequate in most situations.

When it comes to electricity, take special care. The electrical jobs described in this book are suitable only for modern wiring systems. Remember that appearances can be deceptive. You may have a system, for instance, where old rubber-insulated cables in steel conduits have been left in place, even though the old sockets have been replaced by modern square-pin 13 amp versions. In such a case, the rubber insulation may have become hard and started to crumble. If you suspect this might be the case, you should switch off the power supply at the mains and unscrew the sockets, so that you can see for yourself if the cables are new or old and examine the state of the insulation. And, if you find you have a radial socket circuit system rather than a ring one, you should remember that it is unsafe to add extra sockets to it.

What it comes down to at the end of the day is common sense. If you feel that a job is too ambitious for you, or will take too long, the best advice is not to touch it, but to call in the professionals. On the other hand, as this book will show you, there are lots of tasks which you may have thought were beyond your skills that you are perfectly capable of undertaking. It may be something as straightforward as dealing with a blocked sink or a project that is as seemingly complex as planning a new shower. With the aid of this book, either can be tackled with complete success. And, throughout, there's all the practical guidance you'll need – including invaluable hints, tips and tricks of the trade – to become an even more competent do-it-yourselfer.

Fitting latches and locks

FITTING A CYLINDER NIGHT LATCH

You will need
Tools Pencil; drill and large bit (size given on maker's instructions); screwdriver and a steel tape measure. Perhaps twist bits.
Materials Cylinder night latch.

1 Mark the position of the key cylinder at a convenient height on the door stile, using the dimensions or paper template usually supplied with the lock. Alternatively, use the lock mounting plate. The shape of the hole for the cylinder depends on the make of lock; some need a large round hole, others need a shaped hole made by drilling two smaller holes through what will be the circumference of a larger hole, which is drilled afterwards.

2 Drill the hole for the cylinder.

3 Position the cylinder at the front of the door and place the mounting plate on the inside face. Temporarily fix the two together with the screws provided. The cylinder connecting bar will protrude through the mounting plate to engage in the body of the lock.

4 Cut the connecting bar to a suitable length, depending on the thickness of the door, following the manufacturer's instructions.

5 If the lock has a fore-end that screws to the edge of the door, temporarily place the lock assembly on the mounting plate and mark where it will be necessary to cut a recess.

6 Remove the lock and cut the fore-end recess; if necessary, also remove the lock mounting plate.

7 Refit the mounting plate to the cylinder.

8 Put the body of the lock on the mounting plate, ensuring that the cylinder connecting bar engages in the lock.

9 Screw the body of the lock to the door.

10 Check that the bolt works, using the key and the internal knob.

11 Close the door and mark the position of the striking plate on the door jamb.

12 Cut a recess for the striking plate and screw it to the door jamb.

Check that the door closes properly and that the lock operates.

13 If not, recess the striking plate slightly deeper into the door jamb.

FITTING A MORTISE LOCK

You will need
Tools Pencil; try square; carpenter's brace and auger bit – the width of the lock body; adhesive tape; mallet; two chisels (one the width of the lock body and a wider one); pliers; bradawl; power drill or wheel handbrace and twist bits; padsaw; screwdriver.
Materials Mortise lock.

1 Hold the lock in position against the face of the door. Ideally it should line up with the centre rail of the door. On flush doors fixing points are often marked on the edge.

2 Mark the dimensions of the lock casing on the door and with the try square transfer the height marks to the edge of the door.

3 Mark the centre line of the mortise on the edge of the door between the height marks.

WHICH LOCK TO CHOOSE?

Mortise deadlocks are extremely secure because the door frame has to be smashed to get past them. Nor can their bolts be turned back without using the key. The key operates levers, and the more levers the harder the lock is to pick. For the best security, fit a five-lever lock with a box-type striking plate, together with a cylinder nightlatch to ease coming and going. A two-bolt ring lock screws to the inside face of the door. It is simple to install, but provies less security since it can be forced off the door easily. One, two and three-lever actions are unsuitable for external doors.

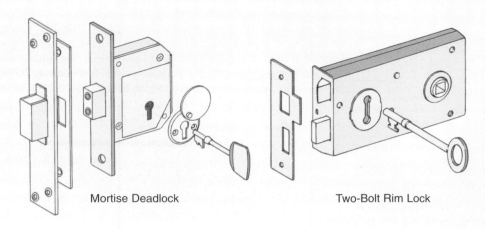

Mortise Deadlock

Two-Bolt Rim Lock

Fitting locks and latches (continued)

4 Mark the depth of the lock body on the auger bit with a strip of tape, and drill an overlapping line of holes through the centre line to the depth of the lock body.

Get someone to check that the bit is horizontal and square-on to the door, so that the hole does not go off at an angle.

5 Use a mallet and the narrow chisel to square up the top and bottom of the mortise slot.

Then use the wider chisel to smooth the sides of the mortise slot so that the lock body will slide snugly into the door.

6 Turn out the bolt of the lock with the key, then push it into the mortise slot and mark the shape of the fore-end (rectangular plate) on the edge of the door. Grip the bolt with pliers to withdraw the lock.

7 Chisel out a recess for the fore-end so that when the lock is in place it will lie flush with the edge of the door.

8 Hold the lock in position against the face of the door, and with a bradawl mark the centre point of the keyhole and the handle spindle (if there is one).

9 Using a drill and twist bit, make holes through the door the same diameter as the handle spindle and the keyhole, at the positions you have marked with the bradawl.

Make the keyhole the correct shape by enlarging the lower part with a padsaw. Or drill a smaller hole below the first and join them with a padsaw.

10 With the bolt of the lock sticking out, push the lock into the slot and check that the key and handle spindle will fit.

11 Insert screws through the fore-end of the lock into the edge of the door.

12 Push the handle spindle through the lock, and screw the handle plates on each side of the door.

13 Screw the keyhole plates on each side of the door.

14 Almost close the door and mark the positions of the deadbolt and latch on the edge of the frame. Continue the mark around onto the jamb.

15 Measure the distance from the outside of the door to the centre of the bolt, and mark that distance on the jamb – measuring from the doorstop.

16 Use the narrow chisel and mallet to cut mortises for the bolts at this position.

Check that the door closes properly. If not, enlarge the mortises as much as necessary.

17 Hold the lock striker plate over the two mortises and mark the outline of the plate on the door jamb with a pencil.

18 Cut a recess for the plate, check that the door still closes properly, and screw the striker plate in place.

Fitting door furniture

The front door of a house usually needs a letterplate, a handle to close the door (which may be built into the letterplate), either a knocker or bellpush, and probably a street number.

All are simple to install, but a power jigsaw makes the job of cutting the letter opening much quicker than doing it by hand with a padsaw.

LETTERPLATE

You will need
Tools Pencil; ruler; drill and twist bits; ½in (13mm) flat bit; power jigsaw or padsaw; chisel; abrasive paper; screwdriver; small adjustable spanner; hacksaw.
Materials Letterplate and fittings.

1 Decide where you want the letterplate. On a panel door it can be fitted horizontally in the middle rail or vertically on the lock stile. On a flush door, fit it horizontally in the middle to coincide with the rail position that is marked on the edge of the door.

2 Hold the letterplate in position on the door and lightly mark its outline with a pencil.

3 Measure the size of the flap and spring mechanism and mark the outline of the required cut-out within the larger outline.

The cut-out may have to be off centre to allow room for the flap mechanism.

4 Using the flat bit, drill a ½in (13mm) hole at each corner of the cut-out position and saw along the cut-out line. Preferably use a power jigsaw with a long enough blade. Alternatively, you can make the cut-out with a padsaw, but it will be slow work.

5 At each side of the cut-out, mark the positions of the holes for the fixing bolts.

6 Working from the front of the door, drill ½in (13mm) diameter holes to a depth of ½in (13mm) to accommodate the fixing lugs of the letterplate.

7 Using a twist bit the same diameter as the fixing bolts, drill from the centre of the holes right through the door.

Smooth the edges of the holes with abrasive paper.

8 Fit the letterplate to the door and tighten the fixing nuts with an adjustable spanner.

9 If the bolts protrude, use a hacksaw to cut them off flush with the face of the nuts.

DOOR KNOCKER

1 Hold the knocker in position and press it hard against the door so that the lugs leave light marks.

2 At these positions, drill holes for the lugs and the bolts.

3 Screw the bolts into the lugs on the back of the knocker, and push them through the holes.

4 Tighten the fixing nuts, and if the bolts protrude cut them off flush with the face of the nuts.

CHOOSING HANDLES, KNOBS, LETTERPLATES AND OTHER DOOR FURNITURE

Door furniture is available in a multitude of designs, from ornate reproductions to simple modern styles. It may be made of cast iron, brass, aluminium, steel, ceramics, glass or plastic. But whatever the design or material, each piece of door furniture has a particular function.

HANDLES FOR A MORTISE LOCK

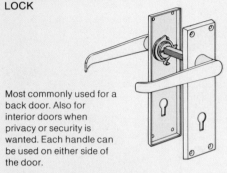

Most commonly used for a back door. Also for interior doors when privacy or security is wanted. Each handle can be used on either side of the door.

HANDLES FOR A MORTISE LATCH

The handle plate has no keyhole because a mortise latch is used on interior doors where no privacy or security is required. Each handle can be used on either side of the door.

HANDLES FOR BATHROOM OR LAVATORY

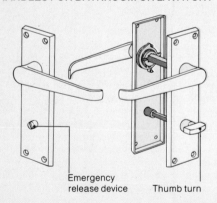

Emergency release device   Thumb turn

A thumb-turn on the inside of the door prevents it from being opened. The outside of the door has an emergency release device. Buy either a right-hand or left-hand opening set, as the handles are not interchangeable.

DOOR KNOBS

Can be used on a mortise lock or latch, provided the spindle is far enough from the edge of the door to allow you to open the door without scraping your knuckles. Can be used for bathroom or lavatory doors with a privacy adaptor kit.

DOOR KNOBS FOR RIM LOCKS

Rose

Designed to fit on a rim lock, with a rose on the outside of the door but no rose on the lock side.

DOOR KNOB FOR BATHROOM OR LAVATORY

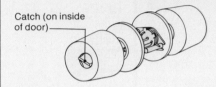

Catch (on inside of door)

The knob has a catch that prevents the door from being opened from the outside.

LETTERPLATE AND INNER FLAP

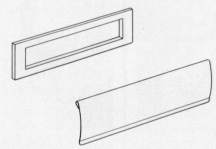

A standard letterplate fits on the middle of the front door. An inner flap fitted on the inside of the door gives a neat finish and helps to prevent draughts.

POSTAL KNOCKERS

HORIZONTAL The letterplate incorporates a handle for pulling the door closed, which can also be used as a door knocker.

VERTICAL Fits on the lock stile of the door. The hole allows a nightlatch cylinder plate to be set into the knocker.

CENTRE KNOB

For closing the front door as you leave the house. It is often fitted to the door above a central letter-plate.

DOOR KNOCKER

Fits to the front door instead of a bell. A wide range of designs is available.

FINGERPLATE

Decorative plate to protect interior doors from becoming grubby with frequent use. Ceramic, brass and plastic are the most common types.

ESCUTCHEON (OPEN OR COVERED)

An escutcheon gives a tidy finish to the keyhole of a mortise lock. A covered escutcheon keeps out draughts.

CYLINDER PULL

Fits under a nightlatch cylinder on the outside of a front door, and is used to pull the door closed.

BELL PUSH

The bell push, which may be made of metal or plastic, is fitted to the door frame.

PULL HANDLE

Can be fitted to either the inside or outside of a front door to provide a grip while opening or closing it.

NUMBERS

The street number of the house can be indicated with brass, iron, plastic or porcelain numbers screwed to the front door.

Curing faults in doors

STICKING ALONG ONE SIDE

Sticking is usually caused by a build-up of paint on the edge of the door and the frame. The problem is often worse in wet weather when the wood swells. If the trouble is not severe, simply rub the edge of the door with a candle or with dry powder lubricant.

If that is not enough, you will have to strip the door edge and frame.

1 Wait for a warm dry spell, and strip off the paint.

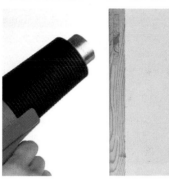

2 It is a good idea to dry out the surface with a hot-air gun before repainting.

3 Rub the stripped surfaces with glasspaper and check that the door opens and closes easily.

4 There should be a slight gap between the edge of the door and the frame, so run a thin knife blade all round the edge of the door when it is closed. Where the gap is insufficient, plane the edge of the door. It may be necessary to take the door off its hinges, and perhaps remove locks and bolts.

5 Sand, prime and paint the edge of the door. Let the paint dry before closing the door.

STICKING AT THE BOTTOM

If an external door sticks along its bottom edge, the problem is often caused by moisture being absorbed by the unpainted edge.

1 Wait for dry weather, then take the door off its hinges and thoroughly dry the bare edges with a hot-air gun.

2 If the binding is severe, hold the door on one of its long edges in a portable workbench. Mark a line to work to, then plane downwards from the edge of the door to the centre; this will avoid splintering the edge.

3 Prime and paint to match the rest of the door.

STICKING AT THE TOP

You may be able to plane the top edge of a door without taking it off its hinges. It will have to be propped open firmly while you work from a stepladder.

Doors stick at the top much less frequently than at the bottom or side.

A SQUEAKING DOOR

Oil the hinge pins with an aerosol lubricant. Work the door backwards and forwards a few times to get the lubricant into the hinge, then wipe away surplus oil with a clean rag.

With rising butt hinges, lift the open door off the hinge pins and lightly smear them with grease or petroleum jelly. Wipe away the surplus after re-hanging the door.

A DOOR THAT SLAMS

The only solution is to fit a surface-mounted hydraulic door-closer.

They are often supplied with a paper template which acts as a guide for the fixing holes to be marked at the top of the door and on the architrave above.

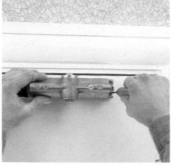

1 If a template is not supplied, hold the door-closer in position on the top edge of the door on the hinge side, and use a long bradawl to mark the screw positions.

2 Drill pilot holes, and screw on the closer. Chisel out a flat recess for the pivot arm fixing plate in the architrave, and screw it on.

3 Fix the pivot arm to the body of the closer, and turn the adjusting screws on the closer so that the door closes smoothly and slowly without slamming.

SPLIT DOOR PANELS

Sometimes splits develop in the panels of old doors. The solution varies according to whether the door is painted or natural wood.

Painted door

On a painted door, fill the crack with a two-part epoxy filler and paint over it.

Natural wood door

On a door where the filler will show, you must drive dowels into the edge of the door to press against the edges of the panel and close the crack.

1 First clean out any old paint and filler from the crack.

2 Using an auger bit, drill two or three ¼in (6mm) diameter holes through the edge of the door stile to line up with the edge of the panel. Measure the thickness of the stile and mark the auger bit with a piece of tape to avoid drilling too far.

3 Cut some ¼in (6mm) dowels about ¾in (19mm) longer than the width of the stiles.

4 Inject PVA wood glue into the crack in the panel and into the holes in the stile. Drive the dowels into the holes so they press against the edge of the panel and close the crack. Sash cramps can be used to squeeze the dowels inwards.

5 Clean off surface adhesive with a damp cloth, and leave the protruding dowel until the glue has set, then trim it off flush with the door.

WHEN THE LATCH WILL NOT ENGAGE

If a door sags a little or becomes slightly swollen, the latch bolt will be out of alignment with the striking plate. A small mis-alignment can be corrected by enlarging the cutout in the striking plate with a file.

Otherwise, remove the striking plate and refix it in the correct position. If the plate has to be moved only a small distance, plug the old screw holes with small wooden pegs and drill new pilot holes for the fixing screws.

LOCK DIFFICULT TO TURN

Spray an aerosol lubricant into the lock using the narrow flexible applicator tube usually provided. Squirt the lubricant through the latch and bolt apertures and through the keyhole.

If this is not sufficient, remove the lock from the door, take off one side of the case, and lightly grease the mechanism.

Before starting work, note the positions of the components so they can be put back if they become displaced.

Do not use oil in Yale-type front-door locks. It attracts grit. Use graphite powder or PTFE dry powder lubricant.

LOOSE DOOR FRAME

Slamming a door often leads to the frame becoming loose.

Make new fixings with three large screws and wall plugs on each side of the frame. Long fixing screws,

part-fitted into a plastic wall plug, are sold for the purpose. The length should be the thickness of the frame plus at least 2½in (60mm).

1 Using a masonry bit, drill through the frame and into the supporting masonry, ideally to coincide with the mid-point of a whole brick rather than a mortar joint.

2 Hammer the screw and plug into the hole so that the plug is fully into the wall, then tighten the screw to hold the frame secure.

A HINGE-BOUND DOOR

A door that is difficult to close, and tends to spring open, is said to be hinge-bound.

The problem is usually caused by hinge recesses being too deep in either the door edge or in the frame. When correctly fitted the hinge flaps should be flush with, or slightly below, the surface of the wood.

1 Open the door and push a piece of wood under the lock stile to take the weight.

2 Clear any paint from the slots in the hinge screws, and remove the screws.

3 Get someone to steady the door while you lever the hinge flap out of its recess.

Pack out the recess with pieces of cardboard, and then replace the screws.

Protruding screw heads

Occasionally the hinges may bind because the screw heads are too large, or have been put in askew, and come into contact with each other when the hinge flaps come together.

Remove the screws and replace them with screws with heads that fit the countersinks in the hinges. One gauge size smaller should be sufficient. If they will not tighten, pack out the holes with matches.

ALTERNATIVELY, deepen the countersinks in the hinge flaps so that the screw head will be flush with the surface. Use a high-speed-steel countersink bit.

If the screws were originally set in askew, plug the screw holes with pieces of scrap wood dipped in wood glue and then re-drill straight pilot holes.

Badly placed hinge flaps

Binding can also be caused by hinge flaps that are set into the frame too near to the door stop. As the door is closed, the face of the

door presses against the stop, preventing it from going farther.

1 Remove the hinges and plug the fixing holes with pegs of scrap wood dipped in wood glue.

2 Re-drill the hinge fixing holes so that they are farther away from the door stop.

When the door is closed the hinge pin should protrude an equal distance from the face of the door and the edge of the frame.

On an internal door it may be possible to move the door stop as it is probably made from a separate piece of wood.

A ROTTEN DOOR

If exterior doors have not been protected with paint or varnish, rot may set in, especially near the bottom and at joints.

If you catch it early, you can patch it with a high-performance filler, such as Ronseal Wood Repair System.

1 On a warm, dry day, dig out the rotten wood and if possible allow the remaining wood to dry thoroughly. Warming with a hot-air gun can help.

2 Treat the area with a wood hardener, and when this has dried fill the cavity with a two-part epoxy

Curing faults in doors (continued)

filler. Build it up slightly above the surface, and sand it flat when it has hardened; hardening will take about 30 minutes.

3 Drill holes in the surrounding wood at intervals of about 6in (150mm).

4 Insert wood preservative pellets in the holes and then fill the holes with more filler.

5 Repaint the door to disguise the repair.

A ROTTEN FRAME

External door frames often rot near the sill. The only satisfactory repair is to insert a new piece of timber. Use an all-purpose saw; the teeth will not be affected by the masonry.

1 Make a sloping cut into the frame about 3in (75mm) above the rotted section. Probing with a screwdriver will reveal where the soft, rotten section ends. Make the cut at about 45 degrees.

2 Prise the rotted part away from the wall, including the base which was probably tenoned into the hardwood sill.

3 Cut a length of new timber to fit into the space, cutting the top at an angle to align with the saw cut.

The old frame was probably a one-piece section, but the matching repair can be made from two or more pieces of wood glued and screwed together. Make up the correct shape and add a door stop.

4 When the new section is a good fit, treat all the new wood and the cut edges with wood preservative, and fix the repair in place with 3½in (90mm) No. 12 screws countersunk into the wood, and wall plugs.

5 Where the old and new frame sections join, drill ¼in (6mm) holes through the joint at right angles to it. Smear glue on ¼in (6mm) hardwood dowels and hammer them into the holes.

6 Trim them level with the surface when the glue has dried.

A SAGGING DOOR

When the bottom corner of the door rubs on the floor, the cause is either faulty hinges or loose joints in the door. Partly open the door and lift the handle or knob to see if there is movement at the hinges or joints.

Faulty hinges

If the hinges are loose, remove them and plug the holes with dowels. Refit the screws, or fit thicker screws. If necessary enlarge the countersunk holes in the hinge to take the larger screw heads. Use a high-speed steel bit.

If the movement is in the knuckle of the hinge due to a worn hinge pin the only cure is to fit a set of new hinges. It may be that the hinges are not big enough to support the weight of the door. In this case fit larger, heavier hinges and perhaps a third hinge midway between them.

Loose door joints

If the door joints are loose, glue and cramp them back into place.

1 Take the door off its hinges, and try to dismantle it by gently prising the loose joints apart.

2 Re-glue the joints and put them together again. If they will not come apart, inject woodworking glue into the joints.

3 On the edge of the door, drive small wooden wedges into the ends of the tenons to prevent the joints from opening up again.

4 Drill through the face of the door and through the tenon and drive a dowel smeared with woodworking glue into the hole. This will lock the tenon in place. On an exterior door use waterproof glue.

5 Cramp the door with a sash cramp or Spanish windlass while the glue sets.

6 Trim off the dowels flush with the door.

A WARPED DOOR

A cure with the door in place

It may be possible to cure a warp, with the door in place – but it will be out of action for at least 24 hours.

1 Close the door, putting blocks of timber behind that part that normally rests against the frame. You will probably need to tape the blocks to the frame while you close the door.

2 Push the part that bows outwards back into place by screwing a length of timber across the frame. You will have to fill the screw holes later.

3 If the door bows out in the middle, put the blocks at the top and bottom of the door and screw the length of timber across the middle.

Taking the door off its hinges

If the correction cannot be done in place, take the door off its hinges and lay it on a flat wooden floor.

Put blocks under the door in the places where the door normally rests against the frame, and correct the warp by forcing the door down to the floor with a length of timber screwed to the floor.

Adjusting the door stop

With internal doors, if the warp is not severe and is merely letting in draughts, a fairly simple cure is available. Prise the door stop away from the frame and re-fix it so that it rests against the face of the door.

This will not work with exterior doors because the door stop is an integral part of the frame.

Replacing a broken window pane

When buying glass, tell the supplier the size of the panes. He will cut them to fit.

Use 3mm glass in very small panes, such as Georgian-style windows. For windows up to about 12sq ft (1sq m) use 4mm glass. For anything larger, use 6mm glass.

When glass is to be used over a very large area such as a picture window, or where it may be mistaken for an opening as in a patio door, or where it will be fitted within 31in (800mm) of the floor, use safety glass.

For wooden windows use linseed oil, universal or acrylic putty; for metal windows use metal casement, universal or acrylic putty. You will need about 2¼lb (1kg) of putty for 12ft (3.7m) of frame. Brown putty is available for windows that are to be finished with preservative stain.

Broken glass in doors is replaced in the same way as for wooden windows, unless the door has been glazed with beads which are replaced as for square-edged double-glazing units.

You will need

Tools Leather gloves; safety spectacles or goggles; glass cutter; hammer; hacking knife or old chisel; pincers; dustpan and brush; paintbrush; putty knife.
Materials Primer paint; putty; glazing sprigs; glass to fit the window.

HELPFUL TIP
Disposing of broken glass can be difficult. The best way is to take it to your local bottle bank. Otherwise, wrap it thickly in newspaper and put it either beside or in your dustbin, clearly labelled 'Broken glass'.

REMOVING THE BROKEN GLASS

1 Lay newspapers on the ground on both sides of the window to catch the fragments of old glass.

2 Put on leather gloves and safety spectacles. Also wear thick leather shoes in case jagged pieces of glass fall to the ground.

3 Using a glass cutter, score the glass all round the window, close to the putty.

4 Working from the outside, tap the glass with a hammer to break it, starting from the top. Try to keep the pieces as large as possible.

5 After breaking out as much of the old glass as possible, remove the remaining putty and glass with a hacking knife or old chisel. Hold a hacking knife in one hand with the point against the putty and tap it on the blunt edge with the hammer.

Look out for old glazing sprigs embedded in the putty – or metal clips in metal frames. Pull them out with pincers.

Leave the rebate in the window as clean as possible, before putting in the new glass.

6 Brush all the dust from the frame and paint a wooden frame with primer, which should be allowed to dry. This is not necessary on a metal window unless it is rusty.

If the window has to be left overnight, cover it with a sheet of polythene or a piece of plywood (see panel below).

PUTTING IN THE NEW GLASS

1 Mould the putty in your hands to get it soft and pliable. If it sticks to your hands, try wetting them, or take some of the oil out by rolling the putty on newspaper.

2 Hold the pliable putty in the palm of your hand and squeeze it out between the thumb and forefinger to form a layer about ⅛in (3mm) thick in the rebate all the way round the window.

3 Press the glass carefully into the rebate so it is well bedded on the putty. Press it round the edges only, taking care not to push too hard in one place – and never in the middle

---

REPLACING DAMAGED PUTTY

As putty hardens it tends to crack and eventually sections fall out. It is best to replace all the putty rather than re-putty the missing sections.

Remove the old putty with a hacking knife or old chisel as shown on this page. If the glazing sprigs have corroded pull them out if possible, and then drive in some new ones as described below. Brush away dust, prime the rebate and then apply and smooth in new putty.

of the glass. It could break and cause a nasty injury.

4 Fix the glass in place with glazing sprigs inserted into the window about 10in (250mm) apart. Knock them in with the edge of the chisel or with the back of the hacking knife, sliding it along the face of the glass.

The heads of the sprigs should protrude about 3/16in (5mm) from the frame.

5 Apply more putty to the front of the glass to fill the rebate, and smooth it off with a putty knife to form a neat triangular line of putty which covers the heads of the sprigs and lines up with the putty on the inside edge. Try to achieve neat mitres at the corners.

6 Leave the putty for about two weeks to harden slightly before painting it. When you do paint it, allow the paint to spread onto the glass by ⅛in (3mm) to keep out the rain.

EMERGENCY COVER FOR A BROKEN WINDOW

It is often impossible to repair a broken window immediately, so carry out an emergency repair to keep out the weather while you arrange to get the new glass.

A cracked pane can be temporarily sealed with waterproof glazing tape, which is transparent.

If the panel is smashed, cover the window with heavy-gauge polythene, secured with timber battens nailed around the edge of the frame. The battens will prevent the sheet from tearing.

If security is important, cut a sheet of plywood to cover the window frame and fix it with either nails or screws.

Replacing double-glazed panes

There are three main ways of replacing broken double-glazed panes, depending on whether they are sealed stepped units, square-edge units, or are in aluminium or plastic windows.

Double-glazing units must be bought ready-made to the size of your window from a glass merchant or double-glazing supplier.

SEALED STEPPED UNITS

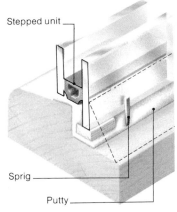

Stepped unit

Sprig

Putty

Replacing sealed stepped double glazing is similar to fitting a single sheet of glass, except that spacer blocks are fitted in the rebate of the window to keep the stepped part of the double-glazed unit clear of the frame.

Retain the old spacer blocks so

they can be re-used, or buy new ones from your glass merchant. Window companies are unlikely to sell them.

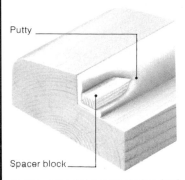

Putty

Spacer block

1 Place the spacer blocks in a bed of putty about 12in (300mm) apart along the bottom of the rebate.

2 Stand the double-glazed pane on the blocks and fix it in place with sprigs all round. Apply putty to the outside of the window in the normal way.

SQUARE-EDGED UNITS

Glazing beads are usually screwed into the outside of the window to hold square-edged double glazing in place.

1 Unscrew the glazing beads before removing the broken glass.

2 Put a bed of non-setting putty (available from glass merchants) around the rebate. Press spacer blocks into the putty (two blocks spaced well apart on each of the four sides).

3 Lift the sealed unit into place on the spacers and press it well back into the rebate.

4 Coat the glazing beads with non-setting putty on the inside face

and press them tightly in place against the glazing units.

5 Fix the beads in place with brass screws.

ALUMINIUM OR PLASTIC WINDOWS

The glass is often in rubber gaskets, making replacement difficult. Call in a glazier, or ask the manufacturer for details on glass replacement for your particular model of window.

HELPFUL TIP
If your double glazing was broken accidentally, your house insurance policy may cover you to have the repair done professionally. Check your policy.

Repairing leaded lights

Doors and windows may have leaded-light panels, consisting of small panes of glass held together with lead strips that are H-shaped in cross section.

DEALING WITH LEAKS

Using polyurethane varnish
1 Mark the leaks with a wax crayon so that repairs can be undertaken in fine weather.

2 Carefully scrape any dirt away from the edges of the lead strips.

3 With a small artist's brush, paint clear, exterior grade polyurethane varnish liberally along the flanges of the strips. Take great care to seal the outside of the glass.

ALTERNATIVELY, inject a bead of the clear sealant used to seal leaks around car windscreens.

4 Press the flanges down, supporting them firmly from the other side. Wipe varnish off the lead and the glass with a cloth moistened with white spirit.

Using putty
If the varnish does not work, the putty in which the glass is set must be replaced. Use soft glazier's metal casement putty. You can colour the putty grey with a little black powder paint.

1 Open up the lead strips slightly on the outside of the window by

levering up the edges with a chisel. To do this it may be necessary to cut through the corner joints with a trimming knife or some side-cutting nippers.

2 Scrape out as much of the old putty as possible and clean out the dirt.

3 Press in the new putty.

4 Press the lead strip back in place, with a helper supporting the glass from the inside.

5 If it was necessary to cut the corner joints, glue them back together with two-part acrylic glue.

6 Wipe the excess putty off the lead and the glass.

Repairing cracked glass
It may not be necessary to fit new glass if the crack is only a minor one. You can try running a few drops of Glass Bond adhesive into the crack.

Replacing broken panes in a leaded-light panel is a difficult job. It would be best if you called in a glazier to do it.

Curing bulges and buckles
Take the complete panel out of the door. It may be held with putty, like an ordinary sheet of glass (page 12), or it may be held with both putty and an outer wood beading. You can remove the beading by unscrewing it or, if it is nailed, by prising it out very gently.

Lay the panel on a flat surface and press the lead strips flat. Be very careful not to press too hard or you are likely to break the glass panes.

If this does not work, it may be necessary to take the panel to a glazier to have it rebuilt. While this is being done, cover the opening in the door or window as explained on page 12.

Patching damaged plaster

Large cracks, holes or crumbling areas of plaster, which may result from dampness or general wear and tear, can generally be repaired quickly and cheaply with plaster. For filling small areas of damage, use proprietary fillers.

There are three types of plaster that can be used: ordinary, quick-setting lightweight gypsum plaster as used by professional plasterers (mixed with water and applied in two coats – an undercoat and a finishing coat); one-coat DIY plaster (mixed with water); and ready-mixed DIY plaster available as two coats (see chart below).

Ordinary plaster is generally the most economical, but is less convenient to use as it has to be applied fairly fast. DIY plasters allow more working time and are easier to use, but usually cost more, especially for large areas.

Do not repair damage caused by dampness until the dampness has been remedied. If large cracks re-open after repair, get the advice of a builder or surveyor, as they may be caused by structural movement of the building.

If the damage reveals a cavity underneath the plaster, the wall material is likely to be plasterboard or – in an old house – lath and plaster. These call for different types of repair (pages 15–16).

USING ORDINARY PLASTER

You will need
Tools Cold chisel; club hammer; hand brush; large paintbrush or house-plant spray; clean plastic bucket; mixing stick or wooden spoon; length of wood; plasterer's trowel; carrying board (also called a hawk).

Materials Undercoat plaster; finishing plaster; supply of clean, cold water for mixing.

1 Chip away loose or crumbly plaster with a cold chisel until you reach firm surface all round.

2 Brush away dust and debris. If bricks or building blocks are exposed, dampen the area with water.

3 Mix the undercoat plaster with cold water in a clean bucket until its consistency is between that of stiff porridge and whipped cream. Use it as quickly as possible after mixing – within 15-30 minutes.

4 Load plaster onto a carrying board. Apply it with a plasterer's trowel held at an angle of about 45 degrees to the wall and sweep it

TYPES OF PLASTER FOR INDOOR USE

Plasters for indoor use are generally gypsum based, and sold in 50kg (1cwt) packs, but smaller packs are usually available for DIY repair work. Cement-based plasters are for outdoor use, or for damp places indoors (page 462).

Working times (the time in which the plaster must be applied before it becomes unworkable) and setting times (the time the plaster takes to become fairly hard) are given as a guide, but vary with temperature. Times are shorter in places where the temperature is high, and longer in low temperatures.

There are different types of undercoat for two-coat ordinary plasters – designed for absorbent or less-absorbent surfaces. The wall material absorbs water from the plaster, and if it is absorbed too fast the plaster will crack.

PLASTER	WHERE USED	DESCRIPTION
Browning undercoat (such as Carlite browning; Blue Hawk undercoat)	On solid, fairly absorbent surfaces indoors, such as bricks or building blocks. The layers should be about $\frac{3}{8}$in (10mm) thick.	A lightweight, quick-setting pink or grey undercoat, mixed with clean, cold water. Apply within 15–30 minutes of mixing. Sets in 1$\frac{1}{2}$–2 hours. 10kg (22lb) covers about 16sq ft (1.5sq m) at $\frac{3}{8}$in (10mm) thick.
Bonding undercoat (such as Carlite bonding)	On dense, not very absorbent surfaces indoors – for example, concrete, engineering bricks, or surfaces treated with PVA adhesive, such as laths. Layers should be about $\frac{1}{4}$in (8mm) thick.	As above. 10kg (22lb) covers about 16sq ft (1.5sq m) at $\frac{1}{3}$in (8mm) thick.
Finishing coat (such as Carlite finish; Blue Hawk finish)	On browning or bonding undercoats. The layers should be about $\frac{1}{16}$in (2mm) thick.	A lightweight, quick-setting pink or grey finish plaster, mixed with clean, cold water. 10kg (22lb) covers about 48sq ft (4.5sq m) at $\frac{1}{16}$in (2mm) thick.
Plasterboard finish (such as Thistle plasterboard finish)	On a plasterboard surface (grey side). Layers should be about $\frac{3}{16}$in (5mm) thick.	As above. Sets in 1–1$\frac{1}{2}$ hours. 10kg (22lb) covers about 16sq ft (1.5sq m) at $\frac{3}{16}$in (5mm) thick.
One-coat plaster (such as Wonderplast, Bixmix)	On most indoor surfaces, such as bricks, blocks or plasterboard. Can be applied up to about 2in (50mm) thick into cavities.	Suitable for filling or finishing in one application. Mixed with clean, cold water; dries white or pink. Workable for 30–60 minutes. 8kg (17$\frac{1}{2}$lb) covers about 7$\frac{1}{2}$sq ft (0.7 sq m) at $\frac{3}{8}$in (10mm) thick.
Renovating plaster (such as Thistle Renovating plaster and Snowplast)	For use in damp conditions (but not below ground level on an unlined background), or slow-drying places. Undercoat layers should be about $\frac{3}{8}$in (10mm) thick, finishing layers about $\frac{1}{16}$in (2mm). Some are one-coat plasters.	A lightweight plaster mixed with clean cold water. Sets in 1$\frac{1}{2}$–2 hours. Treat backgrounds with low absorbency, such as concrete or dense bricks or blocks, with a water-resisting bonding aid first. 10kg (22lb) covers about 12$\frac{1}{2}$sq ft (1.2sq m) at $\frac{3}{8}$in (10mm) thick.

PLASTER	WHERE USED	DESCRIPTION
Ready-mixed undercoat or one coat (such as Polyplasta)	On most indoor building surfaces such as bricks, blocks, plasterboard or laths. Layers can be up to about 2in (50mm) thick into cavities.	A grey paste applied straight from the container. Workable for about 4 hours after application. Slow setting – takes about 24 hours to dry. Can be used without a finishing coat if the surface is to be papered. 10kg (22lb) covers about 8sq ft (0.75sq m) at about $\frac{3}{8}$in (10mm) thick. Available in 2.5kg (5$\frac{1}{2}$lb) packs.
Ready-mixed finishing coat (such as Polyskim)	On ready-mixed undercoat or other plaster surfaces. Layers should be about $\frac{1}{8}$in (3mm) thick.	A creamy-white paste applied straight from the container. Workable for about 4 hours after application. Sets in about 24 hours. 10kg (22lb) covers about 22sq ft (2sq m) at $\frac{1}{8}$in (3mm) thick.

ACCESSORIES FOR USE WITH PLASTERBOARD

PLASTER	WHERE USED	DESCRIPTION
Joint compound (such as Gyproc Jointex)	On plasterboard joints and joint tape.	For filling and embedding joints on plasterboard by hand. In powder form; mixed with clean, cold water. Workable for up to 30 minutes. Sold in 10kg (22lb) or 25kg ($\frac{1}{2}$cwt) packs.
Joint tape	On plasterboard tapered-edged joints before decorating (ivory side out).	A 53mm (2in) wide paper tape for reinforcing plasterboard joints. Corner tape with metal reinforcing strips for strengthening external corners is also available.
Scrim tape	On plasterboard joints before plastering (grey side out).	Jute tape 90mm (3$\frac{1}{2}$in) wide for reinforcing plasterboard joints.
Plasterboard primer/sealer (such as Gyproc drywall topcoat)	On ivory-coloured surface of plasterboard.	For preparing plasterboard surface for decoration. Two coats will give the surface protection against moisture.
Coving adhesive	For fixing coving to walls and ceilings. Also suitable as a plaster filler in repair work.	An adhesive powder mixed with clean, cold water. Workable for about 30 minutes. Sets in 1 hour. Sold in 5kg (11lb) packs.

Patching damaged plaster (continued)

upwards to press the plaster to the surface, flattening it slightly at the end of the stroke. Be careful not to press the trowel flat against the surface, or the plaster will pull away when you lift off the trowel.

5 If necessary, build up the damaged surface in thin layers.

Wait for each successive layer to stiffen (but not to dry) before applying the next.

6 Fill the undercoat to within ⅛in (3mm) of the surface and while it is still wet knock off the high points by drawing a length of wood across it. Rest it on the edges of a firm surrounding surface and work upwards with a slight zigzag motion.

7 When the undercoat is dry (about two hours after application) mix the finishing plaster in a clean bucket to the consistency of melting ice cream.

8 Using a plasterer's trowel held at a slight angle, spread the finishing

coat on top of the undercoat within about 15-30 minutes of mixing. This is a messy job, so make sure the surroundings are protected from splashes, if necessary.

9 When the finishing coat has stiffened – about 20 minutes after application – continually dampen it with a large paintbrush or houseplant spray while you smooth the surface with a plasterer's trowel held at a slight angle, using wide backwards and forwards sweeps.

USING READY-MIXED PLASTER

You will need
Tools Cold chisel; club hammer; hand brush; filling knife or plasterer's trowel. Possibly also fine abrasive paper or electric sander; face mask and safety spectacles large paintbrush; and finally a plastic spreader (supplied with skin-coat container).
Materials Ready-mixed plaster. Possibly also: Ready-mixed skim-coat plaster.

1 Chip away loose or crumbling plaster with a cold chisel until you reach a firm surface all round.

2 Brush away dust and debris.

3 Stir the plaster and apply it to the wall with a filling knife or plasterer's trowel held at an angle.

4 Build up deep areas in layers – applied up to 2in (50mm) deep in cavities. Allow each layer to stiffen before applying the next.

USING ONE-COAT PLASTER

Mix the plaster according to the instructions on the packet – generally up to about 1pt (½ litre) per 1kg (2.2lb) of powder – until it is a smooth paste that is just stiff enough to use.

Apply it in the same way as ordinary plaster (page 14), and finish in the same way (step 9 above).

5 If the surface is to be papered, fill the undercoat to the top of the damaged area. When it is thoroughly dry, smooth it with fine abrasive paper or an electric sander (wear a mask and safety spectacles to protect you from dust).

ALTERNATIVELY, if the surface is to be painted, fill the top ⅛in (3mm) of the area with a coat of skim plaster to give a smooth finish. Apply it with a large brush, in upward strokes, then spread it with light strokes. When it begins to dry, smooth it with the plastic spreader supplied.

Filling holes in lath and plaster

Fill small holes and cracks in lath and plaster in the same way as plaster.

If the hole is large enough to reveal the laths, the method of repair depends on whether the laths are intact or broken.

IF THE LATHS ARE INTACT

1 Paint the laths with a PVA building adhesive and sealer to make the surface less absorbent.

2 Fill the hole with layers of plaster in the same way as patching

damaged plaster (page 14). If you are using ordinary quick-setting plaster, use a bonding undercoat plaster rather than a browning undercoat plaster.

IF THE LATHS ARE BROKEN

Either patch the laths or – if the hole is not more than about 3in (75mm) across – plug the gap before you fill it with plaster.

1 To patch the laths, use a piece of expanded metal mesh, cut to the size you need with tinsnips. Wrap it

round the laths to bridge the gap between broken edges.

ALTERNATIVELY, to plug the gap, use a ball of newspaper soaked in water and then worked round in a bowl of runny plaster.

DEALING WITH LARGE AREAS

Where a large area of plaster has crumbled away from the laths, cut back the damaged area to a regular shape and patch it with a piece of plasterboard in the same way as repairing a hole in plasterboard (facing page).

Use plasterboard of the same thickness as the plaster, if possible. If the plasterboard is much thinner, nail an extra layer of laths across to pack it out so that only a thin layer of surface plaster will be needed. If the plasterboard is thicker, cut away the laths from the damaged area.

Nail the plasterboard patch, grey side outwards, to the timber framework supporting the laths.

Fill the gaps round the edges with interior filler and finish the surface of the patch with a coat of skim plaster.

Repairing and reinforcing corners

When filling an external corner with plaster, it can be difficult to get a level surface and a straight edge. The job is easier if it is done in two operations using a timber batten as a guide.

You will need
Tools Cold chisel; club hammer; softwood timber batten 2in × ¾in (50mm × 19mm) and longer than the depth of the area to be filled; straight-edge; masonry nails; hammer; hand brush; plasterer's trowel. Possibly also: carrying board; large paintbrush or house-plant spray: spirit level with horizontal and vertical vials; corner trowel (see step 9); rubber gloves.
Materials Plaster (page 14). Possibly also: length of expanded metal angle beading (see panel).

1 Cut back crumbling plaster to a firm surface and brush away debris from the damaged area.

2 Drive two masonry nails through the batten, closer to one edge than the other, and position them so that they will either be driven into the mortar between bricks, or fit into firm plaster well beyond the edges of the damaged area, to avoid cracking more plaster.

3 Hold the wood batten vertically against the damaged edge with the nails nearer to the inner side.
Use a straight-edge along the adjacent wall to align the batten with the plaster surface at the top and bottom.

4 Nail the batten gently to the wall, leaving the nail heads protruding.

5 Plaster the area with a suitable undercoat or one-coat plaster (pages 14, 15) to align with the edge of the batten.

6 When the plaster has dried, remove the nails and pull the batten carefully backwards from the wall to avoid crumbling the edge of the new plaster.

7 Nail the batten to the other side of the corner and then plaster the remaining damaged area in the same way.

8 If using a finishing coat, use the batten in the same way to plaster both sides of the corner.

9 Finishing the edge of the corner is easier if you use a corner trowel, if one is available. Otherwise round it off with a plasterer's trowel.
ALTERNATIVELY, before the plaster hardens fully, put on a rubber glove, wet it, and run your fingers down the edge to blunt it slightly.

REINFORCING A DAMAGED CORNER

If an external corner is prone to damage, reinforce it with expanded metal angle beading before plastering the wall.

The beading is formed from two bands of galvanised steel mesh set at right angles to a rounded centre strip. It is sold in lengths and can be cut to the required size with tinsnips and a hacksaw. Treat the cut ends with metal primer – also any areas of the galvanised coating accidentally damaged during installation.

Fit beading against the corner with dabs of plaster about 2ft (600mm) apart on each side. Use a straight-edge and spirit level to make sure it is vertical.

Press the mesh firmly against the wall and check with a straight-edge that the centre

strip will not protrude above the plaster surface.

The centre strip can be used as a guide to forming a straight edge when plastering, instead of using a timber batten.

Repairing holes in plasterboard

Small holes or dents in plasterboard can be repaired in the same way as plaster (page 14).

Medium-sized holes – up to about 5in (125mm) across – need to be fitted with a backing piece to block the cavity at the rear before they are filled with plaster filler.

Larger holes 5in (125mm) or more in diameter, or a severely damaged surface, cannot be satisfactorily repaired with a filler. The damaged section must be removed and a new piece of plasterboard patched in (see page 17).

USING A BACKING PIECE

You will need
Tools Trimming knife; drill and twist bit; filling knife.
Materials A plasterboard offcut; piece of string 6-8in (150-200mm) long; a long nail or wood sliver; interior or plaster filler or coving adhesive. You may also possibly need finishing plaster.

1 Trim the hole with a sharp trimming knife to give it a clean edge.

2 Cut a backing piece from a sheet of plasterboard offcut. It should be narrow enough to go through the hole, but long enough to overlap the hole by about 1in (25mm) on each side.

3 Bore a hole in the middle of the backing piece and thread the length of string through it.

4 Knot a nail or a sliver of wood to one end of the string to anchor it against the back of the offcut. Generally, use the white (ivory) side as the back of the backing piece and the grey (which will be covered with filler) as the front. Make a loop in the front end of the string so that it is easy to hold.

5 Apply some filler or coving adhesive to the front (the grey side) of the backing piece.

Repairing holes in plasterboard (continued)

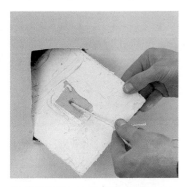

6 Guide the coated backing piece through the hole, then use the string to pull it into position against the back of the hole.

7 Hold the string taut while you fill the hole. Leave room for a finishing coat, if needed to match the surround.

8 When the filler has almost set, cut the string flush with the surface and apply a finish.

FITTING A PLASTERBOARD PATCH

You will need

Tools Trimming knife or pad saw; broad-bladed filling knife or plasterer's trowel; pencil; straight-edge; spirit level; try square; hammer; medium or fine abrasive paper; sponge; steel tape measure.
Materials Sheet of plasterboard or offcut as thick as board on wall (sizes, facing page); two lengths of timber to fit tightly between uprights (studs) – the thickness is usually 2in × 3in (50mm × 75mm) for a stud-partition wall or 2in × 1in (50mm × 25mm) for a dry-lined wall; four 3in (75mm) oval nails; large-head galvanised plasterboard nails; G-cramps; joint tape or scrim tape (page 14); joint compound or plasterboard finishing plaster (page 14).

1 Check that there are no pipes or cables behind the board. Use a trimming knife or pad saw to cut across the plasterboard from the middle of the damaged area outwards to each side until you reach the timber studs supporting the panel.

2 Use the straight edge of a spirit level to draw the edge line of the stud vertically on the plasterboard.

MENDING DAMAGED CORNERS

Damaged external corners of plasterboard can be repaired with battens and filler in the same way as you would do for plaster corners.
Reinforce the corners with joint tape bedded in joint compound. Ideally you should use corner tape, which is reinforced with metal strips. Crease the tape down the centre and fit it so that the metal strips lie inwards, close against the surface of the wall.
The tape gives the corner a clean, sharp edge.

3 Draw horizontal parallel lines across the panel between the studs, about 2in (50mm) above and below the edge of the damaged area. Make sure the lines are at right angles to the studs.

4 Cut out the squared-off section of damaged plasterboard.

5 On each side of the opening, draw a vertical line to indicate half the width – usually about 1in (25mm) of the timber stud, and score it using a straight-edge and trimming knife.

6 Cut back the sound plasterboard down the scored lines to reveal half the width of the studs.

7 Fit the two timber pieces as cross-pieces (noggins) between the studs at the top and bottom of the opening. Position them with the 2in (50mm) thick side outwards so that 1in (25mm) is under the edge of the existing plasterboard and 1in (25mm) is exposed as a nailing surface for the patch.

8 Hold the noggins in position with G-cramps while you drive 3in (75mm) oval nails through the noggins and into the studs at an angle.

9 Measure the area and cut plasterboard to fit. Insert it with the grey side out if the wall is plastered, or the ivory side out if it is not.

10 Nail the plasterboard to the wood surround with plasterboard

nails of suitable length and thickness (facing page).
Set the nails at intervals of 6in (150mm), positioned at least ½in (13mm) from the edge of the patch. Sink them into the surface of the plasterboard so they do not protrude, but take care not to damage the outer layer of paper.

11 Lightly sand the edges of the joint with abrasive paper, if necessary, to remove any burring.

12 Fill the joints according to which side is facing outwards. Then decorate the surface as required.

DEALING WITH DAMAGE ROUND A SWITCH OR SOCKET

Switch off the mains supply at the consumer unit before patching round a switch or socket. Disconnect the fitting, noting the wiring connections, and remove it.
Whether the socket is seated in plaster or plasterboard, fill small cracks or holes with an interior filler in the same way as filling any other small hole or crack, and larger holes by one of the methods described above. Wait for the plaster to dry before refitting the switch or socket.

Filling plasterboard joints

If you are lining a whole wall that will be painted or papered, the ivory side of the plasterboard should face into the room. Use tapered-edged boards to make jointing as smooth as possible. If you have to cut ivory-faced board, joint the squared edge in the same way as a tapered edge.

Do not confuse tapered edges with bevelled edges, sometimes used as a decorative feature.

If you use plasterboard to line a wall that needs a skim coat of finishing plaster to match the surface of adjoining walls, put it up with the grey side facing you.

Tapered edge

Square edge

Bevelled edge

JOINTING TAPERED-EDGED BOARDS

The joint compound is workable for about 30 minutes after mixing. To begin with mix only a small amount so that you can gauge your working rate. If you mix only about a quarter of a bucketful, you can use it all up completing a number of joints up to the feathering stage.

Before you start jointing, fill any gaps more than about $\frac{1}{8}$in (3mm) wide with a stiff mix of the jointing compound.

You will need

Tools Clean bowl or bucket; mixing stick or wooden spoon; plasterer's trowel; broad-bladed filling knife; scissors or trimming knife; sponge; large paintbrush.
Materials You will require some joint compound; joint tape; clean, cold water; and some plasterboard primer/sealer.

1 To prepare the joint compound, sprinkle and stir the powder into cold water in a bowl or bucket. Measure out the quantities as advised on the packet. Then let the mixture stand for two or three minutes before stirring it to a thick, creamy consistency.

2 Use a broad-bladed filling knife or plasterer's trowel to press the compound into each joint, spreading it in a thin band just over 1in (25mm) wide on each side.

3 Cut a strip of jointing tape to length and while the compound is still wet use the knife or trowel to press it on the joint. Press out any trapped air bubbles, but make sure there is enough compound under the tape for it to stick firmly.

4 After five minutes, apply another layer of joint compound over the tape in a wide band. Smooth it flush with the board surface.

5 Before the compound begins to stiffen, moisten a sponge and use it to feather out the edges into the surrounding surface and to remove excess compound without disturbing the tape.

Rinse the sponge from time to time to prevent any joint compound setting in it.

6 Use a filling knife to cover nail heads with a stiff mix of the joint compound.

7 When the layer of compound on the joint has dried, apply another layer in a wider band – 9-12in (230-300mm) – and feather the edges smooth in the same way.

8 When the surface has dried, finish it for decoration by applying one or two coats of plasterboard primer/sealer over the whole board.

JOINTING AND FINISHING GREY-FACED PLASTERBOARD

The grey side of plasterboard is jointed and finished using scrim tape and plasterboard finishing plaster, which is specially designed for the surface, although there is a risk of cracking at the joints.

Apply the plaster in the same way as ordinary finishing plaster. Use within 15-30 minutes of mixing, after which it is too stiff. This is a tricky job and should only be attempted over a small area – a repair in an old plaster wall, for example.

You will need

Tools Plasterer's trowel; scissors or trimming knife; large paintbrush or house-plant spray; clean plastic bucket; mixing stick or wooden spoon.
Materials You will require some plasterboard finish; scrim tape; and clean, cold water.

1 Mix the plaster in the same way as ordinary plaster.

2 Press the plaster into the joint between butted square-edged boards with a plasterer's trowel, and also spread it thinly on each side of the joint to form a band about 3½in (90mm) wide.

3 Cut a strip of scrim tape to length and press it into the plaster along the joint with the trowel.

4 Apply a second thin coat of the plaster along the joint.

5 When all the joints have been scrimmed, apply plaster to the boarding between the joints to cover the whole area with a thin plaster coat about $\frac{3}{16}$in (5mm) thick.

6 When the first coat has set, apply a second coat of the same thickness, and as it stiffens dampen and polish it with the trowel.

Fitting a plasterboard ceiling

The simplest way to fit a new ceiling is to nail sheets of standard plasterboard (page 243) to the ceiling joists. For joists up to 16in (400mm) apart, use plasterboard 9.5mm (⅜in) thick with 30mm (1¼in) galvanised plasterboard nails. For joists up to 24in (610mm) apart, use plasterboard 12.5mm (½in) thick with 40mm (1½in) plasterboard nails.

The plasterboard can be fitted over an existing ceiling as long as it is only cracked, not crumbling or sagging. If the ceiling is covered with polystyrene tiles, they can be left in place for extra insulation under the plasterboard. But you will have to locate and mark the joists in the ceiling (page 249), and use nails long enough to go through all the ceiling material and at least 1in (25mm) into the joists.

Take the old ceiling down, if you can (see right). You can then nail direct to the joists, and see any pipes and electric cables. It puts less weight on the joists and also enables you to treat the joists against woodworm if necessary.

It is best to fit the plasterboard with the ivory face downwards, as it can be painted or papered after filling the joints and applying a special primer-sealer (page 14). The grey face will need a coat of plasterboard finishing plaster before decoration.

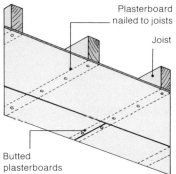

Fix boards with long edges at right angles to the joists, with board ends butted centrally on a joist. Stagger the rows so that adjacent boards do not butt on the same joist, cutting boards as necessary. Boards along the edge of the ceiling may need scribing.

You will need a helper to lift each board into place at one end. To support the board at your end while you nail it, use a T-shaped floor-to-ceiling prop (known as a deadman). You can make it from a length of 1½in (38mm) square timber the height of the room, with a piece of flat timber about 24in (610mm) long – such as a floorboard offcut – nailed to the ceiling end. To reach the ceiling easily and safely, with your head about 6in (150mm) from it, use either the base section of a scaffold tower, if available, or stout scaffold boards resting on two stepladders or stout wooden boxes.

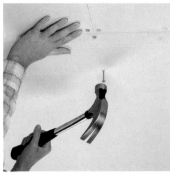

Nail the boards to the joists in the same way as for lining a stud partition wall.

When all the boards have been nailed to the joists, fill the joints between them (page 18) and finish the surface for decoration.

PULLING DOWN AN OLD CEILING

Pulling down an old ceiling is a very messy job (especially if it is lath and plaster). Before you start, clear the room and seal round door, cupboard and drawer openings with masking tape. Wear a face mask and safety spectacles as well as a hat and overalls.

Knock a hole through the ceiling with a hammer, then lever away the old board.

Alternatively, knock out the plaster and laths from above, or break away the laths as you go along. Either pull out lath nails, or drive them flush into the joists. To reduce dust, wet the lath and plaster with a paint roller.

Repairing ceilings and cornices

Modern ceilings are generally made of plasterboard, but lath-and-plaster ceilings are still found in some older houses.

In general, cracks and holes in both plasterboard and lath and plaster can be repaired in the same way as for walls.

CRACKS WHERE WALL AND CEILING MEET

The simplest way to cover cracks between the wall and ceiling is to fit coving – decorative moulding designed for wall and ceiling joints – using an expanded polystyrene or plaster adhesive, according to the coving material. A less effective alternative is to seal the gap with mastic frame sealant.

Another method is to use plasterboard joint or scrim tape along the crack, bedded in with either joint compound or plaster filler.

DEALING WITH A BULGE IN THE CEILING

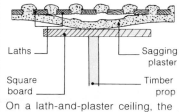

Laths — Sagging plaster

Square board — Timber prop

On a lath-and-plaster ceiling, the plaster sometimes sags away from the laths to form a distinct bulge.

Try to push the bulge back into position using a square of chipboard or plywood nailed to a floor-to-ceiling timber prop (a tool known as a deadman).

To re-fix the plaster, you need to reach it from above – either from the loft or by lifting the floorboards in the room above.

Vacuum clean the area between the joists at the back of the ceiling bulge.

Then pour fairly runny bonding plaster over the affected area. This should bond the ceiling plaster back to the laths, replacing the 'nibs' of holding plaster that have been broken or dislodged.

Leave the supporting prop in place until the plaster has dried.

If this method does not work, or if you cannot get at the ceiling from above, remove the sagging area and patch it with plasterboard (page 16).

A ceiling that sags over a large area should be pulled down and replaced.

RESTORING A CORNICE

Old cornice (ornate decorative moulding) is often clogged with paint – usually distemper, which can be removed with water. If the cornice has been painted with a modern paint, you will have to apply paint remover.

1 Remove accumulations of distemper by soaking a small area at a time with warm water applied from a house-plant hand sprayer. Spray repeatedly for about half an hour until the distemper has been thoroughly soaked.

2 Pick out the paint carefully with an old screwdriver, taking care not to damage the plasterwork.

3 Remove loose material with a brush so that you can see the areas that still need cleaning.

REPAIRING A BROKEN CORNICE

If parts of the cornice have broken away, a repair can often be made with plaster of Paris. Mix the plaster of Paris with water to a stiff paste – only a little at a time as it sets in about three minutes.

Damp the surface of the cornice, then use the plaster of Paris to build up the moulding in layers, using a clay modelling tool or a small knife.

Traditional cornice lengths, ceiling roses and beadings made from fibrous plaster are still available from specialist firms.

CHOOSING A LINING FOR A WALL OR CEILING

Various materials can be used in place of wallpaper or ceramic tiles as a wall or ceiling lining. Some are both decorative and practical, being used to cover an insulation lining or fittings such as water pipes. or to mask a rough or uneven wall. Never use a lining material to mask damp. Get the damp remedied and the wall or ceiling dried out before putting up the lining.

LINING MATERIAL	DESCRIPTION AND USE	TYPICAL SIZE	ADVANTAGES AND DISADVANTAGES
Plasterboard	Used both as a building board and a substitute for plaster, and also as an insulation lining. There are several different types for different uses.	Length 2400mm (about 7ft 10in); width 1200mm (about 3ft 11in); thickness 9.5mm ($\frac{3}{8}$in), 12.5mm ($\frac{1}{2}$in).	The surface can be given a finishing coat of plaster, or can be papered or painted, but joints have to be taped and filled. A lining of plasterboard on battens will be about 1½in (38mm) thick, so that architraves and electrical fittings have to be remounted.
Decorative wallboards (or wall panelling sheets) 	Hardboard or, more expensively, plywood with a patterned or plain face. The facing may be paper, wood veneer, vinyl or a waterproof laminate. Or a pattern may be stove-enamelled onto hardboard. Commonly used in kitchens and bathrooms. Tile patterns are popular, as patterned boards are cheaper, lighter and quicker to fix than ceramic tiles.	Length 2440mm (8ft); width 1220mm (4ft); thickness 3mm ($\frac{1}{8}$in) hardboard or 6mm ($\frac{1}{4}$in) plywood.	Wallboards can be fixed to the wall with a panel adhesive if the surface is virtually flat. Or they can be stuck or nailed to timber battens, or slotted into plastic or aluminium framing. Boards need to be conditioned before fixing.
Timber cladding (or V-joint cladding) 	Narrow boards interlocked along their length, usually with tongued-and-grooved or shiplap joints. Used to panel walls or ceilings. Boards may be solid timber, mostly softwood, or man-made board faced with wood veneer, plastic or patterned paper. Hardwood, which is more expensive, is also available.	Length 2400mm, 3000mm (about 7ft 10in, 9ft 10in); width 100mm (4in) or 95mm (3$\frac{3}{4}$in), with cover width about 90mm (3$\frac{1}{2}$in); thickness 10–13mm ($\frac{3}{8}$–$\frac{1}{2}$in).	Boards are nailed, clipped or screwed to battens. Before fixing, they need to be conditioned to their surroundings. When fixing, allowance must be made for ventilation behind them in rooms subject to condensation. Electrical fittings may have to be remounted, but can be recessed in the panelling.
PVC cladding 	Narrow white, hollow, plastic boards similar to timber cladding. Particularly suitable for walls or ceilings in kitchens or bathrooms. Can also be used outside. Matching coving is available.	Length 2330mm (7ft 6in); cover width 100mm (4in); thickness 10mm ($\frac{3}{8}$in).	Boards are fitted to timber battens with concealed clips, according to the maker's instructions. PVC profiles can be used to neaten joints and corners. Boards can be cut with a fine-toothed saw or trimmed with a sharp knife. They can be wiped clean with a damp cloth.
Brick slips 	Tiles made of fired clay, aggregate or plastic to simulate bricks. Used for decorative wall covering, laid in brick-bond patterns. L-shaped tiles are available for external corners. Can be used on outside walls but should be coated with exterior water repellent after fixing.	Length 215mm (8$\frac{1}{2}$in); width 65mm (2$\frac{1}{2}$in); thickness 13mm ($\frac{1}{2}$in).	Slips are stuck to the wall with the adhesive recommended by the maker, or with sand-cement mortar. Wall surfaces must be flat. Joints of even thickness must be maintained between courses, which must be kept horizontal. Clay slips can be cut with a tile cutter, other types with a hacksaw or power-drill masonry cutter.
Stone cladding	Tiles made from reconstituted stone to simulate quarried natural stone. Used for decorative wall covering, laid in brick-bond or random-bond patterns. Irregular shapes are available for random patterns. Cladding can be used outside but should be coated with exterior water repellent after fixing.	Lengths 300mm (12in), 230mm (9in), 150mm (6in); width 150mm (6in); OR Lengths 200mm (8in), 150mm (6in); width 100mm (4in). Thickness 13mm ($\frac{1}{2}$in).	Cladding is stuck to the wall with the adhesive recommended by the makers or with sand-cement mortar. The wall surface must be flat. Courses of regular shapes must be kept horizontal when fixing. Tiles can be cut with a special grit-edge blade in a hacksaw frame, or a power-drill masonry cutter.
Cork tiles	Thin squares of cork, available either unsealed, or sealed with a washable or steamproof finish. Used as a decorative wall covering where natural colours and texture are desired. A pack of nine covers about 1sq yd (0.8sq m).	300mm (12in) square; thickness 3mm ($\frac{1}{8}$in).	Fixed to the wall with adhesive. The wall must be virtually flat. Tiles give some sound and heat insulation. They should be left in the room for conditioning 24 hours before fixing. Not suitable for kitchens or bathrooms unless steamproof. Should not be fixed close to fireplaces.
Expanded polystyrene tiles	Lightweight white plastic tiles, plain or with an embossed design, used for lining ceilings. Can be over-painted with emulsion, but not gloss, paint. Modern types are self-extinguishing and less of a fire risk than old types, but avoid using where there is a lot of heat, such as less than 4ft (1.2m) above a gas water heater.	300mm (12in) or 600mm (24in) square; thickness 10mm ($\frac{3}{8}$in).	Stuck to the ceiling with ceiling-tile adhesive or as recommended by the maker. The tiles are a cheap and easy way of hiding blemishes and providing some heat and sound insulation (they cut down the noise leaving the room, but not entering).
Fibreboard tiles and plaster tiles 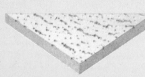	White fibreboard (sometimes perforated) or fibrous or fissured gypsum plaster tiles. May be plain or embossed. Some types have interlocking tongued-and-grooved joints. They are much heavier than expanded polystyrene, and are mostly used with suspended-ceiling framing kits.	300mm (12in) or 600mm (24in) square; thickness 13mm ($\frac{1}{2}$in) or 19mm ($\frac{3}{4}$in).	Square-edged tiles are fixed with the adhesive recommended by the maker. Interlocking types are fixed to ceiling battens with concealed staples or panel pins. Unlike plasterboard, the tiles can be put up singlehanded. They provide good sound absorption and are thicker and more expensive than polystyrene tiles.

Moving switches, sockets and ceiling lights

Where a wall lining such as plasterboard or timber cladding is fixed to a timber frame, switches or sockets on the wall often have to be moved forward and remounted. Before disconnecting and moving any electrical fitting, make sure you switch off the supply at the consumer unit.

If you have to move a socket, it is a good time to replace a single socket by double or treble fittings, if required. Or to add an extra socket on a spur of cable.

FLUSH-MOUNTED FITTINGS

Most switches or sockets are now flush mounted – with only the cover visible on the wall surface and the mounting box carefully recessed into the wall.

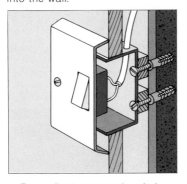

For a flush-mounted switch or socket, the mounting box must be moved forward so that it fully encases the terminal connections

and the cover can be re-screwed to its lugs. If you find that a switch has no mounting box, just long screws into the back of the recess, fit a mounting box.

When moving the mounting box forward, pack the recess behind it with wood as necessary, and screw the box firmly to the wall through the packing into wall plugs in the masonry. The screws should be long enough to penetrate about 1in (25mm) into the masonry.

You may need to fit battens round the cable outlet to support the edges of the wall lining round the hole cut for the mounting box. The mounting box usually has separate lugs for fitting to plasterboard.

SURFACE-MOUNTED FITTINGS

If the switch or socket is surface-mounted with a cable-entry hole in

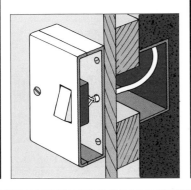

the mounting box, fit battens round the wall outlet to support the box fixing screws. Pierce the lining for the cable.

If the switch is mounted on an open frame, replace the frame with a mounting box to encase the terminal connections safely.

If the cable is too short to be pulled forward, replace with new cable of the right size. Cable can be carried in special trunking for skirting and architraves.

CEILING FITTINGS

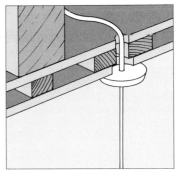

A ceiling light can be dealt with in the same way, with the rose backplate remounted on top of the panelling and screwed to battens fixed on each side of the cable outlet.

The rose position can be altered slightly as long as the cable will not be too stretched and the connections strained. If the cable will not reach the new position, fit a junc-

tion box and an extension cable as for adding a new lighting point on a spur.

RECESSING A SWITCH

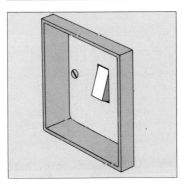

With timber cladding, switches and sockets can be left in position and the panelling boxed round them so that they are in a recess.

Line the edges of the panelling with a thin timber frame.

SAFETY PRECAUTION

Do not move a switch or socket by pulling the cable forward and refitting the cover on the outside of the panelling without moving the mounting box forward.

This contravenes safe wiring practice because it leaves the terminal connections unprotected, and is a fire risk.

Locating joists in a floor or ceiling

Timber framework for supporting a partition wall or a ceiling lining must be fixed to solid timber joists in the floor or ceiling.

Joists are parallel timbers about 2in (50mm) thick stretched across from wall to wall to support the floorboards or ceiling. They are usually 16-24in (400-600mm) apart, but on a top floor ceiling joists may be 13½in (350mm) apart.

LOCATING FLOOR JOISTS

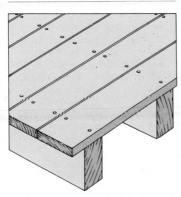

Find the positions of joists by noting the lines of nails where the floorboards are fixed to them. The

joists are always at right angles to the floorboards.

LOCATING CEILING JOISTS FROM ABOVE

One way to locate the ceiling joists in an upstairs room is to get into the loft above and mark their positions through the ceiling.

Use a bradawl to poke down through the ceiling on each side of a joist, at both ends. Measure the width of a joist and the distance between joists, and mark the position of another joist at the far side of the area through the ceiling.

From below, you can join up the marks to show the joist positions,

then measure and mark the positions of the other joists.

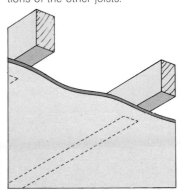

A quick method of marking the position of the joists is with a chalked string line.

LOCATING CEILING JOISTS FROM BELOW

In a downstairs room you will have to find the ceiling joists from below, unless you are prepared to lift the floorboards in the room above. You can get an idea of their positions by lifting only the floor covering and looking for the lines of nails.

On a lath-and-plaster ceiling,

joists can be located from below with a metal detector, which you can hire, or buy from DIY stores. The detector lights up when it passes over metal such as a nail head, so can be used to trace the lines of nails where laths are fixed to the joists. It will also show the paths of any metal pipes or electric cables running alongside the joists.

To find the joists without the aid of a metal detector, tap the ceiling lightly to detect a solid area, then probe with a bradawl. Use the bradawl to trace the position of one joist, and mark it with a chalked string line. From this, you can measure and mark the other joists, testing each surface with the bradawl.

Removing and refitting skirting boards

Wooden skirting board is normally levered away from the wall, but levering can be difficult if it has been screwed or nailed directly into the masonry. If you are going to refit the same skirting board, lever it off with more care than if you intend to fit new board.

REMOVING A SKIRTING BOARD

You will need

Tools Wrecking bar; thin softwood pieces for wedging. Possibly also: Hammer and cold chisel or bolster; torch; hacksaw blade; screwdriver.

1 If plaster juts onto the top of board, chip it away only at the place where you want to lever. The board should pull clear without damaging the jutting plaster.

2 When removing only part of the skirting, note whether the board to be removed is overlapped by another at an internal corner. If it is, remove the overlapping board first. Otherwise, start levering at an external corner or where skirting butts against a door frame.

3 Hold the wrecking bar near its hooked end and insert the blade behind the skirting, then put a thin piece of wood behind the top of the blade to protect the wall.

4 Prise the board away from the wall and wedge it with a piece of wood. Move to a new position about 3ft (1m) or so away and continue in the same way until the whole board is loosened.

5 If a board is difficult to loosen, wedge a gap open to look behind and check the fixing.

6 If the fixing is a screw, gently probe the front of the board to find the head (probably covered with filler). Unscrew it if you can, otherwise cut through from behind with a hammer and cold chisel or hacksaw blade.

7 If the fixing is a large nail, you can usually lever it off but will probably damage the board. If you want to refit the board, cut through it in the same way as a screw.

8 If you want to refit the same skirting board, pull out the nails from behind to avoid damaging the face of the board.

REFITTING A SKIRTING BOARD

Plaster is rarely taken far down the wall behind skirting. When you fit new skirting, buy board of the same height as the old to avoid patching the plaster. Or raise the height of the new board by nailing moulding to the top.

If new skirting board is narrower than the plaster or lining above it, pack behind with an extra piece of timber to bring it out to the required thickness.

If the plaster does reach to the floor, fix the skirting board through it into the brickwork with screws and wall plugs.

Coat the back of new skirting board with clear or green wood preservative to guard against rot. Shape the corners as necessary (see right).

Before refitting skirting board, lay it flat along the floor and mark on the front the positions of the fixing points so that you can nail through the marks.

Refit skirting board to existing fixing points wherever possible.

DIFFERENT TYPES OF FIXING POINT

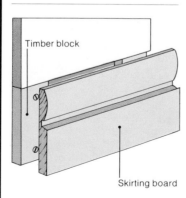

Timber block

Skirting board

The commonest type of fixing point is a timber block called a ground. Grounds are nailed or screwed to the wall at 18-24in (460-610mm) intervals.

Fit new grounds if necessary, using timber treated with wood preservative. Fix them with masonry nails or screws and wall plugs.

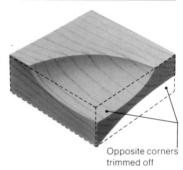

Skirting board

Timber wedge

An alternative type of fixing point is a timber wedge, called a plug. They are inserted into the mortar joints between bricks. If a timber wedge is damaged, remove it by partially driving in a large screw, then pulling it out, together with the wedge, using a wrecking bar claw or claw hammer. You will have to make a new wedge to replace the damaged one.

MAKING A TIMBER WEDGE

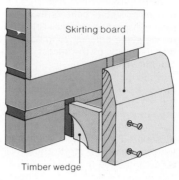

Opposite corners trimmed off

Cut the wedge from a wood block treated with preservative.

Make the size 4in × 3in × ⅜in (100mm × 75mm × 10mm). Plane off opposite corners as shown above to produce a twist in the wedge that will help to grip it firmly in place. Hammer the wedge firmly between the bricks.

SHAPING CORNERS ON NEW BOARDS

Before new skirting is fitted, shape the ends where there are external or internal corners. If a board butts against a door frame that is out of true, measure and mark the angle of the cut with a sliding bevel.

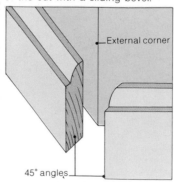

External corner

45° angles

On an external corner, mitre the two boards to meet each other at an angle of 45 degrees.

On an internal corner, one board is shaped to overlap the other, in the manner described below.

1 Fit a board right against the internal corner and temporarily nail it in position.

2 Hold the second board butted at right angles to the first and pencil its profile onto the end of the first board.

3 Remove the first board and cut away the end along the pencilled mark with a coping saw.

4 Refit the boards with the second, uncut board pushed into the corner and the first board lapped over it.

GAPS BELOW THE SKIRTING

A gap of about ¼in (6mm) between the skirting board and the floor can be useful if you want to push fitted carpet or vinyl flooring beneath it.

But if gaps occur below newly fitted skirting because the floor is not true, the simplest remedy is to nail quadrant or scotia moulding to the bottom of the skirting against the floor.

Do not nail moulding to the floorboards, as they expand and contract more than the skirting, and another gap could open up.

JOINING STRAIGHT LENGTHS

When joining two straight lengths of skirting board, do not make straight butt joints, which are impossible to hide.

Instead, make each joint with matching 45 degree cuts using a mitre board.

REFITTING SKIRTING TO A HOLLOW WALL

Skirting board fitted to a hollow wall – a partition or a dry-lined wall – is fixed to the vertical studs and floor rail (sole plate) of the framing. Locate the studs with a metal detector (page 21) or as shown on the same page. Refit the board using 2½in (65mm) oval nails.

REPAIRING MOULDING ON A SKIRTING BOARD

It may be impossible to buy matching moulding to repair a damaged section of skirting board (or picture rail) in an old house.

Getting a similar moulding cut to order by a timber merchant can be expensive. You can do the job yourself by cutting a matching piece with a power router, which can be hired.

Another method possible for replacing a short length is to shape a simple cutter – which is known as a scratch stock – from hard steel such as an old hacksaw blade. Grind the end of the hacksaw blade to the required profile and clamp it between two pieces of hardwood that are cut to an L shape to form an anchor for keeping a straight line.

Scrape the scratch stock slowly along a suitable piece of board to form the shape you want.

Where a small section of ornate moulding is damaged or missing, take an impression from a sound piece by pressing model-casting rubber against it. Or use dental-impression compound. Tack the hardened pressing to a piece of wood to form a mould, and fill it with glass-fibre resin. Smooth the set casting and glue in place.

DEALING WITH ARCHITRAVES AND PICTURE RAILS

Architraves are strips of moulding used to cover a joint between woodwork and a wall – such as round a door frame.

Remove an architrave or picture rail by prising it away from its backing using a mallet and wide wood chisel or bolster.

Start at the centre of the longest length and ease it gently out, working from both sides. Wedge between the backing and the moulding with a scrap of wood or hardboard as soon as possible.

When removing a picture rail, make good any damage done to the plaster.

The gap left by the rail can be difficult to disguise if the plaster is at different levels because the wall has been skim plastered since the rail was fitted.

Refit new or old architrave with thin wire nails. Punch the heads below the surface with a nail punch and fill the holes with wood filler.

Removing an old fireplace

There are three main steps in removing an old fireplace – removing the surround (which may be one of several types), removing a raised hearth if there is one, and sealing off the grate opening.

Old fireplace surrounds can be quite valuable – particularly old cast-iron or timber surrounds. Remove them carefully to maintain their resale value. Modern tile or brick surrounds that have been built since the 1940s are not usually worth preserving.

An unwanted fireplace opening can be permanently bricked up, or it can be boarded up in case you want to reopen it later.

Alternatively, you can keep the fireplace opening as a wall recess by sealing off the top of the grate only. Shelves could then be added, or it could be used to display a vase of flowers.

Before sealing off a fireplace, get the chimney swept and then have it capped by a builder.

A CAST-IRON SURROUND

1 The fireplace surround is normally screwed to the wall through metal lugs positioned at the sides near the top, and hidden under the plaster. Remove the wall covering and carefully chip away the plaster to expose the lugs.

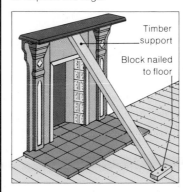

2 Support the surround by wedging a length of timber between the top and the floor. Cast-iron surrounds, particularly, are often top heavy. Without support the surround may fall forward when you undo the fixing screws.

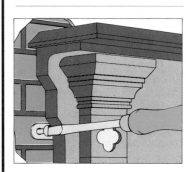

3 Remove the fixing screws if possible. Otherwise, prise the lugs away from the wall, but be very careful as they are brittle and will break easily (this lowers the value of the surround).

4 The grate may be fixed to the surround with screws or bolts, and will come away with it. There is no need to separate them unless you are planning to sell the fireplace surround only.

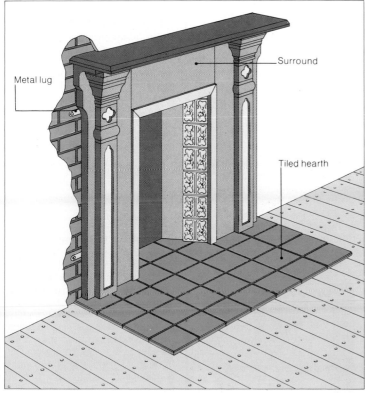

Cast-iron surround Old cast-iron surrounds can be valuable. They are usually fixed to the wall through lugs hidden under the plaster. Sometimes there is an inner surround of tiles.

REMOVING OLD BOLTS OR SCREWS

If you want to separate a cast-iron surround from its grate, you may have to soak the bolts or screws with penetrating oil before you can undo them. Make several applications of oil over about 24 hours, if necessary.

If they are still difficult to undo, use a nut splitter, which can be hired, to cut through the nuts. The splitter clamps round the nut or the bolt head and cuts it off as it is tightened.

Drill out screw heads with a high-speed-steel twist bit of about the same diameter as the screw shank (compare the screw head with loose screws to estimate the size). If necessary for resale, drill screw or bolt stubs from the surround and use a tap wrench to cut new threads.

Removing an old fireplace (continued)

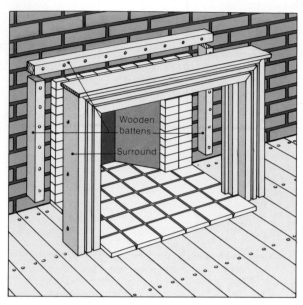

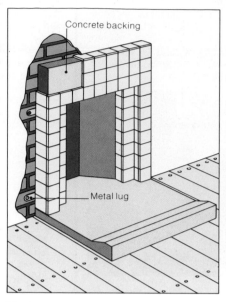

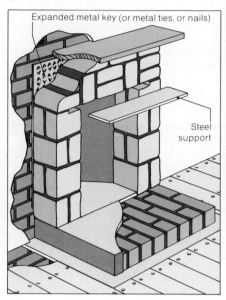

Timber surround The surround is usually screwed to wooden battens fixed to the brickwork.

Tiled surround There is usually a concrete backing, making the surround very heavy.

Stone surround The stones (or bricks) over the opening stand on a steel support.

A TIMBER SURROUND

A timber fireplace surround is usually screwed to battens fixed to the wall behind. There may be a tiled inner surround, which has to be removed separately.

1 Scan the timber surface to find filler covering the screw heads. If necessary strip off the surface with paint or varnish remover to reveal the screw heads.

2 Dig out the filler to clear the screw slots, and undo the screws.

3 Lift away the surround and remove from the wall the battens used for fixing points.

4 Remove an inner tiled surround in the same way as a tiled surround (below). It is usually much lighter, however, and can be handled by one person.

A TILED SURROUND

A tiled surround normally has a concrete backing that is screwed to the chimney breast through metal lugs, in the same way as a cast-iron surround.

It is normally very heavy, and you will need a helper to hold it steady and help lift it away.

If a raised hearth is resting against the front of the surround, move the hearth first (see right).

1 Remove the wall covering and plaster at the sides, near the top, to reveal the lugs. Either undo the fixings or prise the lugs away from the wall with a wrecking bar.

2 Get a helper to steady the surround as it comes away from the wall. If it does not come away easily,

there may be another set of lugs lower down on each side.

3 Lower the surround with the aid of a helper. If possible, take it outside for breaking up.

4 Lay the surround face downwards and cover it with sacking. Put on safety spectacles and protective gloves before breaking it up with a sledgehammer.

A BRICK OR STONE SURROUND

Before you start, check that the surround is not imitation brick or stone with facings bonded to a concrete backing. If it is, remove in the same way as a tiled surround.

Begin removing bricks or stones at the top course, loosening them by chipping away the mortar with a hammer and cold chisel.

There may be metal ties or nails in the mortar joints, linked in to the wall behind. Chip into the wall to remove them, and make good with filler afterwards. Alternatively, an expanded metal key may link the bricks to the wall.

REMOVING A RAISED HEARTH

A raised hearth may be a tiled slab of concrete or a number of stone slabs or bricks. The raised hearth is bonded to a concrete layer flush with the floor (known as the constructional hearth) with mortar.

1 Chip away the mortar with a hammer and cold chisel and prise out stones or bricks individually. ALTERNATIVELY, use a wrecking bar to prise up a solid slab hearth.

2 Leave the constructional hearth in place. Smooth it with self-levelling compound before laying the floor covering.

BRICKING UP A GRATE

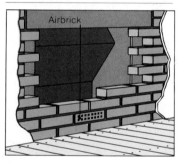

Use bricks or blocks and mortar to block the opening, building them up in courses. The face should be level with the surrounding brickwork – that is, set back slightly from a layer of plaster. Unless the opening is wider than about 4ft (1.2m), there is no need to tooth-in the bricks (that is, remove surrounding half bricks so that new bricks can be linked in).

Insert an airbrick in the centre of the second or third course, to keep the chimney dry.

If you are left with a gap about 1in (25mm) or more deep at the top of the opening, fill it in with a course of slates or part tiles.

Cover the brickwork with plaster to bring the surface flush with the surrounding wall.

BOARDING UP THE GRATE

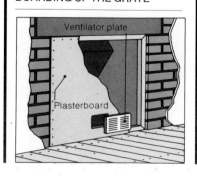

Use plasterboard or incombustible building board such as Masterboard, and cut it to fit flush into the opening. Fit a frame of 2in × 2in (50mm × 50mm) timber battens all round the edge of the opening, set back to allow for the thickness of the board. If the opening is more than about 24in (610mm) wide, fit a central vertical batten to give extra rigidity.

Nail or screw the board to the battens so that it lies flush with the surrounding wall. Cut a hole near the bottom at the centre and fit in a ventilator plate.

Cover top and side joints with scrim tape to reinforce them (page 14). Cover the board with readymixed skim-coat plaster, if necessary, to match the surrounding wall.

SAFETY PRECAUTION

If the grate to be blocked is linked to a common flue serving a grate still in use, do not fit a ventilator plate, through which hot soot may fall. When boarding up such a grate, you should use incombustible building board.

CREATING A WALL RECESS

Screw a framework of 2in × 2in (50mm × 50mm) timber battens to the inside of the chimney, just above the crosspiece supporting the front of the chimney.

Cut a panel of incombustible building board to fit to the frame. Make a hole in the centre, and fit through it a length of 2½in (65mm) diameter rainwater pipe with a bend of about 90 degrees at the top. The pipe keeps the flue ventilated, and the panel prevents soot and debris falling into the recess.

Draughtproofing and ventilation

A simple, inexpensive way to reduce the heat loss from your house is to draughtproof the windows and doors. Draughts are caused by cold air forcing its way into the house – through gaps in the roof, up through floors, through vents or cracks around windows and doors – and then forcing its way out through other gaps. Draughts may also occur when air is sucked in from outside to replace air used by boilers and fires.

If you block the gaps where the air is coming in you will stop the draught. Although the house will be more comfortable if you prevent streams of cold air moving through it, you must have controlled ventilation to keep the air fresh and remove excessive moisture.

Fires and boilers need air to burn efficiently and safely. Vents should be as close as possible to the appliance so that air passing to it does not cause a draught. They must never be blocked off or fumes may be sucked down a chimney, with possible lethal results. If the air has to pass across a room, fit the vent above a door or high in a wall so that air entering is mixed with the warmed air in the room before it moves to the fire.

HOW COST EFFECTIVE ARE HEAT SAVING METHODS?

Heating bills can be reduced by 60 pence in the pound by installing draughtproofing and insulation. But how much you actually save depends on the cost of the work compared to the saving in fuel.

For example, the estimated heat loss through windows can be reduced by half if you install draughtproofing and double glazing. It might take 40 years to recover the cost of custom-made double glazing but only two or three years for a DIY system.

Insulating the loft and draughtproofing doors, windows and floors are the most cost-effective forms of insulation.

Similarly, it is worth paying for cavity wall insulation – the cost will soon be recovered from savings in fuel.

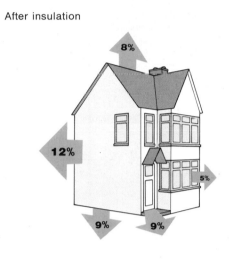
Before insulation

After insulation

Never block out the draught designed to pass under the house – dry rot may develop if the timber is not well ventilated. You can keep cold air out of the house by draughtproofing the floor from inside.

Similarly, there must be some form of ventilation in the loft to prevent condensation.

Draughtproofing a window

A CASEMENT WINDOW

Most of the draughtproofing strips shown in the chart on the opposite page are suitable for use on a wooden casement window; but only the strips with an adhesive backing can be used on a metal casement window.

Rubber sealant for large gaps
For large or uneven gaps, a silicone rubber sealant (also called a frame sealant) is particularly useful.

Both wooden and metal casement windows can be draughtproofed with sealant, and it can be used on doors – interior or exterior. But it cannot be used on sash windows.

Read any advice on the container before you begin.

HELPFUL TIPS
If you cannot find the source of a draught, light a candle and hold it in front of the door or window. Move around the edge of the frame – the frame will flicker at the point where the draught is coming in. Take care not to set curtains alight.

If leaded lights have become draughty, seal any gaps in the lead cames.

---

1 Clean the fixed frame thoroughly with soapy water and a cloth so that the surface is free from dirt. Rinse and wait for it to dry.

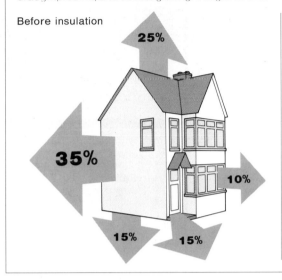

2 Apply a bead of sealant to the rebate of the fixed frame. It should be slightly larger than the gap which needs to be filled.

3 With a clean paintbrush or a cloth, cover the closing edge of the window or door with soapy water which will not act as a release agent.

4 Pull the window or door tight shut to compress the sealant and immediately open it again.

5 Leave the sealant to set – this will take about 2 hours if the weather is warm, but longer if it is cold. The sealant will harden on the surface but will remain flexible underneath,

forming a perfect seal when the window or door is closed.

A SASH WINDOW

Sprung strip is the most suitable material for sealing the sides of a sash window, as the sashes slide over it easily.

1 Remove the staff beads and the parting beads from the window so that both sashes swing free and clean the frame.

2 Measure the height of the sliding sashes and cut four pieces of the sprung strip – two pieces for each sash.

3 Fix the strip to the pulley stiles which run vertically each side of the

sliding sashes. Use pre-holed strip, fixing it with the pins provided and a hammer. Unless the window is rarely opened, self-adhesive strip is not suitable because it is unlikely to withstand the friction from the sashes. Take the strip right into the top and bottom corners so the sashes cannot catch on any sharp edges.

4 Replace the sashes and beading.

5 Seal the gap at the top and bottom of the sashes with any of the more durable foam strips fixed to the frame or the sash.

6 If there is a draught between the top and bottom sashes, fix nylon brush pile strip to the bottom sash at the meeting point.

Draughtproofing a door

Draught excluders can be fitted all round a door, both to the frame and to the threshold – although this should only be necessary on a front or back door.

Draught excluders suitable for doors range from simple foam strip, which is compressed between the frame and the door when it is closed, to weatherbar-and-threshold units which are attached to the bottom of the door and the sill.

Some threshold excluders are designed to deflect in-blown rain as well as to stop draughts.

Threshold excluders are made specifically for internal or external doors and to standard lengths, so choose the appropriate type and size for your doors.

Door edge seals may be self-adhesive or attached by screws; threshold excluders may be in two parts, one section should be screwed to the floor close to the door, the other to the base of the door.

ADDING AN ENCLOSED PORCH TO A DOOR

If you put an enclosed porch around an outside door – especially if it is exposed to prevailing winds – you will greatly reduce the draughts entering the house. You will also help to reduce condensation inside if you can leave wet umbrellas and coats in a porch.

Porches can be bought in kit form from larger DIY stores and builders' merchants for on-the-spot assembly.

Instructions on how to put up each type of porch vary. Follow the instructions supplied with the kit by the manufacturer closely.

HOW DRAUGHT EXCLUDERS ARE FITTED

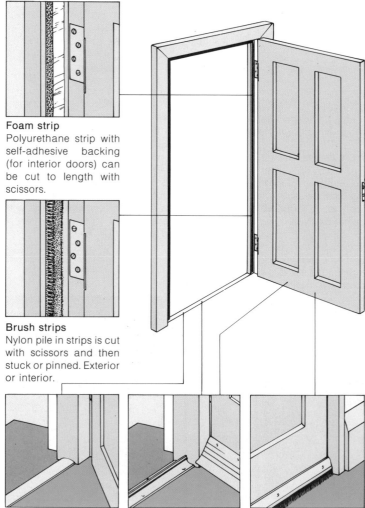

Foam strip
Polyurethane strip with self-adhesive backing (for interior doors) can be cut to length with scissors.

Brush strips
Nylon pile in strips is cut with scissors and then stuck or pinned. Exterior or interior.

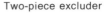

Sill excluder
A plastic or metal-and-plastic bar that is fitted to the sill and seals the gap when the door is closed.

Two-piece excluder
One part is fitted to the door, the other to the sill, and a seal is made between them when the door is closed.

Brush excluder
A rubber, plastic or brush seal attached to the base of the door. Usually adjustable for height.

THRESHOLD AND OTHER EXCLUDERS

Excluders fixed to the door

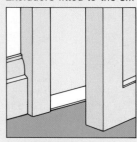

NYLON BRUSH Nylon bristle mounted in aluminium. The excluder is fitted to the base of the door – on the inside if it is an exterior door.

AUTOMATIC FLAP A spring-loaded hinged flap closes when an attachment on one end of the flap strikes an attachment mounted to the door frame.

Excluders fitted to the sill

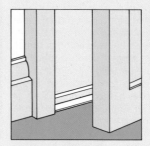

PLASTIC SEAL The plastic strip has a flexible section which compresses under the door when it is closed.

METAL/RUBBER SEAL The metal bar has a rubber insert which seals the gap under the door.

Excluders fitted to the door and sill

WEATHERBAR AND DEFLECTOR The weatherbar is attached to the sill. The deflector is attached to the door base and is shaped to deflect rainwater.

STORM BARRIER Interlocking sill and weatherbar sections, with a rubber seal on the weatherbar, give extra protection in exposed areas.

Keyhole cover and letterbox excluder

KEYHOLE COVER Suitable for the keyhole of a mortise lock, the pivoted cover hangs in front of the hole.

LETTERBOX EXCLUDER A plastic frame with two rows of nylon bristle fits over the inside of a letterbox.

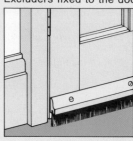

Draughtproofing a timber floor

A well laid tongued-and-grooved floor or one covered with flooring-grade chipboard should not be draughty. But a considerable amount of air can come up into the house if the boards are merely butted together. In older properties particularly, boards may have shrunk so there are gaps between them.

There is no danger that rot will set in after you have sealed gaps in a floor, provided that air can still move freely underneath the floor through airbricks.

The way you choose to draught-proof a floor depends on the size of the gaps. Fill large gaps wider than ¼in (6mm) with wood. For smaller gaps, use a sealant applied with a sealant gun or papier-mâché.

LARGE GAPS

You will need

Tools Mallet; plane; medium-grade abrasive paper and sanding block, or a flapwheel or drum sander in a power tool.
Materials Thin strips of softwood planed to a wedge section; water-proof wood adhesive.

1 Apply adhesive to the two long sides of a wedged strip of wood.

2 Tap the wood into place with the mallet, far enough to fill the gap but leaving the strip a little proud of the floor.

3 When the adhesive has set – this will take about six hours, but it depends on the conditions – plane away the surplus wood.

4 Smooth any rough pieces of wood with a flap wheel or drum

sander in a power tool, working only with the grain of the wood. Or do it by hand with medium-grade abrasive paper wrapped around a wood block.

SMALL GAPS

You can fill the gaps between floor-boards with a coloured acrylic flexible sealant applied with a sealant gun, but this will be expensive in a large room and sealants cannot be stained to match the colour of the floorboards.

It is much cheaper to fill the gaps with papier-mâché.

You will need

Tools Two buckets; trimming knife; putty knife or filling knife; fine or medium-grade abrasive paper; sanding block; rubber gloves.
Materials Old newspapers; glue size or regular wallpaper paste; water.

1 Using the trimming knife, shred the newspaper into small pieces. You need two to three newspapers for half a bucket of water.

2 Soak the paper in water until it is thoroughly wet.

3 Thoroughly work the paper to a pulp and squeeze out the surplus moisture.

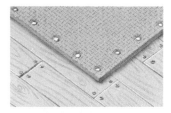

4 In a second bucket, mix up about 4oz (115g) of glue size or wallpaper paste to 1 pint (570ml) of water and work it into the news-paper pulp until it has taken on a thick putty-like consistency.

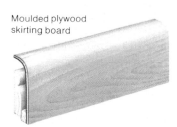
WHEN THE FLOOR IS TO BE COVERED

If you are laying carpet or tiles over a floor, you do not need to fill any of the gaps between the floorboards. A quicker technique, which will provide both draughtproofing and a flat surface for laying the new floor covering, is to put down sheets of hardboard over the whole floor (page 35).

If the cracks are small and the floorboards are level, use reflective foil building paper beneath a carpet. It is cheaper than hard-board. Lay the paper foil side up and fix it with double-sided carpet tape at the edges. The paper will stop draughts and will also reflect a certain amount of warmth back into the room.

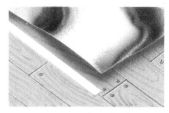

Hardboard covering

Building paper covering

5 Squeeze out the surplus water once again to make the papier-mâché as thick as possible.

6 Fill the gaps between the floor-boards with the papier-mâché, working it well down between the boards with the putty knife or filling knife.

Clean up the surplus to leave the floor as clean as possible.

7 Allow the papier-mâché to set hard – this will take about 24 hours, depending on the temperature of the room.

8 Smooth the surface along the repaired gaps with medium-grade abrasive paper wrapped around a sanding block. The papier-mâché should finally be left level with the floorboards.

CHOOSING INSULATION MATERIAL FOR A LOFT

Whichever type you decide to install, plan to lay at least 4in (100mm) of insulation. If you put down a thicker layer you will prevent more heat loss but the savings are proportionately less.

You may be able to reduce the cost if you buy insulation material in the summer when there is less demand for it and there are often special offers. You may also be eligible for a grant so that you can reclaim some of the money you spend. Contact your local council or Citizens Advice Bureau for details.

Before you buy, find out whether your supplier will deliver the insulation. Blanket rolls and sacks of loose-fill are very bulky for their weight. Even a car with a hatchback will only hold about a quarter of the amount you need to insulate the average loft.

You can insulate a loft yourself with blanket, loose-fill or sheet insulation. Alternatively, you can pay a specialist company to blow loose-fill insulation between the joists. The advantage with blowing is that the insulation can be directed into areas close to the eaves which are otherwise difficult to reach.

In addition to the more usual DIY loose-fill types of insulation, companies use other specialist materials.

BLANKET ROLLS

Mineral-fibre or glass-fibre blanket is supplied in rolls 4in or 6in (100mm or 150mm) thick. It is 16in (400mm) wide and from 17½ft to 26ft (5.3m to 8m) long. If the space between the joists in the loft is narrow and you need to cut the blanket, use a panel saw to cut through the roll while it is still in its wrapper, or you can cut through single widths with sharp scissors. Fibre blanket is cheap and effective, but it tends to compress as it gets older.

Insulation is not effective if water condenses in the material. For this reason, some rolls of blanket are backed with foil or polythene which acts as a vapour barrier – warm, moist air cannot pass into the material and condense. If you are using paper-backed or un-backed blanket, install a vapour barrier before you insulate.

MINERAL-FIBRE SLABS

Multipurpose insulation slabs can be used instead of fibre blanket in any insulation job. They are supplied to a standard thickness of 2in (50mm) so two slabs are needed to meet the minimum depth required for insulating a loft floor. The slabs measure about 45in × 18in (1140mm × 465mm), which makes them much less bulky and easier to handle than blanket rolls – but they are more expensive.

LOOSE-FILL

The material is poured out to a depth of about 4in (100mm). It is supplied in paper sacks each sufficient to insulate 12sq ft (1sq m).

The most common loose-fill materials are vermiculite granules, such as Micafil, and loose mineral wool. Vermiculite is more expensive than mineral wool but it holds its bulk better. It can also be used to top up old blanket insulation.

Polystyrene granules are a third type of loose-fill insulation, but they will blow about in a draughty loft, so pin building paper to the joists over the granules, but leave the top of the joists visible so you can walk safely.

HOW MUCH MATERIAL DO YOU NEED?

Calculate the size of your loft before buying the insulation material. Measure the overall length and width of your house and multiply the two figures.

If you are going to lay loose-fill, you will have to go into the loft to measure the joists. Unless you deduct the amount of space the joists take up you will have sacks left over.

Most suppliers will advise on how much material is needed for a given area. Information is often supplied on the packaging. Check how much it costs for each square metre or square foot – sometimes prices are misleading. For example, rolls of 150mm blanket may appear to be cheaper than rolls 100mm thick, but it is sold in shorter lengths and works out more expensive.

EXPANDED POLYSTYRENE SHEETS

Sheets of expanded polystyrene are particularly useful for sliding into areas which have been boarded over or which are difficult to reach – the flat roof over an extension, for example – but it can cost up to twice as much as insulating with glass fibre. You can also use expanded polystyrene to insulate between rafters and to insulate a cold water cistern, but it is too expensive for a whole loft.

Expanded polystyrene is most commonly available in sheets 6ft × 2ft (1800mm × 610mm) and sometimes 8ft × 4ft (2400mm × 1200mm). Sheets are usually 1½in (38mm) thick, but they are also made in sizes up to 4in (100mm). Thick sheets cost more but provide the best insulation. When buying polystyrene sheets for insulation, ask for fire retardant sheets for domestic use. They are likely to be labelled Type A or FRA. Non-fire retardant sheets are Type N or Normal.

REFLECTIVE FOIL BUILDING PAPER

Supplied in rolls just over 82ft × 3ft (25m × 900mm) and stocked by some builders' merchants. Lay the foil between joists or drape it over them. Acts as a vapour barrier so that moisture cannot condense in the insulation material. Heat also reflects off the shiny surface – either back into the house in winter or back into the loft in summer. If using it between rafters, pin the paper in position, but there is no need to pin it if it is laid on the floor beneath insulation material.

Insulating a loft

Insulate the loft floor, if the space is only used for storage. But if the loft has been turned into a room – or if you plan to convert it into a room – insulate the roof. You can make it easier to store things on the floor if you put down flooring-grade chipboard after you have insulated between the joists, and this also adds an extra insulating layer.

You cannot use the area as a room just because there is chipboard on the floor, although it is safe to walk on the chipboard for short periods of time. Loft conversions involve more complicated work which must be done by professionals and which must conform with building regulations. The joists in the floor, which are in fact only ceiling joists for the room below, must be strengthened, or new floor joists must be inserted. For this reason it is unwise to store too many heavy things, like furniture and piles of books, in the loft.

Before you start work, clear the floor space as much as possible and spring clean the loft to remove accumulated dust – use a vacuum cleaner, if possible. It may be worth hiring an industrial one. At the same time, look for signs of woodworm and rot, and if necessary call in a specialist contractor.

Also, check that the wiring does not need to be replaced. If you encounter rubber-covered cables, you should probably rewire with PVC cables. If in doubt, consult a qualified electrician.

If the loft does not have a boarded floor, you must keep your weight on the joists. Do not step on the plaster or plasterboard – your leg will probably go through and you could injure yourself as well as having to repair the ceiling below. Find a stout board which is thick enough to take your weight and long enough to be laid across at least two joists. It may be easier if you have two or three similar boards so that you do not have to keep moving the one you are on.

If the loft has no lighting, connect a safety light to a socket downstairs or run a table lamp off an extension cable. A torch will not give adequate light.

Opinions vary as to whether gloves are necessary when handling glass fibre and mineral wool products. If the fibre does not cause too much irritation, use bare hands and rinse them with cold water when you stop work. If you decide to wear gloves, tuck them into an old long-sleeved shirt to prevent fibres from getting inside. If they do get into the gloves, loose fibres will cause more irritation than if you wore no gloves at all.

Wear a face mask to keep dust out of your lungs if you are handling mineral wool or glass fibre, or if the surroundings are very dusty. It

is also a good idea to wear a safety helmet to protect your head against the rafters – it is easy to forget that you have little headroom when you are working under the eaves.

FIXING A VAPOUR BARRIER ON THE FLOOR

You will need
Tools Scissors.
Materials Rolls of reflective foil building paper or sheets of polythene; masking tape.

1 Cut the material with scissors so that it is about 2-3in (50-75mm) wider than the gap between the joists.

2 Lay the material in the gap, taking care to keep your weight only on the joists. Reflective foil paper must be laid foil-side down.

3 Seal any overlaps in the material with 2in (50mm) masking tape.

LAYING INSULATION BLANKET ON THE FLOOR

The spacing between joists varies but 13½in (350mm) is about average. Do not cut the excess off 400mm blanket – let it curl up on each side to make a snug fit.

You will need
Tools Scissors; face mask. Possibly also protective gloves.
Materials Rolls of glass fibre or mineral fibre blanket.

1 Start unrolling the blanket between two joists at the eaves at one end of the loft.

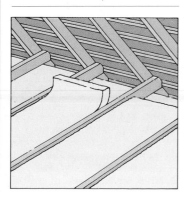

2 Do not take the material right into the eaves; you must leave a

PROBLEMS WITH CONDENSATION

Warm air is moist and if it meets cold air it condenses. Condensation can be a problem in a loft if you insulate the floor. No heat will escape into the loft but moisture will pass upwards and condense in the insulation material, which becomes ineffective if it is damp.

Foil-faced plasterboard is impervious to moisture so if the ceilings have been constructed of this material you do not need to take additional protective

measures. If not, make sure that insulation material is protected by some form of vapour barrier below it so that the risk of condensation is reduced.

Sometimes blanket is supplied with a plastic or foil backing which moist air cannot pass through. But if you are using paper-backed or unbacked blanket or loose-fill insulation, you need to install a vapour barrier first.

LAGGING A LOFT HATCH DOOR

Cut a piece of glass-fibre or mineral-fibre blanket or thick expanded polystyrene sheet to fit above the loft hatch.

To fix the blanket, hammer about two nails along each edge of the door, depending on its size. Tie string over the top of the material and loop it around the nails to hold it in place. Do not pull the string so tight that it squashes the blanket.

Alternatively, cut a piece of tough brown paper large enough to cover the blanket. Fix the paper

over the blanket, holding the edges in place with drawing pins.

If you are using expanded polystyrene sheet, stick it to the door with adhesive designed for the purpose, such as Evo-Stik ceiling tile adhesive or Unibond polystyrene adhesive.

Make sure that the hatch door is a tight fit. Fix a foam, rubber or flexible draught excluder to the rebate so that damp air cannot pass through into the cold loft and cause condensation.

gap of about 2in (50mm) so that air can come in through the soffit and flow through the loft. If the air cannot circulate, condensation may form.

3 Press the blanket down lightly as you unroll it so that it lies flat but do not squash it so that it becomes compressed.

4 When you reach the other side of the loft, cut the blanket with scissors, again taking care not to block where the necessary ventilation comes in under the eaves.

5 Continue to lay the insulation between the other joists.

6 When joining two rolls, make a butt join, pressing the ends close to each other.

7 Cut the insulation so that it fits tight around pipes.

8 Try to place insulation under loose electric cables so that there is no danger of them becoming overheated. Where practicable, fix cables to the sides of the joists to keep them out of the way.

9 Never insulate under the cold water cistern. Leave a gap in the insulation so that warm air from below will keep the chill off the base of the cistern and help to prevent the water from freezing.

HELPFUL TIP
Use a broom to push the blanket into areas which are hard to reach.

INSULATING WITH LOOSE-FILL

It is easy to insulate with loose-fill granules – you pour the material between the joists and level it out. Make a simple levelling gauge so that the granules are at an even depth. Decide how deep the insulation layer is to be – it must be at least 4in (100mm) – and deduct this measurement from the depth of the joists.

Cut a piece of hardboard, chipboard or wood to a wide T-shape which will fit the gap above the loose-fill. The 'arms' should rest on top of the joists, so that when you run the gauge between two joists the granules are spread to a consistent depth.

Insulating hot and cold water pipes

Hot and cold water pipes that are exposed to the cold should be lagged to prevent winter freeze-ups. Pipes in particular danger are those that run across a loft above an insulated floor, and those running along outside walls in unheated rooms.

Overflow and vent pipes that are exposed to the cold should also be well lagged.

To lag pipes that are boxed in, unscrew the box and stuff pieces of glass fibre or mineral fibre all round the pipes.

LAGGING PIPES WITH FIBRE BANDAGE

You will need
Tools Damp rag; scissors.
Materials Strips of glass fibre or mineral fibre; plastic adhesive tape or possibly string.

1 Clean the pipes with a damp rag and allow to dry.

2 For pipes in the loft, begin lagging at the cistern. Wrap the bandage around the pipe two or three times and secure it with plastic adhesive tape or string.

3 Continue to wrap the bandage around the pipe, making generous overlaps of about one-third of the width of the bandage. Take care to ensure that the pipe is well covered at bends – these are the vulnerable areas most likely to freeze.

CHOOSING PIPE INSULATION MATERIAL

Plastic foam tubes
Easy-to-fit plastic foam tubes will bend round pipe curves. The tubing is split down one side and has to be eased open to wrap round the pipe. It is secured with adhesive tape wrapped round at intervals, or placed along the slit; or with purpose made clips; or with a special adhesive. Some types are secured by integral mouldings that interlock. Tubes are available to fit 15mm, 22mm and 28mm pipes. Plastic foam tube is slightly more expensive than glass fibre and mineral fibre or felt, but it is extremely convenient to use.

Self-adhesive pipe wrap
Thin foam insulating wrap, 2in (50mm) wide, is supplied in rolls usually 15ft (4.6m) or 32ft (10m) long. Some types have a metallic finish.

There is no formula for estimating how much pipe wrap to buy – it depends on the size of the pipes and how large you make the overlaps. Buy one or two packs, use the material and then work out how much more you need to complete the job.

To fix the lagging, peel off the backing paper and wind the material round the pipes. It is self-adhesive. Overlap the tape as you wind it, especially at bends.

Glass-fibre and mineral-fibre bandage
An inexpensive form of lagging but not widely available in bandage form. You can make your own bandage from loft insulating blanket by tearing or cutting the blanket into strips 3in (75mm) wide.

Use a panel saw to cut the roll of blanket while it is still in its wrapping, or use a large pair of sharp scissors on the unrolled blanket. It can be difficult to wrap round pipes that lie close to a wall.

To prevent the fibres from irritating your skin, wear gloves while using the material, or wash your hands in cold water after handling.

Sleeved felt lagging
For plumbing in new pipes, sleeved felt lagging can be slipped over a pipe before installation. It is available in packs of about 72ft (22m), in a size that will fit both 15mm and 22mm diameter pipes, and the material is easy to cut to length with scissors.

To fit sleeved felt lagging to existing pipes, run scissors along the sleeve seam to undo the stitches. Wrap the lengths of felt round the pipes and tie them in place with string. This method provides very cheap insulation for pipework.

---

4 To join two strips of bandage, overlap the new piece and fix it with tape or tie with string.

5 Take the bandage around any valves or stopcocks as you meet them, leaving only the handle exposed.

6 If you want to improve the appearance of visible pipes lagged with bandage, build a simple box around them.

LAGGING PIPES WITH FLEXIBLE FOAM TUBE

You will need
Tools Damp rag; scissors.
Materials Foam tube of right size; adhesive tape; clips or adhesive.

1 Wipe over the pipes with the rag to remove dirt and allow to dry.

2 Lag the pipes leading from the cistern first, if you are insulating

---

pipes in the loft. Wrap plastic adhesive tape round the first tube to hold it in place, even if the tube is one of the moulded self-locking types. Push it up tight against the tank so that the tank connector joint is covered.

3 Butt-join the tubes where they meet and wrap tape around the join to hold them tight. Also, secure a tube with tape, clips or adhesive wherever it seems to want to open.

4 Cut the tube with scissors to fit round the body of a gate valve or stopcock as far as it will reach. Make sure the whole of the pipe is covered.

5 If you want to change the colour of the foam – which is only available in grey – coat it with emulsion paint. Never use oil-based paints or cellulose lacquers – they affect the plastic.

Lagging a cold-water cistern

Never lay insulation under the cold-water cistern. Any warmth which comes from the room below will help to prevent the water from freezing. For extra protection, lag the sides of the cistern and its lid. Make a lid if the cistern does not already have one (facing page).

Expanded polystyrene kits are available for lagging rectangular cisterns; if you buy one, make sure it will fit your cistern. Or you can use sheets of expanded polystyrene, which are available from most builders' merchants.

A cheaper alternative – and the only method possible for round cisterns – is to use glass-fibre or mineral-fibre blanket.

USING FIBRE BLANKET

You will need
Tools Scissors; steel tape measure.
Materials Glass-fibre or mineral-fibre blanket; ball of string; plastic adhesive tape; large sheets of brown paper.

1 Measure the sides of the cistern and cut the blanket to fit so that it will be level with the top of the cistern. You will probably need about 1½ widths.

2 Wrap the first piece of blanket round the cistern and tie it – not very tightly – with string at 9in (230mm) intervals.

3 Butt-join the second piece of blanket on top of the first, and make sure that there are no gaps between them. Tie the second piece in place with string also. Do not pull the string too tight and compress the blanket or it will not insulate effectively.

If you wrap a second layer of blanket on top of the first – so that the cistern is doubly protected – tie the string so that it is not above the string underneath.

4 For extra protection, cover the blanket with a large piece of brown paper. Hold the brown paper sheeting in place with plastic adhesive tape and string.

5 Lag the lid with fibre blanket, overlapping the blanket already around the cistern.

6 To make the blanket secure, fix it in place with brown paper and adhesive tape.

USING EXPANDED POLYSTYRENE

This method is only suitable for square or rectangular cisterns.

You will need
Tools Knife with a serrated blade (such as an old bread knife) for cutting sheets; trimming knife; steel tape measure; serrated spreader or old filling knife.
Materials Expanded polystyrene sheets preferably 3in (75mm) thick; eight wooden meat skewers; ad-

hesive for expanded polystyrene (such as Evo-Stik ceiling tile adhesive or Unibond polystyrene adhesive).

1 Measure the sides of the cistern. Cut sheets of expanded polystyrene each about 1in (25mm) wider and higher than each side.

2 Cut holes in the sheeting to accommodate the pipes protruding from the cistern.

3 Place the sheets around the cistern to form a tight-fitting box.

4 Push a wooden skewer through the polystyrene at the corners to hold the sheets in place. You will probably need eight skewers in all. Put two into each corner, one at the top and one at the bottom.

5 Make a lid for the box with two sheets of expanded polystyrene. Cut one piece to cover the box exactly. Make the second slightly smaller – less the thickness of the side pieces – so that it will fit inside the inner edges of the box. Stick both pieces together with adhesive for expanded polystyrene.

6 If there is a vent pipe hanging over the cistern, make a hole in the lid below the outlet of the pipe.

Place a plastic funnel in the hole so that dripping water is directed straight into the cistern.

COLD WEATHER CHECKS

Make sure no tap is left dripping. If that is not possible put a plug in the basin or bath overnight. Drips cause ice to block waste pipes.

Never allow cisterns to overfill. Water in overflow pipes can freeze, causing the cistern to spill over the sides.

In a long cold spell, open the loft hatch occasionally to let in warmth from the house.

If you leave the house for short periods, keep the central heating turned on, turned down to the minimum. For long periods, drain the system by closing the main stopcock and opening all the taps. When water stops running, open the drain cock near the stopcock. For central heating see page 81.

TWO MORE TIPS FOR INSULATING A CISTERN

Making a cistern lid
A cold-water cistern should have a lid to keep out dust and insects and improve frost insulation (new cisterns must have one). Make it from chipboard about 1in (25mm) larger all round than the cistern top. Glue a sheet of expanded polystyrene to the underside, to fit exactly into the top.

Blocking a draught from an overflow pipe
To stop draughts coming up an overflow pipe and chilling the water in the cistern, extend the pipe inside the cistern so that it is just below high water level. To do this, connect a piece of $\frac{3}{4}$in (19mm) flexible plastic pipe to the overflow.

Insulating a roof

If a loft is to be used for storing valuables that could be affected by extremes of temperature, it is better to insulate the roof rather than the loft floor.

DRAUGHTPROOFING BETWEEN RAFTERS

If there is no felt on the underside of the roof, fix building paper between the rafters before putting up any insulation material. This will help to keep out draughts and in-driven rain and snow.

Standard building paper consists of two sheets of tough paper held together by a central layer of bituminised fibre netting. The paper is available in rolls of 30ft × 3ft (100m × 1m) from most builders' merchants.

You will need
Tools Steel tape measure; scissors; pin hammer; waterproof adhesive tape.
Materials Rolls of building paper; brass drawing pins.

1 Measure the gap between two rafters and cut the building paper into strips that are slightly wider than the gap.

2 Start at the top of the roof and pin the paper to the rafters on each side at intervals of about 4in (100mm).

3 Take the paper right down to the eaves. Push out the end of each strip of paper so that any in-blown rain or snow cannot drip onto the loft floor.

4 To join the paper, make an overlap of at least 4in (100mm) and tape over the join with adhesive tape.

FITTING BLANKET INSULATION

If you can find rolls of glass fibre or mineral fibre with backing paper, you will be able to use the paper to fix the material in place. Arrange it so that the paper faces into the loft and use drawing pins to secure the paper at 6in (150mm) intervals.

If the blanket does not have

backing paper, hold it in place with string lengths wound round tacks.

You will need
Tools Heavy-duty scissors or an old serrated knife (such as an old bread knife); hammer; steel tape measure; face mask. Possibly cotton gloves if your skin is sensitive to fibres.
Materials Rolls of glass-fibre or mineral-fibre blanket; tacks; ball of string.

1 Starting at the top, hammer a tack into the side of a rafter. Do not hammer it right in – let it protrude by at least $\frac{1}{4}$in (6mm).

2 On the adjacent rafter, hammer in another tack about 6in (150mm) farther down. Continue in this way, alternating between sides and moving gradually down the rafter until there are tacks sticking out from both sides from top to bottom.

3 Measure the gap between the rafters and cut blanket to fit.

Insulating a roof (continued)

4 Tie the end of the string to the tack at the top of the rafter.

5 Place the insulation material between the rafters. If possible, get someone else to help you.

6 Starting at the top, wind string between the tacks so that it zigzags down to hold the blanket in place.

7 Continue this procedure. If you have to join pieces of blanket, butt them together.

FITTING SHEETS OF EXPANDED POLYSTYRENE

Expanded polystyrene is more expensive than fibre blanket but easier to fit.

1 Cut a sheet of expanded polystyrene to the exact width between the rafters, and push it in so that it fits tightly.

2 Hammer nails or tacks into the rafters below the sheets so that they protrude and prevent the sheets from dropping down.

3 Butt-join the polystyrene sheets whenever you need to use a new piece to make a joint.

IMPROVING THE APPEARANCE OF THE ROOF

After installing the roof insulation, nail plasterboard to the rafters to form a smooth lining. This will provide an extra layer of insulation as well as hiding the insulation material from view.

Choose thermal board with a smooth decorative face, or Duplex plasterboard with reflective foil. Nail it with foil facing towards the roof insulation.

COPING WITH A FLAT ROOF

Flat roofs should be insulated at the time they are built; if you are having an extension added to your house, make sure that insulation is incorporated when the roof is constructed.

If an existing roof lacks insulation, remove a fascia board so that you can see into the space between roof lining and ceiling.

The fascia board will either be nailed or screwed to the ends of the ceiling joists.

Slide sheets of expanded polystyrene – preferably 3in (75mm) thick – into the gap.

If you cannot take off a fascia board, line the ceiling below, preferably with thermal board not the standard variety.

Alternatively, you can glue sheets of expanded polystyrene direct to the ceiling and perhaps stick a layer of expanded polystyrene ceiling tiles on top.

The thicker the layers of expanded polystyrene, the more effective the insulation will be.

Expanded polystyrene tiles by themselves will not be as effective as sheets of expanded polystyrene, but they are cheap and easy to fix.

Insulating the walls of a house

TREATING CAVITY WALLS

It is good practice to insulate cavity walls because it saves heat loss from a house, but it is not a DIY job. To check if the cavities have already been filled, you can drill a hole into the cavity from the outside and feel with a probe. If it is empty, call in a contractor specialising in cavity insulation.

Since it is impossible to check how well the work has been done or how long the insulation will last, you have to rely on the contractor's integrity. You can get advice from the National Cavity Insulation Association, PO Box 12, Haslemere, Surrey GU27 3AH.

First, check that the walls show no sign of penetrating damp. Walls should not be filled while damp is present, so you must eliminate the cause of the damp and wait for the walls to dry out.

There are two main insulation systems to choose between, with

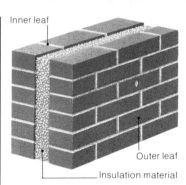

Inner leaf — Outer leaf — Insulation material

similar installation methods. The dry system consists of mineral-wool fibres or expanded polystyrene beads being blown through holes drilled in the outer leaf of the wall until the cavity is filled.

With the second system, the cavities are filled with foam. This is produced on site and pumped through holes drilled in the outer leaf. The foam normally dries after a few days and becomes firm. This system is not suitable for timber-framed houses.

TREATING SOLID WALLS

Insulating the outside
Putting insulation on the outside of the house is another job that is usually done by a specialist company. The walls are clad with insulating slabs which then need decorating. This is an elaborate process because downpipes, windows and doors are affected by the extra thickness of the wall, and pipes will have to be repositioned.

It is an expensive job, only worthwhile in extreme conditions.

Insulating the inside
The extra width of insulation on the inside may bring the wall out beyond skirting boards, picture rails and architraves. Often lights, wall sockets, light switches and radiators will have to be repositioned.

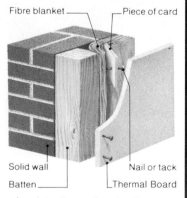

Fibre blanket — Piece of card
Solid wall — Nail or tack
Batten — Thermal Board

Insulate the walls with Thermal Board fixed to battens. Before nailing on the boards, pin fibre blanket to the battens.

ALTERNATIVELY, fix the Thermal Board direct to the walls with the adhesive recommended by the board manufacturer, and a secondary fixing of hammer-in fixings or screws.

THE PROBLEM OF NOISE
It is impossible to prevent noise coming through a party wall. This is because the noise travels through adjoining walls, floor and ceiling as well as the shared wall. And once it gets into the fabric of the house nothing can stop it.

Far more can be achieved from the other side. The re-siting of hi-fi equipment or TV to the far side of the room will achieve much more than spending a lot of money on insulation.

Another way to prevent noise from leaving a room is to fix insulating board, cork or polystyrene sheet to the wall, but this will not stop noise coming in.

On floors, a thick carpet and underlay will prevent most noise from travelling to the room below.

On windows, normal double glazing has little effect on noise from outside. The space between panes needs to be increased to about 4in or 6in (100-150mm). And the weight of glass for the secondary glazing must be heavier so that the two sheets do not vibrate in sympathy.

PREVENTING HEAT LOSS FROM A RADIATOR

A reflector behind a radiator on an outside wall will reduce the amount of heat loss into the wall by about a quarter. It will also reflect some of the heat back into the room.

Rolls of heat-reflecting aluminium foil – easily cut with scissors – are sold with self-adhesive pads.

A cheap way of testing that the job is worth the expense is to make your own reflectors.

Cut one or more pieces of cardboard to fit behind the radiator and glue aluminium kitchen foil to one side. Slide the cardboard behind the radiator with the foil facing into the room. After about a year, the kitchen foil may oxidise and turn black so that it no longer reflects. You can then decide whether to replace it with the special heat-reflecting foil, which does not oxidise. It can also be positioned behind the radiator by sticking it to cardboard.

Lifting and replacing a floorboard

First find out whether the boards are tongued-and-grooved or square edged by poking a thin-bladed knife between them. If they are square edged, the blade will pass right through.

You will need

Tools Thin-bladed knife; drill and twist bits; padsaw; bolster chisel or car tyre lever; hammer; screwdriver. Also for tongued-and-grooved boards: hand-held circular saw (or wide-blade chisel and mallet, or panel saw, or flooring saw).

Materials 2in or 3in (50mm or 75mm) floorboard nails; 3in (75mm) No. 8 screws; pieces of timber about 1½in (38mm) square and 4in (100mm) longer than the width of the boards.

SAFETY TIP

Whenever you do not require immediate access below the floor, put the board back loosely in position, even if only for a few minutes. That will eliminate the risk of someone stepping into the hole.

REMOVING SQUARE-EDGED BOARDS

Before lifting the board, you must cut across it at each end just before it meets a joist. Lines of nails indicate joist centres.

1 Drill a ⅜in (10mm) starting hole near the edge, and complete the cut with a padsaw.

2 Starting at one end, prise out the fixing nails by inserting a bolster chisel or car tyre lever under the board and levering up.

3 Once you have loosened one or two sets of nails, push the handle of a hammer under the board as far from the loose end as possible, and press hard on the end. This sends a shock wave along the whole length, loosening nails farther along which you can remove.

4 Push the hammer farther forward, and repeat the process, until the board is free.

HOW TO REMOVE TONGUES

On tongued-and-grooved boards, the tongues on each side of the board must be removed. If adjoining boards are to be lifted, only the tongues at the outer edges of the group need cutting.

1 The best tool is a hand-held circular saw. Adjust its depth of cut so that the blade just protrudes below the underside of the tongue. Since floorboards are usually ¾in (19mm) thick, the underside of the tongue will be about ½in (13mm) below the surface. This depth of cut will avoid pipes and cables.

2 Place the blade between the boards, switch on the power, and

move the saw along the length of the board.

ALTERNATIVELY, chop off the tongues with your widest-blade chisel and a mallet.

ALTERNATIVELY, try sawing them off, having drilled a starting hole; but this is not easy.

ALTERNATIVELY, special flooring saws are available and can sometimes be hired.

CURING LOOSE AND SQUEAKING BOARDS

A floorboard squeaks because it is not firmly held to its joist. When someone steps on it, it springs under the weight, rubbing against a neighbouring board.

A squeak can be temporarily cured by dusting talc down the side of the board.

Not all loose boards squeak — there may be too big a gap around them — but even so they should be properly secured before a floor covering is laid, otherwise you will feel the movement under new flooring.

A board becomes loose when one or more of its fixing nails is shaken free — by vibration or the movement of the joist below. Prise out the nail if it is still there, starting if necessary with pincers.

Refix the board with a screw big enough to fill the hole left by the nail. A No. 8 screw, 2in (50mm) long, should be suitable.

The screw will hold the board securely in place, and as it goes exactly into the same hole as the nail there should be no danger of striking a cable or pipe.

---

3 With the tongues removed you should be able to see the joists between the boards. Now remove the board in the same way as a square-edged board.

REPLACING THE BOARD

Buy new nails (old ones may be rusty, or may be damaged during the lifting process), and use the proper floorboard type.

You will not be able to nail the board to a joist at its ends — as it has been sawn off before the joists.

1 Screw a short batten to the side of the joist, its top edge jammed hard up against the underside of adjacent floorboards still in position.

2 Nail the board to the batten.

ALTERNATIVELY, if you have old ceilings, it may be wise to screw the boards down. Vibration from heavy hammering can cause ceiling damage. Screws are also useful if access may be needed to pipes or cables in future.

Repairing a damaged floor

Floorboards may be so badly damaged that they have to be removed (page 33) and replaced with fresh ones.

The new floorboards should be exactly the same thickness and width as the old ones. Modern floorboards are usually 4in (100mm) wide and ¾in (19mm) thick, but older ones can be much larger.

You may find it impossible to buy wood of exactly the right thickness (width should be easier to match). If the floor is to be sanded (page 38) it will not matter too much if the new boards are slightly thicker than the existing ones. A heavy-duty floor sander will easily remove the excess thickness.

In all other cases use slightly thinner timber and raise it by laying scraps of hardboard or plywood on the joists, holding them in place with panel pins and nailing the board on top.

If you are replacing only one or two boards, buy square-edged floorboards.

If you have a floor made of tongued-and-grooved boards, and several of them side by side are defective, buy new boards of the same type.

However, do not confuse floorboards with the tongued-and-grooved cladding sold for decorative use on walls and ceilings. It is a much lighter material and not suitable for flooring.

You will need

Tools Saw; hammer; perhaps a chisel; perhaps an electric drill and ₁/₁₆in (2mm) twist bit.
Materials Floorboards; 2in (50mm) or 3in (75mm) floorboard nails; perhaps scraps of hardboard or plywood and panel pins.

LAYING SQUARE-EDGED BOARDS

1 Cut the timber to the same length as the old boards.

2 Lay the new boards in place and nail them to each joist with floorboard nails.

LAYING TONGUED-AND-GROOVED BOARDS

1 Cut the first board to length, and shave off its tongue with a chisel or plane.

3 Cut the second board to length, lay it on the joists and tap it into place so that its tongue locates in

2 Lay it in position, butting its former tongued edge to the groove edge of an existing board. This groove will be filled with the tongue of the old board, which you have removed.

the groove of the first new board. Continue with the other boards.

4 When you come to the final board, you will probably have to shave off its tongue, as it will be too difficult to manoeuvre into place with the tongue attached.
ALTERNATIVELY there is a dodge that sometimes works. Shave off the underside of the groove of the second to last board. It may be possible to tap the last board into place with tongue intact.

5 Fix the boards to the joists with floorboard nails. You will be able to see the positions of the joists from the lines of nails in the existing floorboards.

6 If nails have to be driven in near the end of a board, first drill pilot holes smaller than the nails to avoid splitting the wood.

Replacing a floor with chipboard

If a floor is beyond repair, it can be replaced with chipboard more cheaply than with softwood floorboards.

Flooring-grade chipboard is sold in two thicknesses — ¾in (19mm) and ⅞in (22mm). If the centres of your joists are no farther apart than 18in (460mm), use ¾in (19mm) sheets.

The most common sheet sizes are 8ft × 4ft (2440mm × 1220mm) and 8ft × 2ft (2440mm × 600mm). As chipboard is heavy, use the smallest sheets available, unless you have got a friend to help you.

Flooring chipboard can be bought with either tongued-and-grooved edges — for simpler installation — or with square edges for a saving in cost.

Fix the sheets to the joists with No.10 gauge annular ring nails. Use 2¼in (55mm) nails for ¾in (19mm) sheets and 2½in (60mm) for ⅞in (22mm) sheets.

Before starting the job, find the position of the joists in the floor. The floorboard nails should reveal them, but it is advisable to take up a board to confirm.

Work out the thickness of the

sheets to suit the joist spacing, and the number you will need.

You must be ready to receive the boards when they are delivered; bad storage can distort them. Lay them flat in a pile inside the house. At least 24 hours before you begin work, loose-lay them in the room where they are to be laid so they can adjust to the moisture content.

HELPFUL TIPS

If access may be needed in future to a cable junction or central heating pipe, fix the sheet above it with screws, which are much easier to remove than nails.

If you are flooring an upstairs room or loft, and are worried that the ceiling below is weak, drill pilot holes in the chipboard for the nails. This will avoid unnecessary vibration when you hammer them in.

You will need

Tools Circular saw, panel saw or flooring saw; hammer; brush for

---

A WARNING BEFORE YOU START

The wall on one side of the room may be a hollow partition erected after the floor was installed. It is likely to cover the top of a joist. If so, you must nail a length of 2in (50mm) square timber to the side of the joist to provide a fixing point for the chipboard.

If the partition wall has been built between joists, no fixing point for the chipboard will be available and a new joist would

have to be installed. This is a job for a builder.

Before you start work, you can see the position of the joists by the rows of nails in the floorboards. Joists are usually spaced at regular intervals, so you will be able to judge whether the partition lies on top of one. If it does not, it may be wise not to proceed – or to get a new joist put in before you lay the chipboard.

---

applying adhesive; rag. Perhaps a pencil.
Materials Chipboard; annular ring nails; lengths of 2in (50mm) square timber; 3in (75mm) oval nails; PVA wood adhesive.

1 Start by taking up enough floorboards to give space for the first row of chipboard.

2 If there is not enough space between skirting board and joist to push in the chipboard, the skirting board will have to be removed from the wall.

3 Begin laying the chipboard in one corner.

4 A gap of ⅜in (10mm) must be left around the edge of the room to allow the chipboard to expand in damp weather. If you have removed the skirting, you can see that the correct gap is maintained as you lay the chipboard.

Otherwise push the sheet of chipboard against the wall under the skirting board, draw a pencil line where it meets the skirting and then pull it away by the correct distance.

SQUARE-EDGED SHEETS

1 Lay square-edged sheets with the long edge parallel to the joists. They must be supported on every edge, so the long sides should rest on the centre of a joist, and the ends should rest on a nogging.

2 Make the nogging from a piece of 2in (50mm) square-section wood placed between the joists and fixed with 3in (75mm) oval nails driven down at an angle through the nogging and into the joist.

3 If the width of the sheets does not suit your joists, cut them to fit. However, if this involves too much waste it may be a better idea to use tongued-and-grooved sheets which are laid across the joists and so do not have to be cut to width.

4 Nail the sheets at 12in (300mm) intervals all the way round, putting the nails ⅜in (10mm) in from the edge. On intermediate joists put nails 24in (610mm) apart.

TONGUE-AND-GROOVE SHEETS

1 Position tongued-and-grooved sheets with the long edge across the joists and nail them down. Drive in four nails to each joist, one ⅜in (10mm) from each edge and the others at equal distances.

2 The sheet must be supported at the ends, so saw off any overhang close to the side of the joist.

3 Nail a 2in (50mm) square-section batten to the side of the joist, flush with the top, and fix the next board to it.

COMPLETING THE JOB

Smear the meeting edges of all boards with PVA wood adhesive, then push them firmly together. The adhesive will prevent the floor from squeaking.

Wipe off any glue from the surface with a damp cloth.

If you need to hammer tongued-and-grooved sheets together, use a block of wood to protect the edge from damage.

When you come to the end of a row, cut the sheet to fit.

Use the offcut to begin the next row so that the joins do not co-incide.

Finally, replace the skirting, if you have removed it.

Preparing a wooden floor to lay a covering

Most people know that preparation is needed before they paint a room or hang wallpaper, but tend to think that a floor covering can go down on any old surface.

In fact, preparation is probably more important for floor laying than any other decorative process.

Vinyl or cork flooring will show any ridges in the sub-floor, and will wear unevenly. Even carpet will wear more quickly on the ridges.

Material laid on a properly prepared floor will look far better and will last longer.

Is the structure right?

First, make sure that the floor is in good structural condition.

If it feels unstable as you walk across it, there may be a defective joist, and you should call in a builder. If there is a feeling of sponginess, there could be an outbreak of woodworm or rot below the surface. Take up a board and check, and treat or replace as necessary.

Any damp in the floor must be cured or it will attack the new covering.

Loose boards must be fixed, and badly damaged boards replaced.

Removing old tacks

Most floors are already perfectly sound, but there may be tacks left behind from a previous covering.

Prise them up with a claw hammer, pincers or tack lifter. When using a hammer, put a piece of card or thin wood under its head to protect the floor.

The best tool, however, is the tack lifter. It has a handle and blade rather like a screwdriver, but the blade tip is wider, slightly curved and has a V cut. You slip the V under the head of a tack and give a twist of the handle.

The perfect surface

Now you can create a perfect surface for any sort of covering by lining the floor with hardboard.

This may seem like unnecessary bother and expense. But it is not difficult and does not add much to the overall cost. And it ensures an excellent result.

Hardboard will level off boards that are curling at the edges; it will cover small gaps between boards, and even mask minor damage. It also covers old stains and polishes.

LINING A WOOD FLOOR WITH HARDBOARD

Use ⅛in (3mm) thick hardboard for lining a floor. The largest sheets are cumbersome, so buy boards 4ft (1220mm) square, 3ft (915mm) square, or 4ft × 2ft (1220mm × 610mm).

Lay the hardboard with the mesh side up. This forms a better key for adhesives than the smooth side. And when you nail down the sheets the nail heads will sink below the mesh and not create pimple marks in the final floor covering.

The fixing is best done with annular nails – they have ringed shafts for extra grip. Use nails ¾in (19mm) long so that they will not burst through the floorboards with the risk of causing damage to cables or pipes.

After laying the boards, leave them at least overnight before laying the floor covering.

You will need

Tools Hammer; panel saw; large paintbrush; measuring jug; bowl or paint kettle.

Materials Sheets of hardboard ⅛in (3mm) thick; water; ¾in (19mm) annular nails – probably about ½lb (¼ kilo).

1 The boards must be given a moisture content suitable for the room – a process known as conditioning. Otherwise they may become distorted. Brush ¾ pint (½ litre) of water into the mesh side

Preparing a wooden floor to lay a covering (continued)

of 4ft (1220mm) square boards, and leave them stacked mesh to mesh perfectly flat on the floor of the room they will occupy for 48 hours (not much more or less) before laying.

They will adjust gradually to the humidity of the room, and dry out further when nailed down, tightening up like a drum skin to form a perfect surface for the final floor covering.

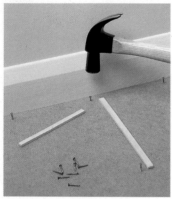

2 Begin laying the boards in a corner of the room, and start nailing along one edge of a sheet, ½in (13mm) in from the edge.

Work sideways and forwards, pyramid fashion (see the diagram). The nails should be 6in (150mm) apart along the edges of the board and 9in (230mm) apart in the middle of the board.

It helps to cut pieces of wood the appropriate length, and use them

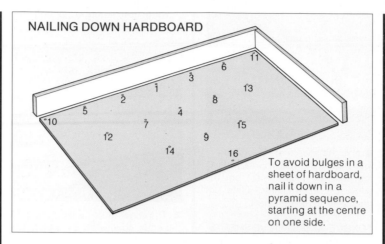

NAILING DOWN HARDBOARD

To avoid bulges in a sheet of hardboard, nail it down in a pyramid sequence, starting at the centre on one side.

as guides to get the nails correctly spaced out.

3 Butt the second board firmly against the first, and begin nailing along the meeting edge.

4 Continue in this way until at the end of the row you will have to cut a board to fit.

You do not need to cut the boards to a perfect fit to the skirting board. Gaps up to ¼in (6mm) do not

matter. They would be covered anyway by tiles or the gripper rod that holds a carpet.

Use the offcut from the previous board to start the next row. This not only avoids waste, but also prevents the joins from lining up across the room.

5 When you reach the end of the room you will have to cut each sheet in the final row to width to fit the remaining space.

HARDBOARD AS A FINAL FLOOR COVERING

Hardboard is an attractive floor covering in its own right – ideal for young couples starting off in a first home that has poor floorboards.

For this use, lay the hardboard smooth side up.

Oil-tempered hardboard is more durable than the standard type. Buy ⅛in (3mm) thick sheets, 3ft (915mm) square or 2ft (610mm) square and treat them like large tiles (page 39), beginning in the middle of the room and working towards the edges.

If you cannot get square sheets, buy 4ft × 2ft (1220mm × 610mm) sheets and ask the supplier to cut them in half.

After they have been laid, apply two or three coats of flooring-grade varnish. Rub on the first with a lint-free rag to spread it. The floor can be given fresh coats as it shows scuff marks.

Preparing a solid floor to lay a covering

A direct-to-earth floor can suffer from three faults that make it unsuitable for a floor covering to be laid. It can be damp; a concrete floor can suffer from a condition called 'dusting'; or the floor could be uneven.

Is the floor damp?

If a floor is damp there is no point in laying a covering. The moisture will eventually destroy the covering itself and any adhesive that was used to hold it down.

Damp in a floor is not always obvious, but if a direct-to-earth floor was laid before the Second World War it is unlikely to have a damp-proof membrane, and will have to be treated.

A cure for 'dusting'

A concrete floor may suffer from a condition known as dusting, in which dust continually forms on the surface, no matter how often you sweep it.

This can be cured by putting on a concrete-floor sealer sold by builders' merchants. Apply it following

the manufacturer's instructions. Alternatively, you can use diluted PVA adhesive.

LEVELLING A SOLID FLOOR

A solid floor with fairly small holes or ridges can be evened out with a floor-levelling compound.

A water-based compound is the easiest to apply, and can be used on terrazzo and quarry tiles, as well as on concrete.

You will need

Tools Bucket; scrubbing brush; steel float; perhaps a trowel.
Materials Water-based levelling compound; sugar soap; water; perhaps sand-and-cement mix and PVA adhesive.

1 Clean the floor by scrubbing with a solution of sugar soap in water. Rinse and allow the floor to dry thoroughly.

2 Any holes deeper than 3/16in (5mm) must first be filled with a sand-and-cement mix; bags of mortar to which you merely add water are ideal.

To ensure a good bond, first brush a priming coat of PVA adhesive on the patch to be filled, and add a little of it to the mortar. Trowel the surface of the mortar patch as smooth as possible.

3 Fill small dents with a little levelling compound, and allow it to dry thoroughly before applying the main coat. Dampen – but do not saturate – the floor before spreading the water-based compound.

4 In a bucket, mix the powder with water to form a slurry. Pour it onto the floor, and smooth with a steel float. Work on a fairly small area of floor at a time; if too much com-

pound is mixed it will stiffen up after about a quarter of an hour.

5 Trowel the compound as flat as you can. The trowelling marks will disappear as it dries out. You can usually walk on the floor two hours after the compound has been laid. It will be ready to receive the floor covering in eight to ten hours.

> **HELPFUL TIP**
> If you do not obtain a good, smooth finish after trowelling the levelling compound, sprinkle water on the surface and try again.

CHOOSING FLOORINGS FOR DIFFERENT PARTS OF THE HOUSE

TYPE OF FINISH		PLUS-POINTS	DRAWBACKS	HOW TO CARE FOR IT
Varnished hardboard Pleasantly coloured surface, achieved by laying hardboard with the smooth surface uppermost, and coating with flooring-grade varnish.		Cheap and simple to do yourself. Durable surface for children's rooms. Oil-tempered grade wears best.	Less sympathetic 'feel' than wood. Some people also think it looks a bit makeshift.	Sweep or vacuum clean frequently to remove grit. Wash with damp mop and mild detergent solution. Lightly sand worn areas and re-varnish when necessary.
Sanded and varnished floorboards Suitable finish for boards in good condition and without gaps. The floor is sanded with a heavy-duty sanding machine that can be hired for a day or weekend.		Cheap, and fairly simple to do yourself. An attractive surface that can be covered with scatter rugs.	Sanding a floor is noisy and dusty work. The finished surface is noisy underfoot. Can be draughty on a ground floor if boards are not tongued-and-grooved.	Sweep or vacuum clean frequently to remove grit which can scratch the surface. Wipe up spillages with damp cloth. Polish regularly. Lightly sand worn areas and re-varnish. Rugs advisable to reduce scuffing.
Vinyl tiles Huge range of colours, patterns and price. Available in imitation ceramic, wood or stone as well as cheaper smooth vinyl.	Plain Patterned	Hygienic, easily cleaned. Resistant to spillages. Good for kitchens, bathrooms, and perhaps nurseries.	Cold clinical 'feel'. Smooth vinyl is slippery when wet. Cushion-backed types – available in a limited colour range – are warmer, safer and quieter.	As for sheet vinyl (below), but beware of using too much water when you wash; it could get under the joins.
Cork tiles Pleasantly coloured natural material, available in various finishes, depending on price. Sold as strips as well as squares.		More sympathetic and warmer material than vinyl. Easily cleaned when varnished or bought factory sealed. PVC-coated cork best but more expensive.	Can become worn in heavy traffic areas, unless PVC coated.	Vacuum clean or sweep regularly to remove surface dirt, and wash with solution of mild detergent. Avoid swamping with water, and do not use abrasive cleaners.
Ceramic tiles The range runs from conventional square quarry tiles to special-purpose ceramics of various shapes. Can be obtained with anti-slip surface.	Quarries Provençal	Long lasting, easily cleaned and highly resistant to stains and spillages. Wide choice of patterns and colours.	Very expensive. Timber sub-floor needs strengthening before laying. Noisy underfoot. Cold if walked on in bare feet. Crockery breaks if dropped on it.	Remove surface grit by sweeping or vacuum cleaning, then wash with non-abrasive detergent in water. Keep water to minimum to prevent seepage under tiles. Scrub stubborn marks, and ingrained dirt round edges of tiles.
Sheet vinyl Two main types available. Smooth vinyl is cheaper; cushioned vinyl is more pleasant underfoot. Wide range of patterns and colours.	 Smooth Cushioned	Hygienic, easily cleaned. Resistant to spillages. Inexpensive flooring for kitchens, bathrooms and perhaps nurseries.	Cold, clinical 'feel'. Smooth vinyl slippery when wet. Cushion-backed varieties are warmer, safer and quieter underfoot than ordinary vinyls.	Vacuum clean or sweep frequently in a kitchen to remove grit, which can scratch. Wash weekly with mop and detergent solution. Apply floor polish when first laid: re-polish regularly. Scuff marks can be removed by gentle rubbing with fine steel wool lubricated with white spirit. Take care not to rub through top surface. Follow with local re-polish.
Carpet Wide range of colour and price. Available as fitted carpet, carpet squares or carpet tiles.		Gives feeling of warmth and luxurious comfort. Graded according to use – from heavily used stairs to under-used spare bedrooms.	Good quality carpet is expensive. Spillages troublesome.	Vacuums clean frequently to remove grit which can harm fibres. Remove stains with proprietary cleaner. Or shampoo the carpet – powered shampoo machines can be hired. Carpet tiles can be rearranged to even out wear.
Wood strip and mosaic Thick wood strip is laid in place of a damaged floor; thin wood strip goes over an existing floor. Mosaic consists of small pieces laid in patterns.	Wood strip Wood mosaic	Luxurious and long-lasting in living rooms, dining rooms and halls.	Expensive. Not very resistant to spillages, so not suitable for bathrooms or kitchens. Noisy underfoot.	Remove surface dirt with vacuum cleaner to minimise scratching. Varnished floors can be wiped over with damp cloth. Waxed floors need repeated re-polishing – an electric polisher makes this easier. Best protected with rugs.

Sanding and varnishing a wooden floor

An attractive floor can be created cheaply by sanding floorboards with a heavy-duty sander, and applying a flooring-grade varnish. Rugs can be laid where people walk most often.

Sanding a floor is a fairly simple job, but it is hard work and usually creates a lot of dust, so wear a face mask (they can be bought in DIY shops). Otherwise the dust will get into your lungs and nose.

Sanding is also extremely noisy, so do it at a time that is least likely to disturb the neighbours, and wear earmuffs, which can also be bought in DIY shops.

The sanding is done with a floor sanding machine, which uses abrasive belts, and an edging sander. They can be hired from a tool hire company – found in *Yellow Pages* under Hire Services, Tools and Equipment. A weekend's hire should be sufficient.

There are various grades of sanding belt. Begin with coarse (you can sometimes skip this if the boards are not in bad condition), then follow with medium, and finish off with fine.

New and damaged boards
On fairly new boards that have not been stained or become too dirty, sanding may not be necessary before applying the varnish. Get rid of surface dirt by scrubbing with detergent in hot water. Pay particular attention to removing dirt from nail holes. When the floor has dried, inspect it to see if it is clean enough.

Any damaged boards will have to be replaced (page 36), but new boards are unlikely to match exactly the colour of the old. For a first-class job, replace a defective board in a prominent position with an existing board from a less obvious spot (one that will be hidden by furniture or a rug, for example). This board can be replaced with a new one.

A sealed floor should be swept regularly, as floor dust contains abrasive grit that scratches the surface. Spillages can be wiped up with a damp cloth. The seal will last longer if it is polished thoroughly once a year, with a light polishing once a month.

If the seal starts to show signs of wear in some areas, lightly sand the affected places by hand, using fine abrasive paper, dust off and apply one new coat of varnish.

You will need
Tools Face mask; nail punch and claw hammer; floor sanding machine; earmuffs; sanding belts (coarse, medium and fine); edging sander; 3in (75mm) paintbrush; fine steel wool (optional).
Materials Flooring-grade varnish (gloss, satin or matt).

HELPFUL TIP
When a floor sander is switched on, the sanding belt starts to move, but does not come into contact with the floor until you operate a lever. Never let a moving belt touch the floor while the machine is stationary, or it will gouge holes in the wood. The moment the belt starts to bite into the wood – and there will be enough noise to indicate this – make sure the machine moves forwards. It will begin to do so anyway, but inexperienced people tend to hold it back.

1 First, punch in all the nails in the floor, otherwise they will tear the sanding belts.

Any tacks left from previous floor coverings should also be removed.

2 If there are any traces of old polish remove them with steel wool dipped in white spirit. Otherwise the polish will clog up the sanding belt. Wear protective gloves.

3 Start at the edge of the room with your back against the wall. Keep the sander slightly away from the skirting board at the side, otherwise you may damage it.

4 It is normal to work along the length of the boards, as sanding across them causes scratches. But if the boards curl up at the edges, make the first runs diagonally across them with a coarse belt. Finish with medium and fine belts along the length of the boards.

5 On a floor where not very much stripping is needed, let the machine go forwards at a slow steady pace to the far end of the room, lifting up the belt before it cuts into the skirting board.

6 Lower it again, and with the belt still moving draw it slowly backwards to the starting point. Lift the belt once more.

On very dirty boards, work backwards and forwards continually over a stretch of about a yard of floor, gradually extending this as the boards become clean.

7 When the strip looks clean, move on to the next one, and continue to the end of the room. Raise the belt as you change direction, otherwise it may damage the boards.

8 You will have started each run about a yard out from the wall behind you. When you have covered the room, turn the machine round, and deal with that area.

SANDING THE EDGES

Eventually, you will be left with a narrow border all round the room that the sander cannot reach. This must be stripped with an edging sander. Do not try to use a disc on an electric drill; it is not powerful enough. The edging tool is a much more powerful disc sander.

1 Use the edging sander all round the edges of the room, taking care

not to damage the paint on the skirting boards.

2 When the sanding is finished, sweep up the floor to get rid of all the wood dust. Do not damp down the floor as the water may leave marks.

3 Finally, go over the floor with a clean, dry, lint-free cloth – shaking it frequently outdoors – to get rid of the last particles.

APPLYING THE VARNISH

To be certain that the floor is ready for sealing, apply a little varnish in an inconspicuous spot and leave it overnight. Next morning rub it with the edge of a coin. If a white powder results, the seal has not 'taken' properly. This means the preparation has not been thorough enough, and more sanding is needed.

1 If the floor is ready, apply the seal according to the instructions on the tin.

2 For a perfect finish, rub down the floor with fine steel wool to get rid of dust specks before applying the final coat.

SANDING PARQUET

Parquet (also called woodblock) and wood mosaic floors can also be sanded. These floors are usually laid in patterns, so the grain lies in two directions. Consequently the floor has to be sanded twice, the second direction at right angles to the first.

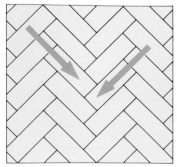

A final sanding with a very fine belt – also in two directions – is needed to remove all scratch marks.

Laying vinyl or cork tiles

Vinyl and cork tiles take longer to lay than sheet material, but they have many advantages. They are less cumbersome to handle; there is less wastage in cutting around awkward obstacles like chimney breasts; they are easier to cut to fit; and, if you make a mistake, ruining one tile is not nearly as serious as damaging a large sheet.

Vinyl tiles are available in a great range of colours, styles and price – from imitation slate to conventional smooth vinyl.

Cork tiles have different surface finishes according to price. The finishes range from transparent PVC coating to no coating at all. Uncoated cork needs to be finished with at least three coats of flooring-grade varnish.

To calculate the number of tiles you need, measure the room and multiply the width by the length to give the area. If the room has a bay or chimney breast, calculate it separately and add or subtract it from the main area.

Each pack of tiles gives the area it will cover, usually a square yard or square metre. Divide the area of the room by the area a pack will cover. The answer – rounded up to the nearest whole number – is the number of packs you need to buy.

Vinyl and cork tiles are both laid in the same way, using the adhesive recommended by the manufacturer. Some vinyl tiles are self-adhesive.

You will need
Tools Tape measure; string longer than the room; chalk; adhesive spreader; rag; pencil; trimming knife; perhaps some scrap hardboard and a metal straight-edge.
Materials Tiles; adhesive (if tiles are not self-adhesive); perhaps white spirit for cleaning up adhesive.

WHERE TO START LAYING

Tile laying always begins in the middle of the room.

Finding the centre point
Measure two opposite walls and mark their centres. Snap a chalk line between these points.

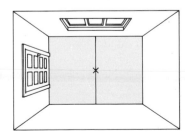

Measure the line and mark its centre. That is the middle of the room.

If the room has a chimney breast, snap the chalk line parallel to that wall.

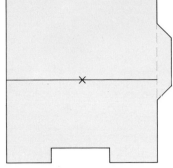

If the room also has a bay, square it off with a line between the ends of the bay and measure along this false wall line.

If the room is even more irregular in shape, choose one wall as the base wall. Snap a chalk line parallel to it, about 3in (75mm) away, and mark its centre point.

Draw a short chalk line at right angles to this base line. To obtain the right angle, use a few tiles as a guide.

Extend this line the full length of the room by snapping a chalk line. Measure this line and mark the centre.

Marking the cross-line

Once the main chalk line has been laid, a second line needs to be drawn across it at right angles. To do this, place two tiles on the floor, each with one side along the centre line and one corner on the centre point. Then snap a chalk line across the room, passing through the centre point and following the edge of the tiles.

PLACING THE KEY TILE

You must now decide the position of the first (or key) tile, which will determine the position of all other tiles in the room.

The last tile in each row all the way round the room will have to be cut to size. So site the key tile to ensure that this border of cut tiles is as neat as possible.

Ideally, all the tiles in the border should be equal in size, and at least a half tile width. Avoid very narrow slivers of tile, as they may not stick properly.

To determine the best position for the key tile, make a series of 'dry' test runs. Without using glue, or peeling off the backing of self-adhesive tiles, lay a row of tiles

SNAPPING A CHALK LINE

For many jobs, you need a line across the room. Rub chalk along a length of string or buy a chalk-line reel (right) which chalks the string for you. Tie one end to a nail in the floor and hold the other end at the far side of the room. Pull the string straight up and let go. It will mark a straight line on the floor.

Sometimes it is possible to lay tiles alongside a string stretched across the floor.

THE FOUR POSITIONS FOR LAYING THE KEY TILE

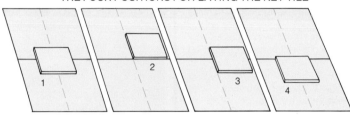

outwards from the centre to all edges of the room.

The key tile can be placed in any of several positions made up in the following ways:
1 Centrally on the middle point of the room.
2 In an angle formed by the two chalk lines.
3 Centrally on the main chalk line, and on one side of the line that crosses it.
4 Centrally on the crossing line, and on one side of the main one.

CENTRING THE TILES ON A FEATURE

1 Some rooms have a dominant feature such as a fireplace, or bay window. To get an attractive result, adjust the appropriate base line – keeping it parallel to the original line – to ensure that the tiles are centred on the feature.

Once again, ensure that you get the biggest possible cut tiles at the edges.

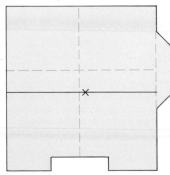

2 A room may have two features. In that case adjust both base lines, so the tiles can be centred on both features.

It is not possible to centre tiles on more than two features, except by accident.

HELPFUL TIP
Sometimes the twin aims of centring the tiles on one or two features, and getting tiles of at least half width round the edges, will conflict.

In that case, go for correct centring.

STICKING DOWN THE TILES

1 Once you have found the best arrangement of tiles, hold the key tile accurately in place, and draw a square around it with a pencil.

2 Give the floor a final dust over, then remove the backing if the tile is self-adhesive. Alternatively, spread a tile-size patch of adhesive on the floor with a plastic spreader.

3 Place one edge of the tile along one edge of the square, and roll it down flat. If you find it is not fitting exactly, pull it up immediately and start again.

HELPFUL TIP
If the tiles have any decorative markings, lay them with the lines of adjacent tiles at right angles to each other.

Laying vinyl or cork tiles (continued)

FIRE HAZARD WITH ADHESIVES

Solvent (or spirit) based adhesives are highly flammable, and give off volatile fumes which may ignite if they come in contact with a naked flame.

When laying a floor with a solvent-based adhesive, open all the windows and doors in the room to get maximum ventilation. Make sure that any pilot lights in the room are turned off, including the pilot lights in a gas stove, gas fire or a central-heating boiler.

Fumes penetrate clothing and remain there for some time. So do not go into a room with a fire or heater to warm yourself in the middle of a job. When you have finished, remove your clothes and hang them up outdoors.

Water-based adhesives are not flammable, however they take longer to dry, which slows a job down in cold weather.

4 With the first tile stuck down, work outwards from it to the walls. Where adhesive has to be spread on the floor, spread a square yard at a time.

The tiles must be positioned very accurately, each one butted up squarely to its neighbour. Take great care that the joins create a straight line, or you will need to trim tiles later to avoid gaps.

5 If any adhesive oozes up through the joins, wipe it up immediately, using a cloth damped with either water or white spirit depending on the manufacturer's instructions.

CUTTING TILES TO FIT THE BORDER

The cut tiles around the edge can be dealt with in two ways. Method 1 is likely to give the better result if adhesive is being used, but Method 2 will have to be used in small areas such as lavatories and narrow corridors.

Method 1

Lay all the tiles except for a border of one whole tile and one part tile all the way round the room.

1 Place the tile to be cut against the last one in the row, and place another tile on top of it, pressed against the wall.

2 Draw a pencil line across the face of the tile to be cut. With some vinyl and cork tiles you do not even need to draw a line; use a knife instead of a pencil, then snap the tile in two.

3 If the tile will not break, cut it on a piece of scrap hardboard, using a metal straight-edge as a guide.

4 The two tiles now change places with the part tile against the wall. Leave the whole and part tile on the end of the row until you have cut the entire border, and are ready to stick it all at once.

Method 2

With this method, you lay all the whole tiles, then deal with the border of part tiles. The disadvantage of the method is that it leaves only a narrow band of floor which may not get adequately covered with glue.

1 Place the tile to be cut squarely on the last tile in the row. Put a third on top, pressed against the wall.

2 Draw a pencil line across the face of the tile to be cut. With some vinyl and cork tiles you do not even need to draw a line; use a knife instead of a pencil, then snap the tile in two.

3 If the tile will not break, cut it on a piece of scrap hardboard, using a metal straight-edge as a guide.

4 The part of the cut tile closer to the centre of the room will fit the empty space perfectly. Leave the cut tile on the end of the row and go on to cut all the other border tiles.

Corner tiles Tiles in a corner will have to be cut to length as well as width, using the same method.

In doorways Around a doorway architrave, you will have to draw three or four lines to create the correct pattern.

CUTTING ROUND A CURVE

In bathrooms and kitchens you may have to cut round an irregular shaped object; a washbasin, for example.

1 To determine the shape of the tiles round the washbasin pedestal, take a sheet of paper a bit larger than a tile. Place it over the area the cut tile will occupy, and fold it along the line of the adjacent tiles, and the pedestal.

You may have to make cuts inwards in the paper if the obstruction is very irregular.

2 Place the completed template on the tile, mark round it, and cut.

CUTTING ROUND A PIPE

A pipe rising from the floor will normally be at the edge of a room, so cut a tile to fit the border.

1 Place the cut tile square on the last whole tile and push it against the pipe. Make a pencil mark where it touches.

2 Put the cut tile against the wall and push it against the pipe. Make another mark where it touches.

3 With a try square, draw a line across the tile from the mark on the side. Then put the try square on the uncut long edge and draw a line through the other mark. (Do not put the try square on the cut edge as it will not be square.)

4 Where the lines cross is the point where the pipe will go. Bore a hole with a brace and bit (with the tile on a piece of scrap wood), or draw round a coin of the appropriate size, and cut with a knife.

5 Make a knife cut from the hole to the wall edge of the tile, and ease it into position.

TILES ON THE DIAGONAL

1 To lay tiles in a diagonal pattern, first make a scriber from a thin piece of batten about 3ft (910mm) long with a nail in each end. A length of softwood or plywood would be ideal. Drill pilot holes, smaller than the diameter of the nails, to avoid splitting the wood.

2 Mark the cross-lines in the middle of the room in the normal way. (See *Where to start laying*, page 39.)

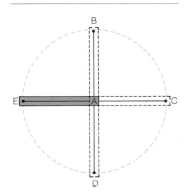

3 Put one nail of the scriber on the point where the lines cross (A), and mark four points on the cross-lines – at B, C, D and E.

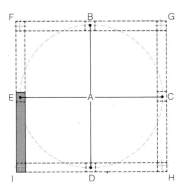

4 Put one nail of your scriber on B and scribe arcs at F and G. Move the scriber to C and scribe arcs at G and H. From D make arcs at H and I, and from E at I and F.

5 Snap diagonal chalk lines on the floor through the points where the arcs meet at G and I and at F and H.

must be the same as the distance across the tiles from corner to corner.

6 Lay out rows of unglued tiles along the diagonal lines to get the largest cut tiles round the border.

7 Glue down all the whole tiles.

Border tiles: Method 1
To cut the border tiles, first make a template.

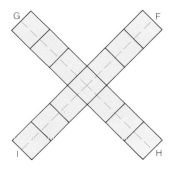

1 Cut a piece of hardboard or card with two opposite edges parallel. The distance between these edges

2 Place the tile to be cut on the whole tile nearest to the wall.

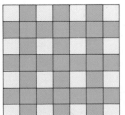

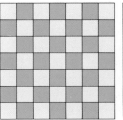

3 Place one parallel edge of your template against the skirting board, and draw or cut along the opposite edge across the face of the tile.

The piece of tile farthest from the skirting board will now fit the empty space.

Border tiles: Method 2
Diagonal tiles can also be finished off with a border of part tiles laid square to the wall.

1 When you are setting out the tiles initially, place the first tile in the centre of the room to ensure a border wider than half a tile.

2 Lay all the whole tiles.

3 Cut some tiles in half from corner to corner and lay them to square off the diagonal pattern.

4 Finally, cut the border tiles square to the wall, measuring each one individually, but sticking them down all at the same time.

HOW TO LIFT A DAMAGED VINYL TILE
To remove a damaged vinyl tile without disturbing the rest of the floor, put a piece of aluminium kitchen foil over it and press with a hot iron.

Wait until the heat penetrates the tile (this will take longer on concrete than wood), then lever up a corner with a filling knife or wallpaper stripper, and pull the tile away.

Lift the remaining adhesive with a filling knife heated with a blow torch or hot-air gun, or over a gas stove.

Lay a new tile with fresh adhesive. Do not slide it in place, or adhesive may be forced up at the edges.

A larger area can be softened with a hot-air gun. The technique will not work on cork tiles, which insulate too effectively against the heat.

PATTERNS IN TILES
You can devise your own floor patterns by combining tiles of two, or even more, colours. The simplest is the 'chessboard' pattern created by using alternative dark and light colours. But many others are possible.

To guard against mistakes in laying the floor, draw a scale plan of the pattern on paper.

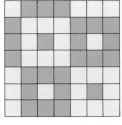

Laying ceramic tiles

Ceramic tiles and quarry tiles are much heavier than other types of floor covering. This is not a problem on direct-to-earth or suspended concrete floors, but a timber floor should be strengthened first.

HELPFUL TIP
Tiles must not be walked on for 24 hours after laying. As few homes can afford to have a kitchen or bathroom out of action for so long, tile only part of the floor at one time.

Special quick-set adhesive is also available for awkward situations.

Strengthening a timber floor
Overlay the existing floor with ½in (13mm) thick exterior grade plywood. This grade of plywood will be capable of standing up to the moisture in the adhesive.

The plywood is laid in the same way as hardboard (page 35) but fix it with screws, not nails, at 12in (300mm) intervals. Use 1in (25mm) No.8 screws countersunk below the surface of the plywood.

Exterior grade plywood of this thickness is expensive, and that may make you decide to choose other forms of floor covering on a suspended timber floor.

Preparing a solid floor
Concrete floors should be thoroughly cleaned, using household detergent in water, and levelled if necessary (page 36).

Ceramic tiles can be laid on old quarry and vinyl tiles, provided these are stuck down properly, but

vinyl needs to be treated first with a special primer, available from the shop that supplies the ceramic tiles.

Calculating the quantity
To estimate the number of tiles, measure the room and multiply the width by the length to give the area. If the room has a bay or chimney breast, calculate it separately and add or subtract it from the main area.

Each pack of tiles gives the area they will cover. Divide the area of the room by the area a pack will cover. The answer – rounded up to the next whole number – is the number of packs you need.

Cutter for floor tiles
Ceramic floor tiles are at least ¼in (6mm) thick, compared to the 5/32in (4mm) thickness of the ceramic wall

tiles sold for DIY use, so you will need a heavy-duty cutter. The tool can be bought or hired. Power-driven tile saws can also be hired. (See *Yellow Pages* under Hire Services – Tools and Equipment.)

PUTTING DOWN THE TILES

You will need
Tools Bucket; trowel; notched spreader; rags; tile spacers or ¼in (6mm) dowel; tile cutter.
Materials Tiles; adhesive (see *Fire warning*, page 40); grout.

1 Set out the tiles in the same way as for vinyl tiles (page 39).

2 Beginning at the centre of the room, pour adhesive on a square yard of floor and spread it evenly with the trowel.

Laying ceramic tiles (continued)

3 Go over it with the notched spreader. This creates a ribbed effect acting as a gauge to leave the right depth of adhesive.

4 Place the tiles in position one at a time, giving a slight twist. This ensures that the whole of the tile is in contact with the adhesive, and no air is trapped underneath.

5 Few ceramic floor tiles are self spacing, yet it is essential to space

them out evenly to get a good appearance. Plastic spacers ⅛in (3mm) wide are sold for this purpose. If you want to make a special feature of wide grouting, take some ¼in (6mm) dowel, cut it into small lengths and use them as spacer guides.

6 Wipe off any adhesive on the face of the tiles. Dampen a cloth with either white spirit or water, depending on the adhesive.

7 To avoid walking over the tiles in the 24 hours before the glue sets, work first on the part of the room farthest from the door. Always leave a passageway of bare floor to allow an exit.

8 Once you have laid all the whole tiles, leave them for 24 hours before laying the cut tiles around the edge of the room. The cut tiles can be laid

in either of the two methods shown on page 40.

9 Mark the face of the tile to be cut in pencil, place it on the tile cutter, and operate the cutter.

10 When all the glue has set, mix the grout into a paste and tip it on the tiles. Work it into the joins with the straight edge of the spreader.

11 Run one corner of the spreader along the joins to give a neat finish. Alternatively use a piece of dowel or the handle of a wooden spoon.

12 Clean off any surplus from the tiles with a damp cloth, then polish with a dry one. Leave the grout to harden for about an hour, then give a final wipe with a damp cloth. Do not put the floor into full use for 48 hours after grouting.

Laying carpet tiles

Carpet tiles are not firmly fixed to the floor – you can take them up and move them at any time. They can be rearranged to equalise wear, or removed while the skirting board is repainted, or lifted for cleaning.

The laying method varies slightly from make to make, so follow the manufacturer's instructions.

Because carpet tiles are not rigid like other tiles, it is not easy to butt them tightly together, and if you are not careful gaps will develop between them as the tiles bed down.

You can use a knee-kicker (page 48), with just hand rather than knee pressure, to push the tiles together.

Or you can improvise a substitute (see panel)

You will need

Tools Tape measure; string longer than the room; chalk; knee-kicker (or substitute); steel rule; craft knife.
Materials Carpet tiles; normal carpet adhesive; metal threshold (page 47).

1 If you begin laying the tiles against one wall, there is a danger that when you reach the far wall

only a narrow strip will be left to fill. Slivers of tile are not stable so start the job by snapping a chalk line down the centre of the room and setting out the tiles in the same way as for laying vinyl tiles.

2 Whatever the method of laying down, apply a carpet adhesive to the first tile in the centre of the room. This will ensure that it is not pushed out of place during the laying process – which would ruin the final effect.

3 Lay subsequent tiles with the pile running at right angles to one another. This gives a chequerboard effect, even though the same colour is used throughout. Some tiles have an arrow on the back to show the direction of the pile, but sometimes you have to 'feel' for the pile – the surface will be smooth when you run your hand across it with the pile, rough when your hand goes against.

ALTERNATIVELY, lay all the tiles with the pile running in the same direction to give the effect of a fitted carpet.

Do not mix the two methods.

4 Put the knee-kicker or improvised tool on top of a tile so that its teeth grip, then push the tile forwards into position.

5 When all the whole tiles have been laid, measure the border tiles for cutting by one of the methods described for cutting vinyl tiles on page 40.

6 Mark the cutting line on the face of the tile by making a nick with a craft knife on each edge. Turn the tile upside down, lay a steel rule across the two nicks, and cut with the knife. Take great care not to cut your fingers.

MAKING A TILE 'KICKER'

Cut a piece of 6in × 1in (150mm × 25mm) wood to 12in (300mm) long. Drill a hole in the centre ½in (13mm) deep and glue in a piece of broom handle. Drive a nail through the wood into the handle. Drive four nails through the front, projecting ⅛in (3mm) to act as teeth.

7 In a doorway, protect the edge of the tiles by fitting a metal threshold, of the kind used for normal carpet.

IF TILES SHIFT IN USE

Should movement dislodge any of the tiles in use – this can happen under chairs – lift the tile, and apply carpet adhesive to the backing.

Laying sheet vinyl in strips

Sheet vinyl is made in several widths, the most common being 2m, 3m, and 4m (about 6ft, 10ft and 13ft).

Covering a room with two or more 2m strips is the easiest technique as each strip is lighter and more manoeuvrable than a width that covers the entire room. But there will be a join which may detract from the appearance, and which could let water seep through when the floor is cleaned.

'Stay-flat' varieties of cushioned vinyl are the easiest of all to lay as they hug the floor and do not need to be glued. If you have to glue sheet vinyl, take care to follow the safety advice on page 40.

Before ordering the vinyl, decide how it will be set out. Ideally, it should run away from the window (or the main window if there is more than one). The joins will be less obvious than if the light strikes them at the side.

It is best to line the floor with hardboard (page 35) before laying the vinyl, but if you decide that your floor is in sufficiently good condition, lay the vinyl at right angles to the floorboards.

If these two recommendations conflict, it is more important that the material should run away from the window. When laying it parallel to the boards, make sure that an edge of the vinyl is not over a gap.

Avoid having a join running into a doorway; this is an area of heavy traffic, and scuffing could occur.

You will need

Tools Steel tape measure; soft pencil; string longer than the room; chalk; small block of wood, or compasses; a second piece of wood about 4in (100 mm) long; scissors or trimming knife; ruler; screwdriver; hammer.
Materials Vinyl to cover the floor; perhaps adhesive and notched spreader; metal cover strip and screws.

MARKING THE BASE LINE

1 Snap a chalk line (page 39) between the middle of the two walls that will be at the ends of the strips. This provides a base line to work from, as the walls will almost certainly be out of true.

2 If the first length of vinyl will cover the line, snap a second line parallel to the first where it can be seen.

3 Cut the first strip to length – the distance across the room plus 3in (75mm) for trimming.

4 Put it on the floor about 1in (25mm) away from the wall on the long side and parallel to the chalk line. Let each end ride up the wall by an equal amount.

SCRIBING THE WALL ON THE LONG SIDE

1 At two or three points, draw a pencil line across the floor and the vinyl. These are crosschecks that will allow you to bring the vinyl back to its original position later.

2 Find out where the gap between the wall on the long side and the vinyl is greatest. Cut a small block of wood slightly longer than that measurement. This will be used for scribing the wall to make the vinyl fit exactly.

Alternatively, use a pair of compasses and set them to the same measurement.

3 Place the wood against the wall, hold a pencil hard against it and move them along the wall, tracing its contours on the vinyl. If you are using compasses, place the point against the wall, and the pencil on the vinyl, keeping the compasses at right angles to the wall.

4 Cut the vinyl along the pencil line with scissors or knife.

5 Put the vinyl back in place – using the check marks for accurate positioning.

SCRIBING THE END WALLS

1 Check that the scribed edge is correctly positioned against the side wall, then draw a chalk line on the floor along the opposite edge. Make a crosscheck on the edge and the floor.

2 Pull the vinyl back from the crosscheck by the length of the second piece of wood.

HOW MUCH TO BUY

Measure the room at right angles to the direction of laying to decide how many strips you will need (As sheet vinyl is made in metric sizes, make your measurements in metric.) Measure right into any alcoves and to the halfway point under a door.

For every 2m, or portion of 2m, you will need one strip of 2m wide vinyl. So if the distance is 3.5m, you need two strips – 0.5m will be waste (in fact, a little less because of trimming).

Then measure in the other direction and multiply by the number of strips. If the length is 3.3m you will need 6.6m (2 × 3.3m), plus 75mm trimming allowance on each strip – a total of 6.75m. Since the shop probably sells to the nearest metre or half metre, you will have to order 7m. Some shops sell in metric widths but imperial lengths. So you may be able to buy to the nearest foot.

If there is a pattern you will also need an allowance for matching up. The exact amount will vary according to the pattern 'repeat', so give the shop your measurements and ask their advice.

Order the flooring well in advance. It can then be stood upright (still tied in a roll) for at least two days in the room where it will be laid in order to reach room temperature. In winter the room should be heated. The vinyl will then be flexible and easy to lay; cold vinyl tends to be rigid.

3 Keeping the outer edge of the vinyl on the chalk line, use the piece of wood and a pencil to trace the contours of the wall onto the vinyl sheet.

4 Cut to this line, then use chalk line and crosscheck to position the vinyl accurately, and it should fit against the end wall.

CUTTING THE SECOND STRIP

1 The second strip will almost certainly have to be cut to width. If the excess is more than about 10in (250mm) cut it back to that to give yourself a workable width. Make the cut on the wall side, not the side to be joined.

2 Put it on the floor with one edge touching the wall where the wall comes nearest to the first sheet. The other edge will be overlapping the first sheet; make sure that this overlap is exactly the same all the way along. Adjust it so that the pattern matches.

3 Cut it at each end, to leave the trimming allowance of 3in (75mm).

4 Make a pencil mark where the second sheet rests on the first. Lift up the second sheet and measure the amount of the overlap.

5 Place the vinyl flat on the floor again and use the ruler and pencil to scribe a line on the vinyl parallel to the wall, and the width of the overlap away from it.

6 Cut to this line.

7 Place the vinyl in position, and scribe the ends.

Laying sheet vinyl in strips (continued)

DEALING WITH DOORWAYS

1 Scribe the vinyl around the door frame and to a line under the door. If a threshold strip has already been laid, scribe up to it.

2 If no threshold strip exists, screw a metal cover strip over the vinyl and the covering beyond the door. If the floor beyond has no

covering, use metal lino edging.

CUTTING AROUND ALCOVES

1 Measure and cut the vinyl to fit the full depth of the alcove, plus the trimming allowance of 3in (75mm).

2 Put it on the floor and allow it to ride up the fireplace wall.

3 Make a cut parallel to the side of the chimney breast, leaving

enough for final trimming. Allow the material to lie on the alcove floor.

4 Cut off the excess material riding up the fireplace, leaving a trimming allowance of 3in (75mm).

5 Trim the edges in the normal way so that the vinyl fits the alcove, and around the chimney breast. If there is a working fireplace, trim the vinyl around the hearth.

STICKING DOWN VINYL

'Stay-flat' vinyl sheeting does not need to be stuck down to the floor, because it hugs the floor closely and does not shrink once it has been laid.

Other types should be glued immediately after laying. If left for any length of time – even overnight – they may shrink slightly and gaps could develop between the strips of vinyl and around the walls.

Use the adhesive supplied, or recommended, by the manufacturer of the sheet vinyl, and apply it to the floor with a notched spreader which can be obtained with the adhesive.

For ordinary vinyl the floor should be glued all over.

Cushioned vinyl needs only to be glued in a 2in (50mm) band around the room and along joins where sheets butt against each other.

Covering a small area with sheet vinyl

A very small room, such as a lavatory or pantry, can be covered by one piece of even the narrowest sheet vinyl. The best way of cutting it is to use a paper template.

You will need
Tools Enough stiff paper (such as paper underlay) to cover the floor; perhaps adhesive tape or stapler; pencil; drawing pins or weights; scissors or knife; block of wood 1½in (38mm) wide; pencil; ruler.
Materials Sheet vinyl; perhaps adhesive and spreader.

1 If the paper is not big enough to cover the room, fasten two pieces together with adhesive tape or staples, but draw a line across both at several points so you can check later that they have not moved out of position.

2 Put the paper on the floor with the edges folded underneath. Fix it in place with drawing pins. On a solid floor use weights.

3 To fit it around obstacles such as a lavatory or a pipe, cut the paper from the wall inwards.

4 When the paper is laid, use scissors or a knife to trim it all the way round the room so that its edge is about ½in (13mm) from the wall or skirting board. Trim it around obstacles as well.

5 Cut a small block of wood about 1½in (38mm) wide, and mark the width on it so there is no confusion later.

6 Put one edge against the wall and hold the pencil against the other edge. Move the block and pencil all the way around the room, tracing an outline of the room onto the paper.

7 Also trace around larger obstacles, such as the bottom of a wash basin.

8 If a pipe comes up through the floor, put a ruler against it on four opposite faces and draw a pencil line along the outside edge of the ruler to make a square.

CUTTING OUT THE VINYL

1 Lay a piece of the flooring material – right side up – on the floor of a larger room and put the template on top, fixing it in place with adhesive tape.

2 Put one edge of the wood block on the pencil line on the template.

Put the pencil against the other edge and draw it along, tracing the shape of the room onto the vinyl. Do the same for large obstacles.

3 Cut the vinyl along the pencil line, using a ruler as a guide on straight lines. Put a piece of scrap vinyl or hardboard underneath to avoid damaging the floor.

4 If you have marked a square for a pipe, draw diagonal lines from the corners of the square. Where they cross will be the middle.

5 Use a coin or other round object to draw a circle the diameter of the pipe. Cut out the circle with the knife.

6 The piece of flooring will now fit the room exactly. To fit it around obstacles, make a cut from the hole to the nearest edge. If you follow the lines of any pattern – for example, the 'grout' lines of imitation tiles – the cut will not be noticeable.

7 Stick down the vinyl in the normal way (above) unless it is a 'stay-flat' variety of cushioned vinyl which does not need to be glued.

Fitting sheet vinyl without a seam

Most rooms can be covered with a single, seamless sheet of vinyl if you use a 4m (13ft) or even a 3m (10ft) width.

Seamless laying gives a neater finish, and will probably last longer because there is no join to come apart and get damaged.

A seamless floor is, however, more difficult to lay. The size of the material makes it cumbersome and very heavy, and you will almost certainly need a helper. Trimming it to the wall also requires greater skill.

Estimate the amount of floor covering in the same way as for narrow vinyl (page 43), except that only one length will be needed. Take the measurements right into any alcoves, and to the halfway point under the door.

To make laying as easy as possible, the sheet should be about 4in (100mm) wider than the floor on every edge – that is, 8in (200mm) wider than the room in both directions. Your supplier should cut it to the required length, even if you have to pay to the next full metre or half metre.

He may also cut it to width. If you have to do it yourself, try to find a large area where it can be laid flat. As a last resort the lawn would do – on a dry day. Make the cut with a trimming knife or scissors.

Re-roll the sheet so the shorter dimension becomes the length of the roll. This makes it easier to get into the room.

Roll it with the decorative side inwards, which is the way you will need it when laying starts.

Keep the roll in the room where it will be laid for two days to reach room temperature. Have the heating on in the room in cold weather or the vinyl will be hard and brittle.

You will need

Tools Soft broom; scissors; trimming knife; small block of wood and perhaps a metal straight-edge.
Materials Sheet vinyl to cover the floor in one piece; adhesive and spreader (except for 'stay-flat' vinyl); cover strip for doorways.

1 The first job is to unroll the vinyl. This is hard work, and you will almost certainly need someone to help you. Make sure that the longer side of the vinyl runs along the longer wall.

2 If the flooring has a pronounced pattern, adjust it so that the pattern lines look to be at right angles to the wall containing the doorway by which you will most often enter the room.

Sight it by eye. If it looks right, it is right.

3 As trimming the edges is quite difficult, put the sheet up against

Trimming vinyl that is bent up a wall is not easy and takes practice. But practising is the last thing you want to do on a large piece of expensive material.

Obtain some offcuts and work on these until you get the knack. After pressing the vinyl against the wall with your block of wood, it may help to hold a metal straight-edge as close to the wall as possible while you cut.

Make sure that the knife cuts away from the hand holding the straight-edge, so that if it slips you will not injure yourself.

the longest wall – then against the other walls in turn, if necessary – to see if there is one wall that is so true that the edge does not have to be cut to fit.

Do not disturb the setting-out so that the pattern is no longer at right angles to the door.

4 For laying, the vinyl must be absolutely flat on the floor. You can ensure this by sweeping over it with a soft broom.

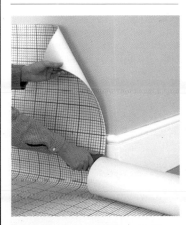

5 To fit the vinyl into an alcove beside a fireplace get your helper to hold it while you make a cut running parallel to the side of the chimney breast.

Take care to leave about 2in (50mm) surplus against each wall for final trimming.

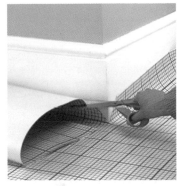

6 Lay the material on the alcove floor, lapping up against the three sides, then cut off the excess riding up the fireplace. Again, leave about 2in (50mm) surplus against the wall for trimming.

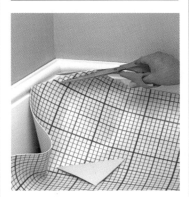

7 To fit into corners, cut off a small triangle at the corner of the vinyl, using scissors. When you push it down to the floor it will form a V, allowing it to hug the skirting. But you must cut off exactly the right amount, so first remove a triangle that is obviously too small. Then take off more small strips until it is just right.

8 To trim to the wall, first run your knife along the vinyl lapping up the wall, taking off the excess so that about 1in (25mm) remains.

9 Push the vinyl firmly against the skirting board with a small block of wood.

10 Place the point of the knife on the vinyl exactly where the skirting board meets the floor, and run it along the skirting with the blade at 45 degrees to the wall. This will trim

the material to fit snugly against the skirting, without leaving gaps.

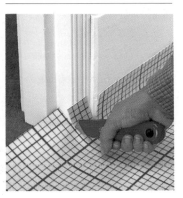

11 To cut around a door frame, make a series of vertical cuts to the point where the vinyl meets the floor, then press it into the angle between door frame and floor. Trim off the excess. In the doorway itself, cut the vinyl so that it ends halfway under the door.

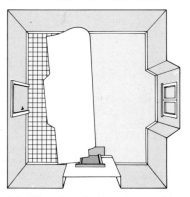

12 When the vinyl has been laid, stick it to the floor, unless it is the 'stay-flat' type which does not need sticking. Glue cushioned vinyls round the edges only. Non-cushioned types should be stuck down all over.

Roll back the sheet over half the room, and put the glue on the floor. (See fire warning, page 40.)

13 Replace the sheet and press it down with the broom. Then glue the other half of the room.

14 Finish off the doorway with metal cover strip.

COVERING LARGE ROOMS

A seamless floor cannot be laid in a room whose width is greater than 13ft (4m). The room will have to be covered with two or more lengths of 2m, 3m or 4m vinyl, depending on which size gives the least wastage of material.

Do not mix different widths on the same floor; they will have been manufactured on different machines, and there will be slight differences in the colours.

Only lengths bought from the same roll should be used on one floor.

Laying foam-backed carpet

Carpet with a foam underlay attached is much easier to lay than hessian-backed carpet, which needs a separate underlay. Not only do carpet and underlay go down in one operation, but foam-backed carpet does not have to be stretched.

Another advantage is that foam-backed carpet is held to the floor with double-sided carpet tape, eliminating the need to install gripper strip around the room.

Carpet tape can be stuck to either wood or concrete floors. It can be bought in two widths – 1in (25mm) and 2in (50mm). When you are covering a floor with a single piece of carpet, the narrow tape will do.

The laying technique for foam-backed carpet differs according to whether the carpet is in one or two pieces. The job will be easiest if you can use a single piece of carpet, a few inches bigger all round than the floor.

If you are laying carpet on floorboards that have not been overlaid with hardboard, it is advisable to fit a paper underlay to stop dust and grit from blowing up between the boards and harming the carpet.

You will need
Tools Trimming knife; clean bolster chisel or wooden kitchen spatula. *Materials* Enough carpet to cover the room; double-sided carpet tape; perhaps carpet adhesive.

HELPFUL TIP
When cutting the carpet to fit exactly against the skirting board, there is a danger that a gap will be created between the carpet and the wall. For maximum accuracy, hold the knife at an angle, with the point of the blade against the skirting and the handle leaning away from the wall.

A ONE-PIECE CARPET

1 If you are using a paper underlay, put it down first (see panel). It must stop short of the walls by the width of the carpet tape so that the tape will stick to the floor, not to the paper.

2 Place the carpet loosely in position. If possible, have its pile running away from the window (or away from the main window if there is more than one). The surface should feel smooth when you run your hand away from the window (with the pile); if you feel resistance, you are going against the pile.

3 If the carpet has a pattern, adjust it so that it looks true when seen from the door.

4 To lay the carpet into an alcove, make a cut at a right angle to the back of the alcove. Take care not to cut too far, and to leave a 1in (25mm) trimming allowance. Cut off the flap riding up the fireplace.

5 Trim off the excess all round the room, so that the carpet is the size of the floor plus a trimming allowance of at least 1in (25mm) on each wall.

The surplus is cut away later to give an exact fit.

6 Re-roll the carpet and lay it diagonally across the room, so that the space all round the wall is clear for laying the tape.

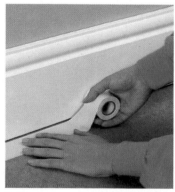

7 Fix the tape round the perimeter of the room.

Some manufacturers also recommend additional tapes across the middle of the room. Follow their instructions.

8 Unroll the carpet to its correct position.

9 Peel off the tape's backing paper, and press the carpet firmly in place all round the room.

10 Push it well into the join between floor and skirting board with a clean bolster chisel or a wooden kitchen spatula so you can see where the knife blade should go.

11 When the carpet is fixed all round, trim off the surplus with the knife.

12 Finally go all round the room making quite sure that the carpet is

---

PAPER UNDERLAY FOR CARPET

On smooth floorboards, paper underlay can be substituted for hardboard. It will prevent dirt from blowing up between the boards and harming the carpet.

Paper underlay is sold in rolls by carpet shops.

You will need
Tools Knife or scissors; stapling hammer or electric staple gun (from a hire shop) or a hammer. *Materials* Paper underlay; staples or large-headed tacks.

1 If gripper strip is being used, lay it first (facing page).

2 Beginning in a corner of the room, unroll about a yard of the paper so that it lies against the

side wall (or the gripper strip) and fix it in place with a stapling hammer, staple gun or hammer.

3 Trim the end of the paper to the end wall (or gripper strip) and fix it in place.

4 Roll the paper out to the far end of the room, smoothing it as you go, and fix it along both edges, making sure it stays perfectly flat. Fix and trim it at the other end.

5 Fix parallel strips of paper to cover the entire room, overlapping each length by about 1in (25mm). The last length will have to be cut to width as well as length.

---

still adhering firmly to the tape, and pressing it back into place wherever necessary.

FOAM-BACKED CARPET IN TWO PIECES

A wide room can be carpeted with two lengths of foam-backed carpet, joined together with carpet tape. The strip of floor where the two pieces of carpet will meet must be left clear of paper underlay so that the tape can be stuck down directly to the floor.

Make sure that the pile of both pieces lies in the same direction, and – if possible – away from the main source of light. The surface should feel smooth when you run your hand with the pile; if you feel resistance, you are going against the pile.

1 Cut the first piece of carpet to length, leaving a trimming allow-

ance of at least 1in (25mm) against all three walls for the final fitting.

2 Cut the second piece of carpet – to width this time as well as length – leaving a similar allowance for final trimming.

3 Butt the two pieces of carpet together on the floor at the meeting point.

If they fit together without any gaps, go ahead with laying the carpet (step 7).

4 If the edges of the two pieces are not straight, and gaps occur between them, snap a chalk line across the room at the meeting place.

5 Place the wider length of carpet along the chalk line, and trim it to the line with the knife.

If you have a metal straight-edge you can use it as an extra guide to get a perfect cut.

6 Place this trimmed edge on the meeting edge of the second length of carpet, and use it as a guide to trimming so that you get the best possible join.

7 Turn back the edges, and place the carpet tape on the floor, centrally along the meeting place of the two pieces. Use 2in (50mm) tape positioned centrally on the join, or two pieces of 1in (25mm) tape side by side. Peel off the backing.

8 Lay the larger piece of carpet down first, and press it into place on the tape.

9 Apply a continuous bead of carpet adhesive all along its edge.

10 Place the second length in position and press it onto the tape, and against the edge of the first. Wipe up any adhesive.

11 Deal with the edges as for *A one-piece carpet* (steps 7-12)

Laying carpet with separate underlay

Carpet with a separate underlay is much more difficult to lay than foam-backed carpet. If it is to lie flat and to wear well, it must be stretched during the laying.

The stretching is done with a tool called a carpet stretcher (or 'knee-kicker').

Achieving the correct tension is the trickiest part of the job. If you stretch the carpet too much you risk tearing it; if you stretch it too little it will not lie flat and will ruck up when furniture is pushed over it. And a bumpy carpet not only looks bad, but may also become worn on the high spots.

It is probably not worthwhile laying a new carpet yourself. The price of good-quality carpet is so high that a fitting fee adds little to the overall cost. And carpet shops often include free fitting.

Used carpet, however, is easier to lay as it has already been stretched once. So if you obtain some second-hand carpet, or move house and take the carpet with you, the job is worth trying.

But it is only possible if the carpet is wide enough to cover the room without joins. Joining a carpet that has to be stretched is skilled work.

For best results, line the floorboards with hardboard (page 35), or with paper underlay (facing page), before laying the carpet.

You will need
Tools Hammer and nail punch (or carpet-layer's hammer); tenon saw or hacksaw; vice or bench hook; protective gloves; trimming knife (preferably with a hooked blade) or scissors; perhaps an electric staple gun (from a hire shop); carpet stretcher (from a hire shop); clean bolster chisel or wooden kitchen spatula.
Materials Gripper strip and nails or adhesive; threshold strip and screws or adhesive; underlay (felt or foam rubber); staples or tacks; carpet to cover the room in one piece.

HELPFUL TIP
If you are laying carpet on a concrete floor, test first to make sure that central heating pipes are not lying too close to the surface. Switch the heating full on until the radiators are hot, and then walk over the floor in bare feet. If you feel heat, do not nail gripper strip; glue it.

FIXING THE GRIPPER STRIPS

1 Measure the perimeter of the room to work out how many gripper strips you will need. The gripper strips are usually sold in 30in (760mm) lengths.

2 Put down the grippers with the pins pointing towards the wall. Leave a space slightly less than the thickness of the carpet between the gripper and the wall. This is for the trimmed carpet to be tucked into later.

3 Nail them to the floor, using a small-headed carpet-layer's hammer. This will enable you to drive in the nails without hitting the pins. Alternatively, start off with a claw hammer, then use a nail punch when the nails get close to the pins.

CHOOSING CARPET FIXINGS

The old way of laying a carpet was to fold it under by about 2in (50mm) all round the edge of the room and tack it in place. The method can still be used, but it has been superseded by the smooth-edged method. The carpet is held by gripper strips – thin lengths of wood or metal containing two rows of angled pins.

Grippers
Some grippers come with nails ready to be hammered into the floor. Wood or concrete nails are available. Or they can be stuck to solid floors with glue sold by the makers.

Threshold strips
In doorways, threshold strips (also called carpet edgings) are screwed, nailed or glued to the floor. They grip the carpet with spikes and fold down over the edge to protect it.

Double threshold strips
To cover the edges of two carpets laid in a room and an adjoining hall, double threshold strips can be used.

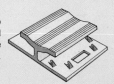

Angled grippers
For staircases, angled grippers are fitted at the junction between tread and riser. They can be bought to fit standard-width stair carpet.

Stair rods
Stair rods are again being made, and old ones can be found in secondhand shops. Make sure you have enough for your stairs. The method of fixing is usually obvious.

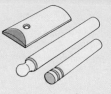

Laying carpet with a separate underlay (continued)

CARPET-LAYING TOOLS

The carpet layer's main tool is called a carpet stretcher or 'knee-kicker'. It has a flat sole with teeth at one end, which grips the carpet. At the other, there is a large pad which the layer 'kicks' with his knee.

Carpet stretchers are expensive to buy, but they can be hired quite cheaply by the day from tool-hire shops, found in *Yellow Pages* under Hire Services – Tools and Equipment.

A staple gun is needed for fixing underlay to a timber floor. Both manual and electrically operated types can be hired from tool hire shops. Use double-sided carpet tape to fix underlay to a solid floor.

A carpet-layer's hammer, which has a narrow heavy head, is useful for fixing gripper strip to a floor or stairs, as it will drive in the nails without hitting the pins on the gripper. It will probably have to be bought from a carpet shop. Alternatively, use a hammer and nail punch.

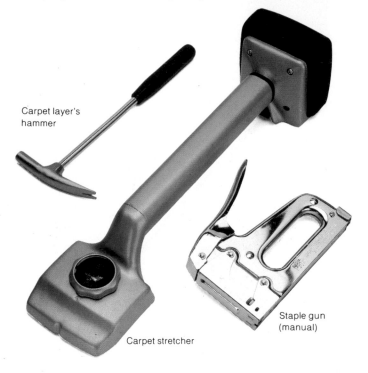

Carpet layer's hammer

Carpet stretcher

Staple gun (manual)

4 When a radiator prevents you from getting close to the wall, fit the gripper as close as the radiator will allow.

5 When you reach a corner of the room, cut the strip to length, using a tenon saw on wood or a hacksaw on metal. Hold the strip in a vice or bench hook and be careful not to hurt yourself on the pins. Heavy gloves will help to protect your hands.

6 When you come to a corner, simply butt-join two pieces of gripper. There is no need to cut mitre joints at the ends.

7 In a curved area, such as a bay window, cut the gripper into short pieces to follow the curve.

8 At a doorway, fit a metal or plastic threshold strip (also called carpet edging) midway under the door.

PUTTING DOWN THE UNDERLAY

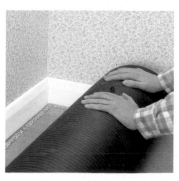

1 Unroll a short length of underlay in a corner of the room so that the end and the side lie against the gripper strip.

2 Fix the edges of the underlay to the floor with the staple gun, or with hammer and tacks. On a concrete floor, use double-sided carpet tape.

3 Roll out the underlay along the edge of the room, smoothing as you go, and fixing along both edges. Make sure it is perfectly flat on the floor.

4 It is not necessary to stretch the underlay, but it helps to push it in position with the carpet stretcher.

5 Where a radiator is fixed to the wall, lay the underlay up to the edge of the gripper, even if the gripper has been fitted a little way out from the wall.

6 At the end of the room, trim the underlay against the gripper strip with a trimming knife or scissors.

7 When you have almost covered the room, you will have to cut the last length of underlay to width as well as to length.

LAYING THE CARPET

1 In a larger room – or on the lawn if it is a dry day – cut the carpet to the size of the room to be covered. Add a trimming allowance of 6in (150mm) on all sides – even more if the carpet has a pattern.

Keep the waste; it may come in handy for patching later.

If possible the carpet should lie with the pile running away from the main or only window; this stops uneven shading in the daylight. The surface should feel smooth when you run your hand away from the window, but give some resistance when you run your hand towards the window.

2 Put the carpet in place on the floor of the room where it is to be laid. If it has a pattern, adjust it so that the pattern looks true, and does not run off when seen from the doorway.

3 Make release cuts to allow the carpet to lie flat in any alcove. Cut the carpet at a right angle to the back of the alcove and take care not to cut too far. Leave some excess for trimming around the alcove.

4 Cut off the surplus riding up the fireplace, leaving some excess for trimming.

5 Trim off the excess all round the room, leaving an allowance of about ⅜in (10mm) along two adjacent walls, and an allowance of about 1½in (38mm) along the other two.

HELPFUL TIP

When trimming into an alcove it helps if you make vertical cuts at the corners. You can then press the carpet down onto the floor before cutting off the excess. This makes it easier to judge the appropriate allowance to be pushed down later.

6 Start the fixing in the corner of the room with the smaller allowance. Working along one wall, run your fingers along the top of the carpet so that it engages on the gripper pins farthest from the wall. Take care not to injure your fingers on the spikes.

7 Do the same along the second wall with the smaller allowance.

8 Run the head of your hammer flat along the top of the carpet, pushing it onto the other row of pins and forcing the excess carpet into the space between the gripper strip and the skirting board.

9 When the first two edges have been fixed, kneel on the carpet with your back to one of the completed walls.

Push the teeth of the carpet stretcher into the carpet ahead of you and 'kick' the padded end with your knee to force the carpet forwards.

Move forwards and repeat once or twice until you are close to the opposite wall.

10 Stretch the carpet again, and hook it onto the gripping pins with your hand. It will immediately contract and be firmly fixed in place. Carpet fitters know from experience when the maximum stretch has been reached. You will just have to experiment until you get the tension of the carpet firm and even all across the room.

11 Repeat this process three or four more times across the room until the carpet is fixed all along one wall.

Then turn 90 degrees and fix it along the fourth wall.

12 When the hooking is complete, excess carpet will be left lapping up the walls. Trim this off to about ⅜in (10mm).

13 Push the remainder into the space between the gripper and skirting, using a clean bolster chisel or a wooden kitchen spatula. Take care not to scratch the paintwork if you are using a bolster.

14 Check that the excess carpet on the other two walls of the room is properly pushed down, and use the bolster or spatula where necessary.

15 Finally, tap down the cover of the threshold strip at the doorway, using a piece of waste wood or carpet to protect the metal from becoming dented.

CUTTING A DOOR TO CLEAR A CARPET

After fitting a carpet, the base of the door may drag on the surface. One cure is to change the hinges for rising butts.

Alternatively, the bottom of the door can be trimmed off. With the door in place use a thin block of wood as thick as the amount of wood to be removed. Put it on the floor with a pencil on top and run it along the door to mark the cutting line.

Take off the door and either saw or plane off the base. If you use a hand saw, work slowly to avoid splintering the face.

If you use a plane, hold the door upright on its long edge in a portable work bench and plane downwards. Work inwards from each side to avoid splintering the stiles at the end. Sand the bottom of the door so that it will not damage the carpet.

It is also possible to hire a door trimming saw from tool hire shops, and trim the door without removing it from its hinges.

Patching a damaged carpet

To repair a hole or a frayed patch in a carpet, you need a piece of the same carpet slightly bigger than the damaged area.

The piece may have been left over when the carpet was laid, or you can cut it from under a large piece of furniture where it will not show. That hole could then be filled with different carpet.

The joins of the repair should not be visible. At first, there will be a colour difference between the patch and the rest of the carpet, but in time this will become less obvious.

You will need
Tools Trimming knife; hammer.
Materials Carpet patch; latex-based carpet adhesive; 2in (50mm) self-adhesive carpet tape (possibly double-sided); a piece of hessian larger than the patch (except for foam-backed carpet).

CUTTING THE NEW PIECE

1 Place the new piece over the damaged portion, ensuring that the pile runs in the same direction. (Run your hand over both carpets to feel the direction in which they feel smoothest.)

2 Hold the patch firmly on the carpet and cut through both at the same time with a sharp knife. This ensures that the patch and hole are exactly the same size.

Take care not to cut through a separate underlay as well.

LOOSE-LAID CARPET

1 In the case of a loose-laid carpet, roll it back and apply a carpet adhesive round the edge of the hole and the edge of the patch to about halfway up the pile. This prevents fraying.

2 Leave the adhesive to dry, then insert the patch in position.

3 On a foam-backed carpet, fix the patch in place with 2in (50mm) self-adhesive carpet tape on all the edges.

With other carpets, spread carpet adhesive on a piece of hessian 2in (50mm) bigger all round than the patch. Stick it over the back of the patch and over the surrounding carpet.

4 Turn the carpet right side up and pinch the edges of the patch and the carpet between your fingers to make quite sure they stick well together.

5 Finally, tap the join all over lightly with a hammer to disguise the join as much as possible, although the colour difference will probably still be visible.

FITTED CARPET

1 Apply a carpet adhesive round the edges of the hole and the edge of the patch to about halfway up the pile, working from the back, and leave it to dry.

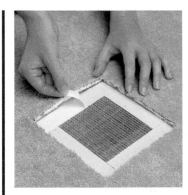

2 Take four lengths of double-sided carpet tape, push them through the hole, and stick them to the floor or the underlay where the patch will join onto the main carpet. Remove the backing from the tape.

3 Place the patch in position and press it firmly down.

4 Push the joins together, and tap lightly with a hammer.

Fitting a stair carpet

Staircases are often covered with a central strip of carpet, with the wood on each side either painted or varnished. The carpet is sold ready made to width – normally 27in (690mm).

Take care when laying a stair carpet; if it is not done properly the carpet can work loose, creating a risk of injury. Laying a central strip is fairly easy, but laying fitted carpet on stairs should be left to a carpet layer.

The carpet wears very unevenly because people walk on just a small part of it – near the front of the tread. You can prolong its life considerably by laying it with stair grippers or stair rods so that it can be repositioned regularly, and leaving some surplus at the bottom.

Stair carpets need an underlay, like room carpets, and it is normal to use stair pads, not a continuous roll. The pads, which will be cut for you by the supplier, are slightly bigger from front to back than the depth of the tread, so that they overhang the nose of the tread.

You will need

Tools Tape measure; pencil; hammer and nail punch, or carpet layer's hammer; trimming knife or scissors; wooden spatula or spoon. *Materials* Carpet to cover the stairs; carpet adhesive; carpet tacks; stair pads; narrow strips of hardboard or plywood; metal stair grippers the width of the carpet; and nails for fixing.

SAFETY TIP
Walking up a staircase with only pads in position can be dangerous, as the pads hang loosely over the edge of the tread. Also the pins on the grippers are very sharp. In a house that is occupied, carpet should be fitted over the pads as quickly as possible. Anyone who has to use the stairs in the meantime should take care.

ESTIMATING LENGTH OF CARPET

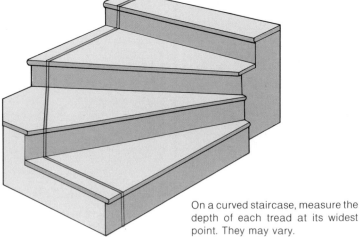

ESTIMATING THE CARPET

1 To decide the length of the carpet, first measure from the front to the back of one tread (the part you walk on) and multiply the figure by the number of treads in the staircase.

2 Where a curving staircase has treads deeper at one end than the other, take the larger measurement. In some cases, the bottom tread may be deeper than the rest; also allow for this.

3 If the stairs turn a corner on a half-landing, measure the length of the half-landing and add it to the total. If you wish the carpet to run to the far end of any landing at the top of the stairs, add this measurement as well.

4 Now measure the height of the riser (the vertical part of each step) and multiply the figure by the number of risers.

5 Add this to the figure you already have. The total is the length of carpet needed to cover the stairs. But an allowance for moving the carpet to even out the wear is also needed, so add the depth of the bottom tread and the height of the bottom riser.

You will probably have to buy to the next metre or half metre.

On a curved staircase, measure the depth of each tread at its widest point. They may vary.

PREPARING THE STAIRCASE

1 If an old carpet has just been removed, inspect the staircase for defects, and carry out any necessary repairs.

2 Remove old nails or tacks left over from the old carpet. A tack lifter is the best tool.

3 Put a pad centrally on the top tread (the one below the landing) with one edge resting against the riser and the other overhanging the front of the tread.

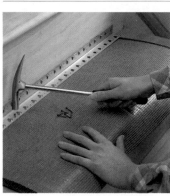

4 Place a stair gripper where the tread and the riser meet. Nail it to the tread through the pad. A carpet-layer's hammer, which has a small head, will drive in the nails without hitting the teeth of the gripper. Alternatively, use an ordinary hammer and finish off the nails with a nail punch. Nail the gripper to the riser as well.

Repeat on the other stairs, except for the bottom one. And do not fit a gripper where the bottom riser meets the floor.

LAYING THE CARPET

1 Unroll the carpet and run your hand over it. It will wear better if the direction which feels smooth runs from the top to the bottom of the stairs.

2 Re-roll it from the top, with the decorative side inwards.

3 Working from the bottom of the stairs, unroll a little of the carpet. If the end is starting to fray, spread a

little carpet adhesive on the edge, taking care not to get any on the top of the carpet.

4 Cover the bottom tread with carpet, laid face down. Make sure to keep the carpet parallel to the sides of the tread.

5 Fix the stair gripper on the tread, trapping the carpet in place with the nails.

6 Bring the carpet over the nose of the tread and down the riser.

7 Fix it at the bottom of the riser with a strip of hardboard or plywood nailed in place through the carpet.

8 Bring the carpet back up the bottom riser to the starting point so the decorative surface is uppermost. Fix it to the gripper by pushing with a wooden spatula, or even a wooden spoon, onto both rows of spikes. Make sure the carpet is firmly fixed.

9 Continue up the stairs, fixing the carpet to each gripper.

A CURVED STAIRCASE

Laying carpet on a curved staircase is difficult unless you use a woven carpet such as Wilton or Axminster. Other types are extremely stiff.

1 Nail wooden gripper strip to both the rise and the tread.

2 Cut the stair pads to shape; they will have to be wider at one end

than the other. Staple or tack them in place, butted up against the gripper on the tread.

3 Begin laying the carpet at the bottom of the staircase. (See Laying the carpet, facing page.)

4 Push the carpet onto the grippers with a spatula or a piece of wood ¼in (6mm) thick. Professionals use a blunted brick bolster.

5 On the first curved stair bring the carpet up the riser and nail it with 1in (25mm) tacks.

6 Fold it down so that it meets the tread below and tack it in place.

FIXING A CARPET ON A CURVED STAIRCASE

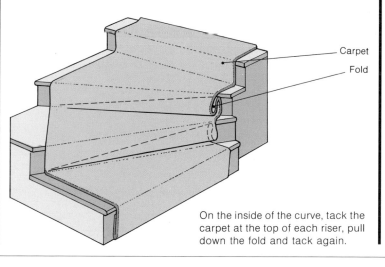

Carpet

Fold

On the inside of the curve, tack the carpet at the top of each riser, pull down the fold and tack again.

7 If the curve is sharp, you may have to lay the carpet in pieces — two or three stairs for each piece.

USING STAIR RODS

1 When buying a set of stair rods, make sure there will be enough for the staircase.

2 Rods do not alter the principles of fixing stair carpet, but their fixing clips will probably not be able to hold the underlay pads, which will need to be fixed with tacks.

Put the clips for the rods at the edge of the carpet to prevent it moving sideways.

3 For the sake of appearance, fix rods on curved stairs and perhaps between the hall floor and the bottom riser, although the carpet will actually be held by the tacks.

Dealing with landings

WALL-TO-WALL CARPET

If the landing is to have wall-to-wall carpet, finish the stair carpet at the top of the last riser. Cut off any surplus, leaving about 1in (25mm) to fold under. Fix it with tacks along its top edge.

Lay the landing carpet in the same way as a room carpet, but take it over the top step and tack it to the top riser.

A HALF-LANDING

Where a staircase makes a 90 degree turn, treat it as two flights of stairs. Cover the half-landing with one of the stair carpets. Butt the other one up to it, turn under the end and tack it down.

If the staircase makes a dog-leg

(180 degree) turn, there may be a wide landing to be covered with a separate strip of stair carpet laid at right angles to the two flights of stairs.

Carry both stair carpets to what will be the far edge of the landing carpet, cut them off and tack them in place without putting underlay beneath them. This surplus can be used for moving the carpet to avoid wear in future years.

Lay a third strip of carpet across them to cover the landing.

There will be a gap under the landing carpet in the middle between the two strips of stair carpet. So fit underlay — perhaps some stair pads tacked in place and trimmed to fit the space.

Tack down the landing carpet all the way round, folding under the two ends.

A FULL LANDING

On a full landing that is not to have wall-to-wall carpet, you can simply run the stair carpet to the far end without a break.

Cut it off and seal the edge with adhesive.

Put underlay beneath the carpet, overlapping the top riser. Finish off the end of the carpet with a metal threshold strip. Tack down along the edges.

FULL LANDING WITH WALL-TO-WALL CARPET

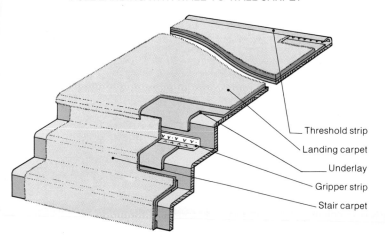

Threshold strip

Landing carpet

Underlay

Gripper strip

Stair carpet

CARPET ON A DOG-LEG TURN

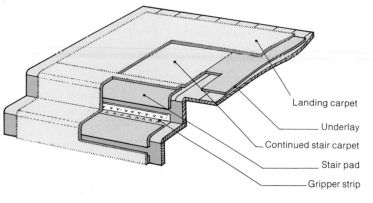

Landing carpet

Underlay

Continued stair carpet

Stair pad

Gripper strip

Moving stair carpet to avoid wear

People walking up a staircase tread on the front of each step, so that the carpet on the edge of the steps can become worn very quickly, particularly if it is not a heavy-duty grade.

Wear can be equalised by moving the carpet up the stairs by about 3in (75mm) every year, so that all parts of the carpet get the same amount of wear over a period of several years. The job is easiest if the carpet is held with stair rods rather than grippers.

You will need

Tools Tack lifter; hammer; wooden spatula.
Materials Narrow strip of underlay; carpet tacks.

1 Release the carpet from the tacks or metal strip holding it in place at the top, using a tack lifter.

2 Fold the end into a roll, and work down the stairs, rolling as you go. This should free the carpet from the top teeth of the grippers, but you may have to lift it from the bottom teeth. Do not just drag the carpet away from the teeth, as it may get damaged.

If the carpet is held with stair rods, simply remove them.

3 With the carpet rolled up, start to re-lay it in the same way as laying it originally (page 50), except that on the bottom tread begin about 3in (75mm) away from the riser, and tack it down.

4 Fill the gap that is created with a strip of carpet underlay fixed under the gripper.

5 Where the carpet ends at the top, turn under the excess of 3in (75mm) and tack it.

6 Year by year, the surplus carpet at the bottom will become shorter, until it will all be transferred to the top, where a double pocket may be needed. At the foot of the stairs it will be tacked to the bottom of the lowest riser.

If the carpet is still in good condition the following year, start off as you began – with a double layer of carpet on the bottom tread and bottom riser.

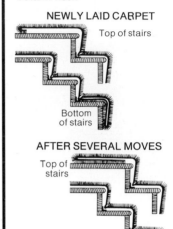

NEWLY LAID CARPET

Top of stairs

Bottom of stairs

AFTER SEVERAL MOVES

Top of stairs

Bottom of stairs

REMOVING STAINS FROM CARPETS

Try to treat stains immediately they occur. The longer they are left, the more difficult they will become.

You should not add extra liquid of any sort and do not rub the carpet. If you do so, you will only drive the stain deeper, or spread it.

First scrape off any solid matter with a spoon or blunt knife. Mop up liquid by pressing on it with a dry towel or wad of tissues. Use different areas of the towel or tissues until no more moisture can be lifted.

If a stain still remains, treat it according to whether it is water-based or grease-based. A water-based stain – a drink, for example – can be removed with a carpet shampoo; a grease-based stain, such as gravy or fat, can be removed with a dry-cleaning solvent. Brand names of dry-cleaning solvents include Dabit-off, K2r and Carpet Devils.

When applying the shampoo or solvent use just enough on a cloth to moisten the area. If you use a saturated cloth you are likely to drive the stain deeper. Turn the cloth to a dry side as soon as it becomes dirty. Work from the outside of the stain towards the middle to avoid spreading it.

Finally, cover the area with a thick wad of tissues weighed down with something flat and heavy, such as a phone book. The remaining moisture will be absorbed by the tissues, further reducing the risk of a permanent stain.

When the treated patch has dried out, it may be necessary to shampoo the entire carpet to ensure uniform colour. Carpet-cleaning firms will do the job for you, or you can hire carpet-cleaning equipment by the day from firms listed in *Yellow Pages* under Hire Services – Tools and Equipment.

Be careful not to over-wet the carpet, and never allow the back of the carpet to get wet. Do not try to dry carpets artificially, as heat may damage the pile.

Smooth the carpet pile in its natural direction and keep it well ventilated until dry.

Proprietary carpet spot-removing kits can be bought, containing bottles of chemicals appropriate for different stains. They are available from Service Master outlets. Kits cannot be sent by post.

Getting professional help
The National Carpet Cleaners' Association will provide lists of member companies in your area who will advise on the removal of stains and carry out cleaning work. The association's address is 126 New Walk, Leicester LE1 7JA (telephone 01533 554352).

SAFETY TIPS

Many solvents are potentially harmful. Some are flammable; many give off poisonous fumes. So treat all stain-removing solvents with extreme care.

Work in a well ventilated room.

Never smoke or work near a naked flame while using a solvent.

Remove children and pets from the room.

Never pour dry-cleaner solvent into a second container. It may later be mistaken by another member of the family for some sort of drink.

Always wear rubber gloves to protect your hands when using solvents.

Keep all solvents locked away from children.

Switch off warm-air ducted heating.

Alcoholic spirits
Mop up with a dry towel or wad of tissues. Sponge with warm water. Allow to dry. Then clean with carpet shampoo. Treat any remaining stain with methylated spirit.

Animal stains (excreta, vomit, urine)
Remove loose solids with paper. Scrape the residue with a blunt knife or spoon. Blot dry with a cloth or wad of tissues. Lightly sponge with a carpet shampoo (add acetic acid for urine). If the stain is serious call a professional carpet cleaner. The most serious stains penetrate the back of the carpet and the underlay.

Ball-point pen
Speedy action is essential. Dab with methylated spirit on a cotton wool bud. Take care not to spread the stain.

On vinyl upholstery or wall coverings, immediately scrub with a nail brush and warm soapy water (the ink will cause a permanent mark if left).

Beer
Mop up with a towel and leave to dry. If there is still a mark, treat with carpet shampoo.

Blood
FRESH STAINS Sponge with cold water. Blot dry. Clean with carpet shampoo if necessary.

DRIED STAINS May not clean completely.

Candlewax
Scrape off as much as possible. Cover remainder with blotting paper or brown paper. Apply the point of a warm iron. Do not allow the iron to touch the carpet; it may cause it to melt. Move the paper about until the wax is absorbed into it.

Clear any remaining traces with a dry-cleaning solvent.

Chewing gum
Freeze the chewing gum with blocks of ice wrapped in a plastic bag, or a proprietary chewing gum remover.

Then break it up into pieces and brush up the bits by hand – chewing gum clogs up vacuum cleaners.

Chocolate
Scrape off the chocolate with a knife, and clean the area with carpet shampoo.

Treat stubborn stains with dry-cleaning solvent when the shampoo has dried.

Cocoa
Mop up the worst and dry off with a towel or wad of tissues. Clean with carpet shampoo. Treat any remaining stain with a dry-cleaning solvent when the shampoo has dried.

Coffee
Mop up the worst of the liquid. Blot dry. Treat any remaining stain with a carpet shampoo. When dry use dry-cleaning solvent to remove grease from milk or cream.

Curry
An extremely difficult stain. Large marks should be treated professionally. With small marks, scrape off the deposit and rub lightly with borax solution (15ml borax to 500ml water). Stubborn stains can sometimes be helped with a little neat glycerine rubbed into the carpet and left for about 10 minutes. Then sponge out with warm water, and blot dry.

Dyes
Have the stain treated by a carpet-cleaning firm.

Egg
Scrape off the deposit. Treat with dry-cleaning solvent or with a proprietary carpet spot-removing kit.

Eye make-up
Moisten the area, then treat with a drop of liquid detergent on a cotton wool bud. Rinse. Treat stubborn stains with dry-cleaning solvent.

Fats, grease and oil
Mop up the worst. Scrape off any deposit. Apply dry-cleaning solvent.

Heavy deposits often respond to the blotting-paper-and-iron technique (see Candlewax).

Felt-tip pen
Some felt-tip pens have spirit-based ink, some have water-based ink. Methylated spirit on a cotton wool bud will remove spirit-based ink, which has a pungent smell. But do not allow it to penetrate to a foam backing. The methylated spirit may stain a light coloured carpet. For water-based ink, use carpet shampoo.

Foundation cream
FRESH WET STAINS Mop up any deposit and apply dry-cleaning solvent. Allow to dry, and treat with carpet shampoo. Stubborn stains can be treated with a proprietary carpet spot-removing kit.
DRY STAINS Brush off powder, then use a proprietary carpet spot-removing kit.

Fruit juice
Mop up with a clean cloth or paper towels. Clean with carpet shampoo.

Gravy
Mop up with paper towels. Treat with dry-cleaning solvent. Clean with carpet shampoo.

Hair oil
Mop up as much as possible and then apply a dry-cleaning solvent.

Ice cream
Scrape up and wipe with paper towels. Treat with a dry-cleaning solvent when dry. Clean with carpet shampoo.

Ink (fountain pen)
Must be tackled immediately. Blot with absorbent paper. Sponge with warm water to remove further ink. You may need more than one application. Blot well each time.

Treat remaining small stains with a proprietary carpet spot-removing kit.

Jam/marmalade
Spoon up deposits. Wipe area with cloth wrung out in warm water. Clean with carpet shampoo. Remove any remaining stains with a proprietary carpet spot-removing kit.

Ketchup
Scoop up or wipe away excess deposits. Take care not to spread the stain. Gently rub with lather made up from carpet shampoo. Wipe with cloth wrung out in warm water. Work in direction of the pile. Treat any remaining stain with a dry-cleaning solvent.

Lipstick
Scrape off with a knife, and use a dry-cleaning solvent. Alternatively, use a proprietary carpet spot-removing kit or a little Polyclens Plus paintbrush cleaner.

Metal polish
Scrape or blot up any deposit. Treat with carpet shampoo containing a few drops of household ammonia.

Milk
Immediate action is essential to prevent milk penetrating down into the carpet where it will give off a smell indefinitely. Blot dry. Clean with carpet shampoo. If a stain remains use a dry-cleaning solvent. May need professional attention to prevent smell recurring each time room warms up.

Mud
Allow to dry. Brush, then vacuum. Clean with carpet shampoo if necessary.

Mustard
Scrape off deposits. Sponge with damp cloth. Treat with carpet shampoo.

Nail varnish
Spoon up deposit; avoid spreading the stain. Moisten a pad of cotton wool with amyl acetate or acetone (non-oily nail varnish remover), and dab on affected area. Use it only in a well-ventilated room, and do not smoke. Do not use oily nail varnish removers – usually the more expensive brands. First test on a hidden corner of the carpet as the acetone may damage man-made fibres. Use as little as possible, as over-soaking can damage the backing. Remaining traces of colour can be removed with methylated spirit. Apply a dry-cleaning solvent if necessary.

On a carpet made of man-made fibres, use the least possible amount of the solvent, and dab dry frequently.

Paint
All paint must be dealt with immediately. Once it has dried it is almost impossible to remove. Scrape up and wipe off as much as possible, then treat according to the type of paint.
EMULSION Mop with cold water, working from the edges inwards. Large areas of dried-on emulsion should be left to professional carpet cleaners.
ACRYLIC Mop up with tissues. Sponge with warm water. Finish with methylated spirit or dry-cleaning solvent.
GLOSS OR OIL-BASED PAINT Sponge with white spirit or a dry-cleaning solvent. If dry, soften with paintbrush cleaner.

Large areas need professional attention.

Paraffin
Mop up spillage immediately. Treat the area with a dry-cleaning solvent.

Paraffin stains are very difficult to remove. Get help from a professional.

Perfume
Clean with carpet shampoo, and allow to dry. Use more shampoo if the stain persists.

Plasticine
Scrape off as much as possible, then treat the remainder with a dry-cleaning solvent.

Scorch marks
Bad scorch marks are impossible to remove as the fibres are damaged. For repairing a carpet, see page 49. For slight marks trim the pile with scissors, or lightly shave with a disposable razor. Or remove loose fibres with a stiff brush, then make circular movements with a wire brush or abrasive paper to disguise the area.

Shoe polish
Scrape off and dab with dry-cleaning solvent. Finish with methylated spirit. Clean with carpet shampoo if necessary.

Soft drinks
Mop up. Treat with carpet shampoo. Stubborn marks often respond to methylated spirit.

Soot
Vacuum the area with a suction-only type cleaner, not a brush type. Or shake a rug outside. Do not brush or the mark will spread. Use a dry-cleaning solvent to remove any small marks. Get professionals to treat large areas.

Tar
Very hard to remove. Scrape away any loose deposit. Treat with a dry-cleaning solvent. If the surface is hard, scratch it to allow the solvent to penetrate.

On stubborn stains try dabbing with eucalyptus oil or Polyclens Plus paintbrush cleaner.

Tea
Mop up as much as possible. Treat with carpet shampoo. Treat any left-over stain when dry with dry-cleaning solvent which will remove the grease from milk.

Toothpaste
Scrape up any deposit and treat with carpet shampoo.

Treacle
Scrape off, then treat with carpet shampoo.

Wine
FRESH SPILLS Blot dry, then clean with carpet shampoo. Do not put salt on the carpet; it may affect the colour.
OLD STAINS May respond to glycerine solution (equal parts of water and glycerine) left for an hour, then rinsed off. Sponging with methylated spirit may reduce very old stains.

STAINS ON UPHOLSTERY
Speed is vital in removing all stains, so there is a great advantage in having a proprietary spot-removing kit in the house (see details of manufacturers on the opposite page).

Specific stains on upholstery can be given much the same treatment as described for carpets.

Where possible, treat stains from the back of the fabric. Loose covers, for example, should be removed before treatment. Lay the fabric on a clean cloth face down and apply the solvent on the reverse side.

All velvet, except acrylic velvet such as Dralon, should be treated by a cleaning firm.

Do not dry the fabric artificially. The heat may shrink the fabric or damage some fibres.

Plumbing emergencies: What to do

WATER POURS FROM THE ROOF SPACE

1 Turn off (clockwise) the main stop-cock. It is usually under the kitchen sink (if it is jammed or broken, see below right). Put buckets under the leaks, then turn on all the taps in the house and flush all the toilets to drain the cold-water storage cistern.

2 Find the cause of the trouble. It may be a burst pipe in the loft, or a cistern overflow caused by a failed ball-valve or float and a blocked over-flow pipe.

Repairing a burst pipe, page 65. Adjusting the cistern water level, page 78.

NO WATER COMING FROM A TAP

1 Check the kitchen sink cold tap. If no water flows from it, make sure the main stopcock has not been turned off by accident. If the stop-cock is on, call the regional water authority.

2 If the kitchen tap is working, check the cold-water cistern. It may have drained because of a jammed ball-valve. If it is drained, move the float arm sharply up and down to free the valve, then clean the valve (page 76).
ALTERNATIVELY, in frosty weather there may be an ice plug blocking a supply pipe. If the kitchen cold tap is working, check the flow into the cold-water cistern by pressing down the ball-valve. If there is no inflow, the rising main is blocked, probably between the ceiling and the cistern inlet.

3 If the cistern is filling, check the bathroom taps. If there is no flow from one tap, a supply pipe from the cistern (either hot or cold) is blocked, probably in the roof-space section.

4 To thaw a pipe, strip off any lagging from the affected part and apply hot water bottles, or cloths soaked in boiling water and then wrung out.

5 If a pipe is difficult to get at, blow warm air onto it from an electric hair dryer. Do not use a blow torch – you may set the roof on fire.

LEAKING HOT-WATER CYLINDER

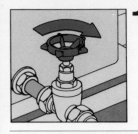

1 Turn off (clockwise) the gate valve, if there is one, in the feed pipe from the cold-water cistern to the hot-water cylinder.
ALTERNATIVELY, turn off the main stopcock and turn on all the taps in the house to drain the cistern. (This will not drain the hot-water cylinder, but will stop water flowing into it.)

2 Switch off the immersion heater, if there is one.

3 Switch off the boiler, or put out the boiler fire.

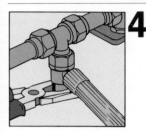

4 Connect a hose to the cylinder drain cock, if there is one (it will be on the supply pipe from the cold-water cistern). Put the other end of the hose into an outside drain.
ALTERNATIVELY, connect the hose to the boiler drain cock (on the return pipe near the bottom of the boiler) and direct the other end of the hose to an outside drain.

5 Open up the drain cock with a drain-cock key or pliers.

6 Get the hot-water cylinder repaired or replaced by a plumber.

IF THE STOPCOCK IS JAMMED OR BROKEN

Use the outside stopcock, if you know where it is. If you have no key, try reaching down to turn the tap by hand or with pliers.
ALTERNATIVELY, for a burst lead pipe in the roof, use a heavy hammer to flatten the pipe between the burst and the cistern, where it crosses roofing timber.
Or for a burst copper pipe in the roof, stuff towelling into the cistern outlet to the pipe, if you can, and raise and tie up the float arm to stop the cistern filling.

How water is supplied to the home

Most British homes have a mains water supply. This is provided by the regional water authority, which distributes the water through iron or heavy plastic water mains.

From these mains, a pipe known as a communication pipe takes the water to the water authority's stopcock – a control valve about 3ft (1m) below the ground at or near the boundary of each property. The

stopcock, which is turned with a long key, is at the bottom of a stoneware guard pipe under a small metal cover set into the surface of the garden or the public footpath outside. This is where the householder's responsibility for his water supply begins.

From the water authority's stopcock, a service pipe carries water into the home. This pipe should rise

slightly towards the house to allow air bubbles to escape; but to avoid frost damage it should be at least 2ft 6in (750mm) and not more than 4ft 5in (1.35m) below the ground surface. The service pipe rises into the house, usually beneath the kitchen sink, and from there is usually referred to as the rising main. Another stopcock for cutting off the household water supply (page 58)

should be provided where the pipe enters the house.

Make sure that you know where the main stopcock is in your house. In a well-appointed house, there will be a drain cock (page 58) immediately above the stopcock, for draining the rising main.

The layout within the house depends upon whether the cold-water system is direct or indirect.

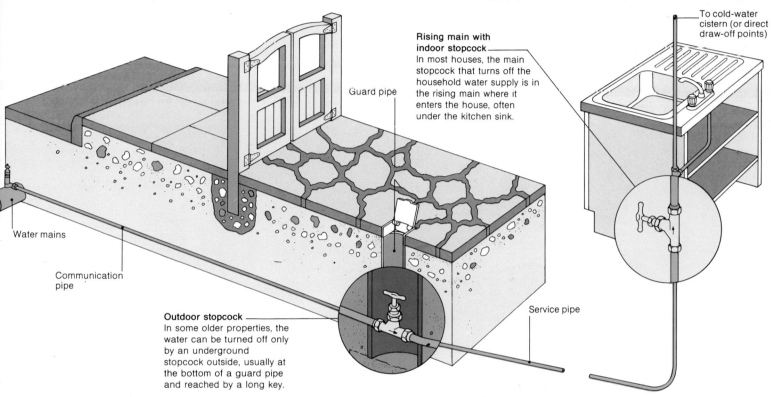

Rising main with indoor stopcock
In most houses, the main stopcock that turns off the household water supply is in the rising main where it enters the house, often under the kitchen sink.

Guard pipe

To cold-water cistern (or direct draw-off points)

Water mains

Communication pipe

Outdoor stopcock
In some older properties, the water can be turned off only by an underground stopcock outside, usually at the bottom of a guard pipe and reached by a long key.

Service pipe

What type of water system do you have?

The cold-water supply
A direct cold-water system is most likely to be found in a dwelling built before 1939 or in a rural or semi-rural area. All the draw-off points to cold taps and lavatory cistern are taken directly from the rising main.

With an indirect system, only the drinking water in the cold tap over the kitchen sink (and possibly pipes to a washing machine and an outside tap) are branched directly from the rising main.

The rising main then goes upwards, preferably against an inside wall, to discharge into a cold-water storage cistern, normally in the roof space. The cistern has distribution pipes that supply the bathroom cold taps and lavatory cistern and feed the hot-water system.

A direct cold-water system is simpler and cheaper to install than an indirect system. It can avoid having pipes or other plumbing fittings in the roof space, where they are vulnerable to frost damage.

Most regional water authorities, however, prefer the provision of an indirect cold-water system in

new properties so that each house has a large cold-water cistern. Otherwise, at times of peak usage, the demand direct from the mains could exceed the supply.

An indirect system has advantages for the householder, too. One advantage is that the stored water is usually high enough to give sufficient head pressure for a conventional shower, and allows for the use of basin and bath mixers instead of individual taps. Also, lavatory cisterns that fill under low pressure from a storage cistern are usually quieter than those connected directly to the rising main, and a leak or burst pipe will be less catastrophic under low pressure than under mains pressure.

And on occasions when the water supply is temporarily cut off – for work on the mains for example – the householder with an indirect system still has plenty of stored water for essential uses.

The hot-water supply
There are two systems for providing hot water. All hot taps may be

supplied from a hot-water storage cylinder, fed from the cold-water cistern and heated by a boiler or immersion heater. Alternatively, hot taps may be supplied from an instantaneous gas multipoint water heater, or a cistern-type electric heater (immersion heater) connected directly to the rising main. This is the usual method of obtaining hot water when all the cold water is direct from the rising main. A gas heater has the advantage of economy, as it heats only the water that is actually drawn off, but delivery is usually slower than from a hot-water cylinder.

Hot-water systems with a storage cylinder heated directly by a boiler were installed extensively in the late 1940s and early 1950s. The boiler is either a back boiler behind a gas fire or open fire, or a separate solid-fuel boiler in the kitchen. In summer the heat is normally supplied by an immersion heater fitted within the cylinder.

Back boilers and separate kitchen boilers have largely been replaced by high-performance

boilers designed for both water heating and central heating. These heat the hot water indirectly through a separate water circuit that acts as a heat exchanger.

Combined units supplying hot and cold water
Some homes have two-in-one plumbing systems, with a cold-water cistern and hot-water cylinder fitted together in one unit. Because they are easy to install and do not need much space, they are often used in self-contained flats where a large house has been converted.

Because of their compact design, two-in-one units can be fitted into a cupboard on the landing or in the bathroom. However, with the cistern at such a low level they cannot usually provide enough pressure for a conventional shower, and there may also be poor pressure to taps and lavatory cisterns on the same floor. Lavatory cisterns need to have full-way ball valves to speed up refilling (page 76).

The tools for the job

Most of the basic tools needed for plumbing are general-purpose tools such as spanners and pliers.

For major additions or alterations, however, you will need extra tools, some of them specialised and expensive and not worth buying for occasional use. They can generally be hired from firms listed in *Yellow Pages* under Hire Services – Tools and Equipment.

A KIT FOR BASIC PLUMBING

Spanners
An average set of open-ended spanners (usually up to 1in or 22mm) can be used for many jobs. You will need both metric and imperial sizes. For larger nuts use a 12in (300mm) adjustable spanner or a pipe wrench. Use a spanner that fits the nut exactly, or it will slip and round off the edges.

Pipe wrenches
For gripping pipes, circular fittings or hexagonal nuts that have been rounded off at the edges. Two wrenches are needed for some jobs. Some pipe wrenches, such as Footprint wrenches, are operated by squeezing the handles together, but the Stillson type has an adjuster nut for altering the jaw size. Useful Stillson wrench sizes are 10in (250mm) and 14in (360mm), with jaw openings up to 1in (25mm) and 1½in (38mm) respectively. For a cistern-retaining nut you may need a wrench or adjustable spanner that will open to about 2½in (60mm).

When using a wrench, always push or pull in the direction of the jaw opening. Pad the jaws with cloth if they are likely to damage the fitting – if it is plastic, for example.

Pliers
A pair of 7in (180mm) standard combination pliers is useful for jobs such as removing split pins from cisterns, and long-nose pliers for gripping a sink or washbasin outlet grid. Mole grips will be useful, also a pair of slip-joint pliers.

Plunger (force cup)
For clearing blockages from a sink or lavatory waste pipe. A medium-sized plunger with a cup about 4in (100mm) across is usually suitable.

Sink-waste cleaner (sink auger)
Used to draw out or dislodge blockages from pipework. A 6ft or 8ft long, ⅜in or ¼in diameter tool (or a 2.4m long, 9mm diameter tool) is

BASIC HOUSEHOLD PLUMBING TOOLS

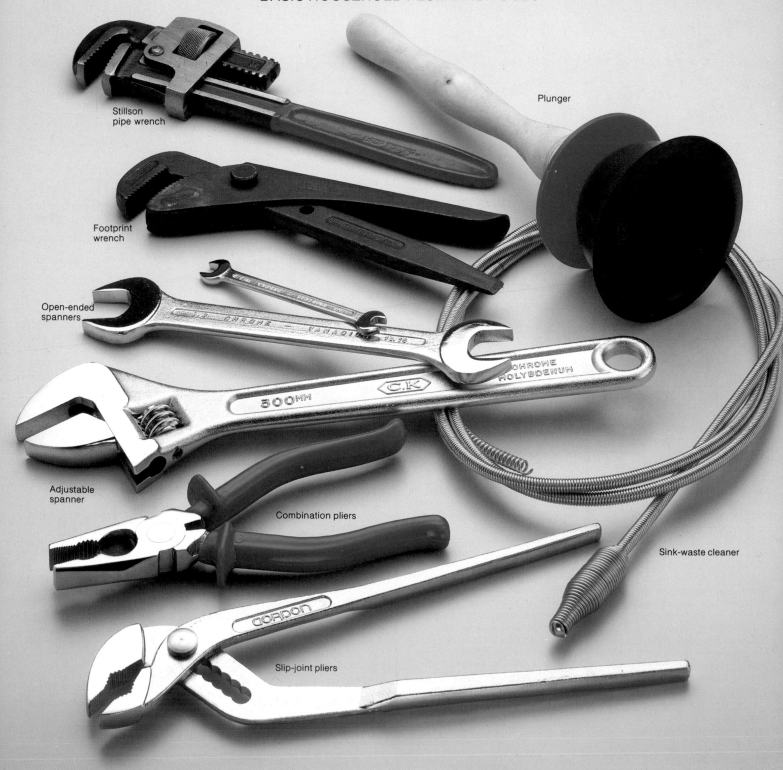

Stillson pipe wrench

Footprint wrench

Open-ended spanners

Adjustable spanner

Combination pliers

Slip-joint pliers

Plunger

Sink-waste cleaner

usually sufficient. A length of expanding curtain wire serves the same purpose, but use an eye end – a hook can catch in the pipe.

What you may also need

SCREWDRIVERS Two flat-bladed screwdrivers – one large, one small – are sufficient for most plumbing jobs. The large one should have a blade about 10in (250mm) long and ⅜in (10mm) wide, the small one a blade about 3in (75mm) long and ³⁄₁₆in (5mm) wide.

BLOWTORCH Needed for soldering capillary joints in piping. The safest and easiest type to use is a gas blowlamp fed by a butane cartridge. Use a fire-resistant mat between the torch flame and flammable material.

VICE AND WORKBENCH Not essential, but useful for some jobs, such as dismantling a ball-valve plug. An engineer's or mechanic's vice, which has serrated jaws, is best for gripping metal pipes – pad the jaws for copper, plastic or chrome fittings. Use a jaw lining on a woodworker's or lightweight portable vice. A Workmate has grooves for holding a pipe.

LADDER Plumbing emergencies usually occur in the loft. A retractable loft ladder is the best means of access. Alternatively, use a ladder that reaches right into the loft.

ELECTRIC TORCH Plumbing is often in dark places. Keep a powerful torch handy – preferably one that is square-shaped so that it will not roll away when put down, or one that is designed to strap to your head.

EXTRAS FOR MORE ADVANCED WORK

Hacksaw

For cutting metal or plastic pipes; a large or small saw is suitable. Most hacksaws are sold with medium-cut general-purpose blades with 24 tpi (teeth per inch). For copper or plastic pipes a blade of 18 tpi is best. For steel pipes use a fine blade of 32 tpi.

File

For smoothing the burred edge of a cut pipe. A half-round 8in (200mm) second-cut file is suitable.

Pipe or tube-bending springs

Hardened steel bending springs allow you to support the inside of copper tubing while bending it by hand. Separate springs are needed for 15mm and 22mm diameter tubing, the common sizes.

Pipe or tube-bending machine

A lightweight machine is useful if you have a number of bends to make in a 15mm or 22mm diameter pipe, and can be hired. It incorporates a curved former for shaping a bend, and separate guide blocks for piping of the two diameters. It can be used in a vice or in the hands.

EXTRA TOOLS FOR MAJOR JOBS

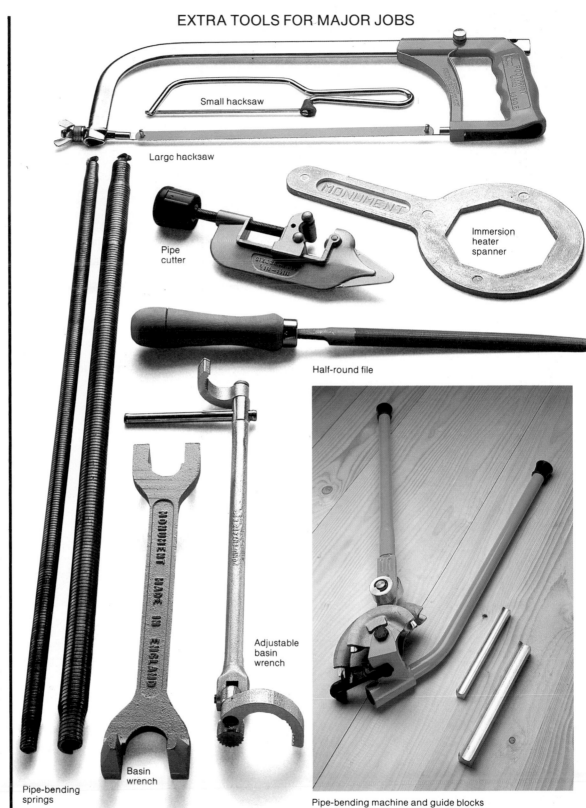

Small hacksaw

Large hacksaw

Pipe cutter

Immersion heater spanner

Half-round file

Pipe-bending springs

Basin wrench

Adjustable basin wrench

Pipe-bending machine and guide blocks

Pipe or tube cutter

Quicker and more accurate than a hacksaw for cutting copper, brass, aluminium and plastic (but not steel). It may have an adjustable slide for cutting tubes of different diameters, and a fixed cutting wheel. The tapered reamer on the front is for removing the burr from the inside of the pipe. A size 1 reamer takes pipes up to 28mm outside diameter.

Basin wrench

The basin wrench (or crowsfoot spanner) will reach the back nuts of bath and basin taps. It fits flat nuts of standard ½in and ¾in taps. The adjustable type, which can be hired, will reach nuts or fittings in awkward places. The swivel jaw is serrated for gripping uneven shapes, and is reversible for loosening or tightening. Different-sized jaws can be fitted for nuts up to 1in (25mm), 1¼in (32mm) and 2in (50mm) across.

Immersion-heater spanner

A very large spanner that will fit the securing nut of a standard immersion heater. It can be hired.

What you may also need

POWER DRILL For drilling through floorboards or walls to fix screws. A variable-speed hammer drill is best, and both wood and masonry bits are necessary. Useful attachments are a wire brush for cleaning metal, and a hole cutter for cutting metal and plastic. The diameters needed for a hole saw are 18mm and 25mm (if hiring, ask for cutters suitable for making holes for 15mm or 22mm tank connectors).

WIRE BRUSHES Useful for cleaning inside pipe ends before making joints, and for removing rust.

Cutting off the water supply

In many homes only the kitchen tap is fed from the rising main, others from the cold-water cistern. But it depends whether the plumbing system is direct or indirect (page 55).

TAPS FED FROM THE CISTERN

1 To isolate a hot or cold tap supplied from the cistern, turn off (clockwise), the gate valve or mini stopcock in the appropriate distribution pipe.

2 Turn on the tap until the water stops flowing.

Alternatively, if there is no gate valve or mini stopcock on the pipe, you will have to drain the cistern:

Draining the cistern

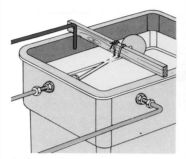

1 Tie the ball-valve arm to a piece of wood laid across the cistern. This stops the in-flow from the mains.

2 Turn on the bathroom cold taps until the water stops flowing, then turn on the hot taps – very little water will flow from them. (You need not turn off the boiler, as the hot-water cylinder will not be drained.)

TAPS FED FROM THE RISING MAIN

Turn off (clockwise) the main indoor stopcock, then turn on the tap until the water stops.

DRAINING THE RISING MAIN

You may want to drain the rising main to take a branch pipe from it or repair the stopcock.

If there is a drain cock above the indoor stopcock, open it with a drain-cock key or pliers. Catch the water, usually only a pint or two, in a bucket or pan.

TURNING OFF THE OUTDOOR STOPCOCK

You may need to turn off the outdoor stopcock if the indoor one is broken, jammed, or has a leak from the spindle. Stopcock keys can usually be bought from hardware shops, but first check the type needed – the tap may have a crutch handle or tapered knob.

Alternatively, make your own.

1 Locate the stopcock, which is under a cover about 4in (100mm) across just inside or just outside the boundary of your property. (If there are two close together, test to find out which is yours, but tell your neighbour.) If you cannot find the outdoor stopcock, call the regional water authority.

2 Raise the cover. This may be difficult if it has not been raised for some time.

3 Insert the stopcock key into the guard pipe and engage the stopcock handle at the bottom. Turn it clockwise.

MAKING YOUR OWN STOPCOCK KEY

If you have no stopcock key, take a piece of strong wood about 3ft (1m) long and in one end cut a V-shaped slot about 1in (25mm) wide at the opening and 3in (75mm) deep.

Securely fix another piece of wood as a cross-bar handle at the other end. Slip the V slot over the stopcock handle to turn it. It should turn a crutch handle or tapered knob.

HELPFUL TIP

If a stopcock is difficult to turn, do not force it – apply a few drops of penetrating oil round the base of the handle and leave at least ten minutes before trying again. Repeat as necessary.

A stopcock that has been open for a long time may be jammed. This can be disastrous in an emergency.

To guard against this, close and open a stopcock fully once or twice a year. After opening a stopcock, give the handle just a quarter turn towards closure. This will prevent jamming without affecting the water flow.

TYPES OF STOPCOCK AND VALVE

Stopcock
A tap with a valve and washer that is inserted into a run of pipe – normally mains pipe – to control the water flow through it. A stopcock is usually kept turned on, being turned off only when necessary to cut off the water. It must be fitted the right way round (an arrow mark shows the flow direction). Most stopcocks have a crutch handle.

Gate valve
A tap, usually with a wheel handle, in which the water flow is controlled by raising or lowering a metal plate (or gate). It can be fitted either way round and is normally used in low-pressure pipes such as cistern distribution pipes. With the gate open, the flow is completely unrestricted. When it is closed, the seal is not as watertight as a stopcock.

Drain cock
A tap without a handle, opened by turning the spindle with a drain-cock key. It is normally kept closed, but has a threaded outlet for attaching a hose when draining is necessary. A drain cock is fitted in those parts of the plumbing system that cannot be drained through household taps – for instance in the boiler or central-heating systems and in the rising main.

Mini (or isolating) stopcock
A small stopcock without a handle, operated by turning a slot screw to open or close a hole to control the water flow. Normally used in a low-pressure supply pipe to a tap or ball valve to cut off the water for repairs. An in-line tap is very similar but has a lever handle and may have a threaded end. It is used to control the flow to a washing machine, for example.

CHOOSING A TAP

Whatever their appearance, most taps work in the same way – turning the handle opens (raises) or closes (lowers) a valve that fits into a valve seat. The valve – a rod and plate known as a jumper valve – is fitted with a washer that has to be replaced when it is worn (when the tap starts dripping).

Some of the latest designs operate differently. The water flow is controlled by two hard-wearing ceramic discs – one fixed, one moving. When the tap is turned on, openings in the disc line up so water can flow through. The discs become smoother and more watertight with wear, so the taps seldom need a new disc. They also open or close with only a quarter turn (through 90 degrees) of the handle.

Taps for washbasins and sinks normally have a $\frac{1}{2}$in diameter inlet that fits into a 15mm pipe. Bath taps usually have a $\frac{3}{4}$in diameter inlet that fits a 22mm pipe. Most taps are made of brass and plated with chromium, but modern designs have a wider range of finishes. Some have plastic handles, others are all plastic.

Two taps with a common spout are known as a mixer. Adjusting the hot and cold handles produces a flow at the required temperature. The taps are linked either by a deck block (flat against the surface) or a pillar block (raised). Most mixers are two-hole types that fit into a standard two-hole sink – one for the hot tap and one for the cold. Some mixers, however, need three holes (a centre hole for the spout) and some (monobloc types) only one.

Pillar tap
The type still often used in the home, with a vertical inlet that fits through a hole in the sink, basin or bath. The conventional tap has a bell-shaped cover – generally known as an easy-clean cover – and a capstan (cross-top) handle.

Handwheel handle
Many modern taps have the cover and handle replaced by a shrouded head that commonly forms a handwheel (a fluted knob) handle – although some shrouded heads are moulded like crosstop handles. Shrouded heads not only give a neater appearance but also prevent water from wet hands going down the spindle and allowing detergent to wash the grease out of the tap mechanism.

Lever handle
Another type of shrouded head has a lever handle, which is easy for elderly or handicapped people to use as it can be pushed rather than gripped. Lever-handle taps usually need only a quarter turn of the handle. Many, but not all, have ceramic discs in place of a valve and washer.

High-neck taps
Ordinary pillar taps have the spout opening about $\frac{7}{8}$in (22mm) above their base on the sink, but high-neck types stand well clear of the sink – with the spout about $3\frac{3}{4}$in (95mm) above the base. With a shallow sink this allows room for filling a bucket or rinsing a large pan under the tap. The handles may be any of the standard designs.

Bib tap
A tap with a horizontal inlet, once commonly fitted into the wall above a sink or basin. Bib taps are now used mainly outdoors, in the garden or a garage. Many are of unadorned brass with a crutch (straight) handle, but some are chromium plated with a capstan handle or shrouded head.

Hose nozzle
Some bib taps have a threaded nozzle for fitting a hose. A tap installed against an outside wall should have an angled head, otherwise you will graze your knuckles when you turn the handle.

Kitchen mixer
The spout has separate channels for hot and cold water which mix only as they emerge. This is because the kitchen cold tap is fed direct from the mains, and it is illegal to mix cold water from the mains and hot water from a storage cistern in one fitting. The spout usually swivels and should be able to reach both of the bowls in a two-bowl sink.

Bath or basin mixer
The hot and cold water merges within the mixer body, as both taps are usually fed from a cistern. It is against the law to fit this type of mixer in a direct system with cold water from the rising main and hot water from a cylinder. This is because mains pressure can alter, and differences in pressure might cause stored – and maybe contaminated – water to be drawn back into the mains. When a mixer is used with an instantaneous gas water heater, both of the taps are fed from the rising main.

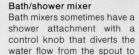

Bath/shower mixer
Bath mixers sometimes have a shower attachment with a control knob that diverts the water flow from the spout to the shower sprinkler. Do not buy a bath/shower mixer unless your storage cistern can supply adequate pressure.

Monobloc mixer
A single-hole mixer having a compact body with the handles and spout very close together. Some types have very narrow inlet pipes. There are monobloc designs for both kitchens and bathrooms. Kitchen monobloc mixers often include a hot-rinse spray and brush fed from the hot-water pipe by a flexible hose, so that the spray can be lifted from its socket for use.

Repairing a dripping tap

A dripping tap usually means that the washer needs renewing. but can also result from a damaged valve seating. Unless the drip is stopped, it will eventually stain the sink or bath. In very cold weather, the constant dribble of water through the outlet pipe is likely to freeze and cause a blockage. If the drip is from a mixer spout, renew both tap washers.

You will need

Tools One large open-ended spanner, normally $\frac{13}{16}$in for a $\frac{1}{2}$in tap or $\frac{15}{16}$in for a $\frac{3}{4}$in tap (or an adjustable spanner); old screwdriver (for prising). Possibly also: one small spanner (normally $\frac{5}{16}$in); one or two pipe wrenches; cloth for padding jaws; one $\frac{3}{16}$in (5mm), one $\frac{3}{8}$in (10mm) screwdriver.
Materials Replacement washer, or a washer-and-jumper valve unit; alternatively, a washer-and-seating set (see below); petroleum jelly. Possibly also: penetrating oil.

REMOVING THE HEADGEAR

1 Cut off the water supply (page 58). Make sure the tap is turned fully on, and put the plug in the plughole to stop any small parts falling down the waste pipe.

2 Unscrew the bell-shaped cover of a conventional tap to expose the hexagonal headgear nut. This can usually be done by hand. If it is stiff, and you have to use a spanner or pipe wrench, pad the jaws with a rag to avoid damaging the surface. ALTERNATIVELY, with a shrouded head, prise off the top plate and undo the retaining screw. Then lift off the handle to expose the headgear nut. If the handle has no retaining screw, it may pull straight off, or pull off after you have given it a half turn. Or there may be a small screw in the side of the head.

3 Undo the headgear nut with a spanner. With a conventional head, the gap between the base and the lifted cover when the tap is turned fully on should be about $\frac{1}{2}$in (13mm) – not wide enough for most adjustable spanners. You will need an open-ended spanner to get at the nut. With a shrouded head you can use an adjustable or ring spanner.

4 If the nut is difficult to turn, do not force it – you may twist the base of the tap and strain the inlet pipe, and perhaps crack the basin. Instead, apply penetrating oil round the joint, wait about ten minutes to give it time to soak in, then try turning the nut again. You may have to make several applications. To guard against cracking the basin, hold the tap base steady with a padded pipe wrench, and use it to counteract the force applied to the nut by pushing in the opposite direction.

Another way is to make a gripping tool from two lengths of wood

joined together at one end with a bolt; use it to hold both the body and the nozzle steady while you apply counterpressure.

FITTING THE WASHER

With a tap fed from the cistern, the jumper valve and washer will probably be fixed in the removed headgear. With a tap fed from the rising main, the jumper valve and washer will probably be resting on the valve seating when you remove the headgear.

1 If there is a small nut holding the washer in place, unscrew it with a spanner (normally $\frac{5}{16}$in). If it is difficult to undo, put penetrating oil round it and try again when it has soaked in. Prise off the washer from the jumper-valve plate.

ALTERNATIVELY, if the nut is impossible to remove, you can replace

---

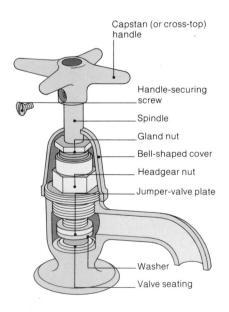

Top plate
Retaining screw
Headgear nut

Jumper valve
Washer

Capstan (or cross-top) handle

Handle-securing screw
Spindle
Gland nut
Bell-shaped cover
Headgear nut
Jumper-valve plate

Washer
Valve seating

Shrouded-head tap

The valve and washer are the same as in a conventional tap (below), but the spindle is sealed by an O-ring rather than a gland. The tap handle and headgear has to be removed both to change a washer and to renew an O-ring.

Conventional tap

The jumper valve is in the shape of a rod and plate, and the washer is attached to the base of the plate. When changing a washer, the handle is lifted off with the headgear. When adjusting the gland, the handle has to be removed so that the bell-shaped cover can be pulled off out of the way.

REPAIRING THE VALVE SEATING

When renewing a washer, look at the base of the tap, in which the valve is seated. If it is rusted or scored by grit, the watertight seal will not be effective and the tap will keep on dripping, even with a new washer.

The simplest repair is with a washer-and-seating set. This has a plastic seat to fit into the metal seat, and a washer-and-jumper unit to fit into the headgear. When the tap is turned off, the plastic seating is forced firmly in. It may take a few days for the new seating to give a watertight fit. An alternative repair is to buy or hire a tap reseating tool and grind the seat smooth.

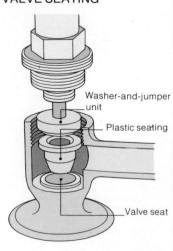

Washer-and-jumper unit
Plastic seating
Valve seat

both the jumper valve and washer in one unit.

2 After fitting a new washer or washer and jumper, grease the threads on the base of the tap before reassembling. Make sure the tap is turned off before you turn on the water supply.

HELPFUL TIP

If you cannot undo the peg or grub screw securing a fixed jumper valve and washer, shear it off by force. Insert a screwdriver between the base of the headgear and the washer plate and prise out the jumper. Before you fit the new jumper and washer, roughen the surface of a metal (but not a plastic) jumper rod with a coarse file. This helps it to grip when you refit the jumper into the head.

Tap conversion kit

A tap with a crutch or capstan handle and a bell-shaped cover can be given a newer look with a tap conversion kit. The kit contains a shrouded-head handle and new plastic headgear for one size of tap, and is available from most DIY stores. Some kits have bushes to fit ½in, ¾in or ⅜in taps (imported taps may be ¾in, or sometimes ⅝in).

The conversion can prove disappointing, because the gleaming new handle may show up the worn condition of the tap nozzle. But a conversion kit is convenient for replacing a broken shrouded-head handle without removing the tap. Fitting instructions are given with the kit.

FITTING A WASHER UNIT TO A SUPATAP

There is no need to turn off the water. The tap has a check valve that drops to stop the water flow as the nozzle is unscrewed.

1 Use a spanner to loosen the hexagonal retaining nut at the top of the nozzle by turning it anticlockwise (it has a left-hand thread).

2 Hold the loosened nut with one hand while you turn the tap on. Keep turning it to unscrew the nozzle. At first the water flow will increase, but will stop just before the nozzle comes off in your hand.

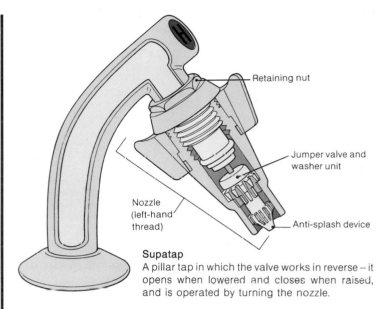

— Retaining nut

Jumper valve and washer unit

Nozzle (left-hand thread)

Anti-splash device

Supatap
A pillar tap in which the valve works in reverse – it opens when lowered and closes when raised, and is operated by turning the nozzle.

3 Tap the base of the nozzle against something firm – not the washbasin, or you may chip the surface. This will loosen the anti-splash device that projects slightly from the top. Then turn the nozzle upside down. The anti-splash device, which contains the jumper and washer unit, will fall out.

4 Prise out the jumper valve with a screwdriver blade inserted between the lip of the anti-splash device and the washer plate.

5 Snap the new washer and jumper unit into place, then reassemble the tap by screwing the nozzle clockwise (left-hand thread).

Leakage from the body of the tap – from round the spindle, the base of a swivel spout, or the diverter knob on a shower – is caused by a faulty gland or O-ring seal.

This sort of leak is most likely to occur on a kitchen cold tap with a bell-shaped cover and visible spindle. Detergent-charged water from

wet hands may have run down the spindle and washed the grease out of the gland (or stuffing box) that makes a watertight joint round the spindle. If the tap is used with a hose for filling a washing machine or watering the garden, back pressure from the hose connection will also weaken the gland.

With a stopcock, leakage round the spindle is commoner than a worn jumper-valve washer.

On a modern tap, especially one with a shrouded head, there is an O-ring seal instead of a gland, and it rarely needs replacing. O-ring seals are also used on a mixer swivel spout or a shower/mixer diverter mechanism, and they may occasionally become worn.

You will need
Tools Small spanner (normally 11⁄16in) or adjustable spanner. Possibly also: one 3⁄16in (5mm) and one 3⁄8in (10mm) screwdriver; penknife or screwdriver for prising; two small wooden blocks about 3⁄8in (10mm) deep (such as spring clothespegs). *Materials* Packing material (either knitting wool, graphite, or O-ring). Possibly also: petroleum jelly; O-rings (and possibly washers) of the correct size – take the old ones with you when buying, or give the make of tap.

ADJUSTING THE GLAND

There is no need to cut off the water supply to the tap.

1 With the tap turned off, undo the small screw (facing page) that secures the capstan handle and put it in a safe place (it is very easily lost), then remove the handle. If there is no screw, the handle should pull off.

HELPFUL TIP

If a conventional tap handle is difficult to pull off after you have removed the screw, turn the tap fully on, raise the bell-shaped cover, and put a block of wood on each side between the raised cover and the tap body. Then turn the tap off (in a clockwise direction). The pressure from the raised cover will force the handle off. Remove the blocks of wood and temporarily slip the handle on again just far enough to fully close the tap.

Curing a leak from a spindle or spout (continued)

2 Remove the bell-shaped cover to reveal the gland nut – the highest nut on the spindle. Tighten the nut about half a turn with a spanner.

3 Turn the tap on by temporarily slipping the handle back on, then check whether there is still a leak from the spindle. If there is not, turn the gland nut another quarter turn and reassemble the tap. Do not overtighten the gland nut, or the tap will be hard to turn off.

4 If there is still a leak, give another half turn and check again.

5 If the gland continues leaking after you have adjusted it as far as possible, repack the gland.

CHECKING THE PACKING

1 With the tap turned off and the handle and cover removed, use a spanner to remove the gland nut.

2 Note the type of packing used in the gland. In an older-style tap it may be string or hemp, in a modern tap graphite or a rubber O-ring. String can be replaced with wool (see below). Replace other packing with the same material.

RENEWING THE O-RING ON A SHROUDED-HEAD TAP

1 Cut off the water supply to the tap (page 58) and remove the tap handle and headgear in the same way as for renewing a washer.

2 Hold the headgear between your fingers and turn the spindle clockwise to unscrew and remove the washer unit.

3 Prise out the O-ring at the top of the washer unit with a screwdriver.

4 Grease the new O-ring with petroleum jelly, fit it in position, and reassemble the tap.

RENEWING SWIVEL SPOUT O-RINGS

1 With both taps turned off, remove the retaining screw at the base of the spout. Ease out the spout by lifting and twisting it from side to side.

2 Note the position of the O-rings (probably two) and remove.

3 Grease new O-rings of the correct size with petroleum jelly and fit them in position.

4 Smear the inside of the spout end with petroleum jelly, then refit.

REPLACING SHOWER-DIVERTER O-RINGS

Although diverters vary in design, all have a sprung rod and plate attached to the diverter knob. When the knob is lifted, the plate opens the shower outlet and seals the tap outlet for as long as the shower is turned on.

1 With the bath taps turned off, lift the shower-diverter knob and undo the headgear nut with a spanner (probably ½in size).

2 Lift out the diverter body and note the position of the washers and O-rings.

3 Remove the knob from the diverter body by turning it anticlockwise. You may need to grip it with a wrench.

4 Withdraw the rod and plate from the diverter body and remove the small O-ring at the top of the rod.

5 Grease a new O-ring of the correct size with petroleum jelly and fit it in place.

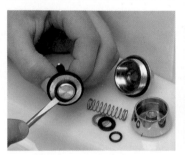

6 Replace all other rubber washers and O-rings on the base of the rod and plate. Old ones may have to be prised out.

REPACKING A STOPCOCK WITH WOOL

The gland on an old capstan-handle tap or a stopcock is the type most likely to need repacking with wool.

handle and cover as for adjusting the gland. Undo the gland nut and slide it up the spindle out of the way.

1 Turn off the stopcock. If it has a bell-shaped cover, remove the

2 Rake out the gland packing below the nut with a penknife or similar tool.

3 To repack with knitting wool, steep a length in petroleum jelly and wind and stuff it into the gland with a screwdriver blade. Continue until the packing material is caulked down hard, then reassemble the tap.

Dealing with an airlock

If the water flow from a tap (usually a hot tap) is poor when fully turned on, then hisses and bubbles and stops altogether, air has somehow entered the system and there is an airlock in the supply pipe.

This is most likely to occur after the water system has been partially drained for repairs or improvements, or after a lot of water has been drawn off – perhaps for a bath or for washing clothes – and temporarily emptied the cistern.

You will need
Tools Length of hose with a tap adaptor at each end. Possibly also: dishcloth; screwdriver.

1 Connect one end of the hose to the tap giving the trouble. If it is a ¾in bathroom tap and the hose is difficult to fit, connect to the nearby washbasin hot tap instead.

2 Connect the other end of the hose to the kitchen cold tap or another mains-fed tap. Turn on the faulty tap first, then the mains-fed tap. The pressure of the mains water should blow the air bubble out of the pipe.

AIRLOCK IN A SUPATAP

Unscrew and remove the nozzle from the faulty tap (as for *Fitting a*

washer, page 61), then connect the hose to the outlet. Do not touch the protruding, pin-like check valve, or water will spray out. Fit the other end of the hose to a mains-fed tap and turn the tap on.

AIRLOCK IN A KITCHEN MIXER

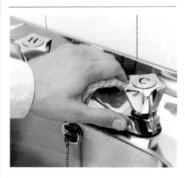

If the hot tap will not work, remove the swivel spout (page 62) and hold a cloth firmly over the spout hole while you turn on first the hot tap then the cold tap.

IF AIRLOCKS KEEP OCCURRING

There are a number of ways that air can be drawn into the water system and cause airlocks. If airlocks occur continually, check:

1 Is the cold-water cistern too small for the household's needs? If

it is smaller than the standard 50 gallons (227 litres), replace it with one of standard size.

2 Is the ball valve in the cold-water cistern sluggish? Watch the cistern emptying while someone fills the bath. If the valve does not open wide enough as water is drawn off, there will be a slow inflow and the cistern will empty before the bath is filled, allowing air to be drawn into the distribution pipe. Dismantle and clean the ball valve (page 76).

3 Is the supply pipe from the cold-water cistern to the hot-water cylinder obstructed or too narrow? Check that any gate valve is fully open, and that the pipe is at least 22mm across. Replace it if it is narrower, as hot water drawn off for a bath is evidently not being replaced quickly enough, allowing the water level in the vent pipe to fall below the level of the hot-water distribution pipe, and air to enter.

Different ways of joining pipes

PREPARING THE PIPE ENDS

Before two pipe lengths of any material can be joined, the ends must be cut square and smooth. Copper and plastic can both be dealt with in the same way, as described here. You may be able to cut polybutylene with a sharp knife.

You will need
Tools Hacksaw or pipe cutter; half-round file. Possibly also: vice.

1 Cut the pipe ends square using a pipe cutter or hacksaw. Holding the pipe in a vice while sawing helps to ensure a square cut. For a plastic pipe, pad metal vice jaws to prevent damage to the pipe surface.

2 Smooth away burrs inside and outside the cut ends with a file or the reamer of the pipe cutter.

MAKING A COMPRESSION JOINT

A strong and easy method of joining copper piping and some plastic pipes. Tightening the nuts is critical – the joint will leak if it is loose, and also if it is strained through over-tightening.

You will need
Tools Two adjustable spanners (with jaw openings up to 1½in wide for fittings on 28mm piping); OR, if you have any that fit, two open-ended spanners – cap nut sizes on different makes of fittings vary.
Materials Compression fitting; pipe jointing compound.

1 Unscrew and remove a cap nut of the compression fitting. Note which way round the olive is fitted, then remove it also.

2 Take one of the cut and smoothed pipe ends (see left) and slide the cap nut over it, then the olive. Make sure the olive is the same way round as it was in the fitting (with some makes this is crucial; with others it is not).

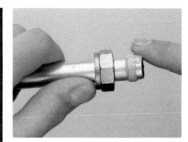

3 For a copper fitting, smear jointing compound on the pipe end and the outside of the olive.

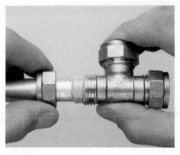

4 Thrust the pipe end into an opening of the sleeve as far as the pipe stop. Then slide the olive and nut up to the connector and hand-tighten the cap nut.

Continued on page 64

Different ways of joining pipes (continued)

5 Hold the sleeve securely with one spanner while you give the cap nut one and a quarter turns with the other. Do not overtighten.

6 Fit piping into other openings of the fitting in the same way.

HELPFUL TIPS
Until you have had some practice in making compression joints, take care not to overtighten a cap nut on copper piping. One way to do this is to make a scratch along the sleeve and cap nut before dismantling it. When you refit and tighten the nut, you will have made a complete turn when the marks meet.

When fitting a sleeve to a vertical pipe, use a spring-clip clothes peg to stop the olive and cap nut slipping down the pipe while you push it in.

MAKING A SOLDERED JOINT

A strong, neat method of joining copper piping so that the joints are not easily seen.

You will need
Tools Wire wool or fine emery paper; blow torch; clean rag.
Materials Tin of flux; soft lead-free solder wire for end-feed joints only. Possibly also; clean paint brush; sheet of glass fibre or other fireproof material for placing between the joint and woodwork while using the blow torch.

1 Clean the ends of the cut and smoothed pipes (page 63) and the inside of the fitting thoroughly with wire wool or fine emery paper. They must be completely clean to make a successful joint.

2 Smear the cleaned surfaces with flux. Use a clean brush, not a finger, for a lot of joints. Push the pipe into the fitting as far as the pipe stop. For an integral-ring fitting, push piping into all the openings because all the solder rings will melt once heat is applied.

3 Wipe off excess flux with a clean rag, otherwise the solder will spread along the pipe surface.

4 Fix the pipe securely in position with pipe clips.

5 For an integral-ring fitting, heat the joint with a blow torch until a silver ring of solder appears all round the mouth of the joint. Solder all the joints on the fitting in the same operation.

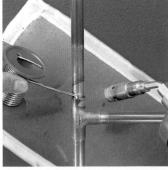

ALTERNATIVELY, for an end-feed fitting, heat the joint until you see flux vapours escaping. Then remove the heat (otherwise the solder will melt too fast and drip) and apply soft solder wire round the mouth of the fitting and heat again until a silver ring of solder appears all round. If you have to leave some joints of the fitting until later, wrap a damp cloth round those already made to stop the solder re-melting.

6 Leave the joint undisturbed for about 20 minutes while it cools.

MAKING A KONTITE PUSH-FIT JOINT

A quick and simple method of joining copper piping. The only tools needed are those for preparing the pipe ends (page 63).

1 Take one of the cut and smoothed pipe ends and push it into the connector sleeve until it meets the built-in tube stop.

2 Fit piping into the other openings of the sleeve connector in the same way.

MAKING AN ACORN PUSH-FIT JOINT

A quick and simple method of joining polybutylene, copper or CPVC piping. To fit piping of Imperial size you will have to remove the end cap and O-ring seal and replace the seal with an adapter ring. Consult the fitting maker's instructions.

You will need
Tools Pencil; measuring tape.
Materials Silicone lubricant or petroleum jelly.

1 Check that the cut pipe end is well smoothed (page 63), otherwise it could damage the O-ring seal in the fitting, allowing leakage.

2 For plastic piping, push the support sleeve into the pipe end.

3 Mark the pipe 25mm from the end. This is the insertion depth into the fitting.

4 Smear the pipe end as far as the insertion line with lubricant. Use silicone lubricant for plastic piping, petroleum jelly for copper piping.

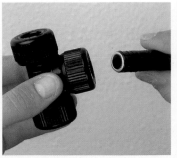

5 Push the pipe into the fitting up to the insertion mark. If it is not pushed fully home the pipe will blow out under pressure.

MAKING A SOLVENT-WELDED JOINT

The only method for joining CPVC piping. Work in a well-ventilated place if possible because the solvent gives off strong fumes. Do not run water through the jointed pipe for at least 1 hour for a cold-water pipe or 4 hours for a hot-water pipe.

The instructions given by the pipe manufacturer may vary slightly from those given below; follow the manufacturer's instructions where available.

You will need
Tools Pencil; medium abrasive paper; clean rag; clean tissue.
Materials Degreaser or spirit cleaner recommended by the pipe manufacturer; recommended solvent cement for piping (brush usually supplied).

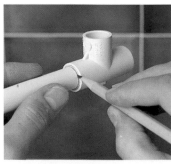

1 Insert one of the cut, smoothed pipe ends (page 63) into the opening of the fitting as far as the pipe stop (do not force it). Mark the insertion depth with a pencil.

2 Withdraw the pipe and roughen the surface as far as the pencil mark with medium-grade abrasive paper. Do not use steel wool, which would polish rather than roughen.

3 Roughen the inside of the fitting in the same way.

4 Clean the pipe end and inside the fitting with rag and spirit cleaner or degreaser. Wipe dry with a clean tissue.

5 Use a brush to apply a liberal, even coat of cement to the pipe end. Apply more cement sparingly into the opening of the fitting.

6 Stroke the cement along the surface rather than round it.

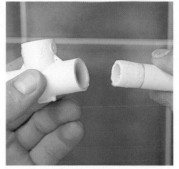

7 Push the pipe fully into the fitting with a slight twist.

8 Hold in place for about ten seconds. Do not remove surplus cement.

Bending copper piping

Never try to bend rigid copper piping by hand without a spring to support the pipe walls – the pipe will lose its shape.

You will need

Tools Bending springs of the required diameter (15mm or 22mm); OR pipe-bending machine with 15mm and 22mm formers and guide blocks; metal bar such as screwdriver shaft; length of string. *Materials* Petroleum jelly.

BENDING WITH A SPRING

1 If the pipe is longer than the spring, tie string to the spring end.

2 Grease the spring well and push it into the pipe.

3 Bend the pipe across your knee with gentle hand pressure to the required angle.

4 Overbend the pipe a little more, then ease it gently back again. This action helps to free the spring and makes it easier to withdraw.

5 Insert a bar through the spring loop. Twist the spring to reduce its diameter, then pull it out.

BENDING WITH A MACHINE

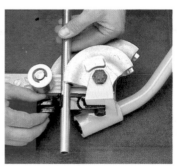

1 Clamp the pipe against the correct-sized semicircular former.

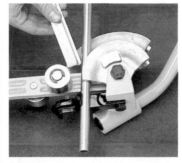

2 Place the guide block of the correct diameter between the pipe and the movable handle.

3 Squeeze the handles together until the pipe is curved to the required angle round the semicircular former.

Repairing a burst pipe

Pipes may burst in very cold weather because water expands by about 10 per cent as it changes into ice. If expansion along the pipe is prevented – perhaps by two ice plugs forming – the pressure can split the pipe or force open a joint.

Metal pipes are more likely to suffer than plastic pipes, and copper and stainless steel pipes are less vulnerable to frost damage than old lead piping. Lead, being a soft metal with little elasticity, expands to accommodate an ice plug but does not contract completely when the ice melts. After a number of freezes the pipe wall will have expanded and thinned to such an extent that it bursts. Lead piping looks silver-grey when scratched.

A split or damaged copper or plastic pipe can be temporarily repaired with a proprietary burst-pipe repair kit such as epoxy putty. Or, in an emergency, a pipe not under mains pressure can be patched with a length of hose.

Make a permanent repair as soon as possible – cut off the water supply (page 58), drain the pipe and replace the damaged length. For a split less than 3½in (90mm) long in a copper pipe, you may be able to make a permanent repair with a slip coupling (see right).

For lead piping, use a tape-repair kit for a strong temporary repair that will allow you to restore the water supply without waiting for a plumber (see next page).

USING A SLIP COUPLING

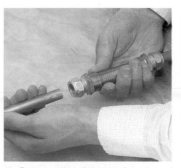

1 Cut out the damaged part and slide the slip end of the coupling (with no pipe stop) onto a pipe end. Then push it onto the other end.

2 Unscrew the compression nuts and slide the nuts and olives at each end along the pipe. Then apply pipe jointing compound.

3 Refit the nuts and olives and screw finger tight. Then tighten with a spanner (facing page).

Repairing a burst pipe (continued)

PATCHING A SPLIT BRANCH PIPE

1 Cut a length of hose to cover the pipe for at least 2in (50mm) beyond the ends of the damage. Split the hose down its length.

2 Wrap the hose round the pipe to meet at the edges. If the pipe is 22mm and the hose will not meet, ensure that the split is covered.

3 Secure the hose round the damaged pipe with three or more hose clips or a series of wire loops.

BANDAGING A LEAD PIPE WITH A TAPE-REPAIR KIT

1 Cut off the water supply (page 58) and drain the pipe.

2 Hammer the ends of the split together, as far as possible.

3 Clean the pipe around the split with fine abrasive paper or wire wool. Make sure the pipe is dry.

4 Cover the split in the pipe, and 1in (25mm) beyond the split at each end, with reinforcing tape. Wind the tape round with a half overlap on each tape width.

5 Cut a 6in (150mm) length of amalgamating tape and remove

the backing film. Do not lose sight of which side is exposed (both sides look the same).

6 Wrap the amalgamating tape (exposed side down) round the pipe for 1in (25mm) beyond each end of the reinforcing tape, stretching it nearly three times its own length as you do so.

7 Wind a final layer of reinforcing tape over the taped area.

8 Allow 2 hours before running water through the bandaged pipe.

9 Get a plumber to repair the pipe as soon as possible.

10 When the pipe has been permanently repaired, lag it with pipe insulation to guard against it freezing again.

Installing an outside tap

A tap with a threaded nozzle against an outside wall can be useful for connecting a hose. Tell your regional water authority before making the installation. There will be an extra charge on your water rate for the tap, and, to prevent the risk of contamination by back-siphonage, you must insert a double check valve as close to the new tap as practicable. Taps incorporating check valves are also available.

Installation involves running a branch pipe from the rising main through the wall to the tap. Take into account that the interior floor level could be 6-10in (150-250mm) above the damp-proof course, and that the branch pipe needs to be higher than the main stopcock and its drain cock.

The instructions given are for fitting copper piping run from a 15mm rising main with compression joints; other materials or joints could be used. Make compression joints as described on page 63. You need not fit a stopcock into the branch pipe, but it allows you to do the job in two stages, and in winter you can cut off the water supply to the tap and drain it to prevent frost damage. Garden plumbing kits are available containing all the necessary parts.

The best way to make a hole through the brick wall of a house is with a heavy-duty power drill equipped with a 6mm diameter, 14in (360mm) long pilot bit for masonry and a 16mm diameter, 8in (200mm) long masonry bit.

You will need
Tools Two adjustable spanners; hacksaw; half-round file; power drill with masonry bits for fixing screws; heavy-duty power drill with masonry bits; screwdriver; two spring-clip clothes pegs; soft pencil; measuring tape; spirit level. Possibly also: shallow pan.
Materials PTFE thread-sealing tape; jointing compound; mastic wall filler; angled ½in bib tap with threaded nozzle; 15mm stopcock with compression ends; 15mm double check valve with compression ends; 15mm copper piping, length according to tap location – normally about 4ft (1.2m); compression fittings as follows: 15mm equal tee (preferably with one slip end), two 15mm 90 degree elbows, one 15mm wallplate elbow (or bib-tap flange).

POSITIONING THE TAP

1 Mark the required position on the outside wall of the kitchen, as

near as possible to the rising main.

2 Check that the mark is high enough for putting a bucket underneath the tap, and is at least 10in (250mm) above the damp-proof course (recognised by a wide line of mortar in the brickwork).

3 Make another mark for the hole through the wall about 6in (150mm) above the tap mark.

4 Take measurements from the hole mark to a point such as a window, so that you can locate and check the hole position inside.

5 Mark the position of the hole on the inside of the wall. Check that it will not interfere with any inside fitting and will be above the position of the main stopcock on the rising main.

FITTING THE BRANCH PIPE INSIDE

1 Turn off (clockwise) the main stopcock, then turn on the kitchen cold tap to drain the pipe.

2 If there is a drain cock above the stopcock, turn it on to drain the rising main. A shallow pan should be sufficient to catch the amount of

water (usually less than a pint) that will run out.

CHECK THE RISING MAIN
Although the rising main is normally 15mm copper piping, in some older houses it could be made of lead or galvanised steel. Get connections to a lead pipe made by a plumber. To join copper piping to galvanised steel, you will need a special tee connector.

If the rising main is 22mm, use a 22mm tee connector with a reduced 15mm branch.

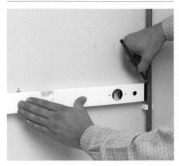

3 Mark the rising main at a point level with the hole mark on the inside wall. Make a second mark ¾in (19mm) higher.

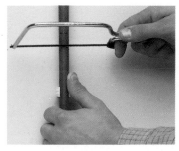

4 Cut through the rising main squarely with a hacksaw at the lowest point marked. If there was not a drain cock above the main stopcock, a small amount of water will run out as you saw through.

5 Cut through the second mark on the rising main and remove the segment of pipe.

6 Use a file to smooth the pipe ends and remove burrs, and to square the ends if necessary.

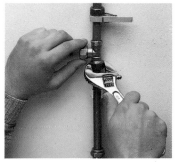

7 Using spring-clip clothes pegs to stop the caps and olives slipping down the pipe, fit the tee connector to the rising main with the branch outlet pointing towards the hole mark. Fitting will be easier if the tee has one slip end (with no pipe stop), otherwise you will have to spring the cut ends into the fitting.

8 Cut a 3in (75mm) length of piping and connect it to the branch of the tee.

9 Connect the stopcock to the piping, with its arrow mark pointing away from the rising main. Angle the stopcock with its handle leaning away from the wall.

10 Close the new stopcock by turning it clockwise. You can now turn on the main stopcock and restore the water supply.

11 Cut a 3in (75mm) length of piping and connect it to the outlet of the stopcock.

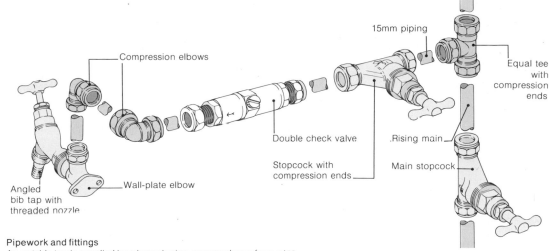

Compression elbows

15mm piping

Equal tee with compression ends

Double check valve

Rising main

Stopcock with compression ends

Main stopcock

Angled bib tap with threaded nozzle

Wall-plate elbow

Pipework and fittings
An outside tap is supplied by a branch pipe, commonly run from a tee connector fitted into the rising main. Instead of a tee connector, you can use a self-boring tap, which can be fitted without turning off the water. No separate stopcock is then needed in the branch pipe.

12 Connect the check valve to the pipe, making sure that its arrow mark points in the same direction as the stopcock arrow.

CONNECTING THE OUTSIDE TAP

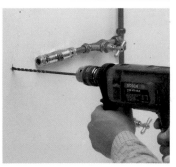

1 Use the pilot bit to drill through the wall from the inside first, making sure to keep the drill at right angles to the wall.

2 Withdraw the bit at intervals to cool it and to pull out dust.

3 Use the larger bit, working from both ends, to make a hole wide enough for a 15mm diameter pipe to fit through easily.

4 Measure the distance from the hole to the newly fitted check valve.

5 Cut a length of pipe to reach between them, allowing extra for fitting into the check valve and an elbow connector (push the pipe into each fitting as far as it will go to check the amount). Cut a second

length to go through the wall – 14in (360mm) will be long enough unless the wall is exceptionally thick.

6 Join the two lengths with an elbow connector and push the 14in (360mm) length out through the wall hole.

7 Connect the free end to the check valve. If this is difficult, undo the pipe at the wall hole and connect the check valve first.

8 Outside the house, cut the projecting piping to leave only 1in (25mm) sticking out from the wall.

9 Fit an elbow connector to the projecting pipe, making sure that the other end of the elbow points towards the tap position mark.

10 Measure from the elbow to the tap mark and cut another length of piping to fit the distance; again allow for fitting into the connectors.

11 Fit the pipe to the inlet of the wall-plate elbow.

12 Fit the other end of the pipe temporarily into the projecting elbow, then hold the wall plate against the wall and mark the position of the screw holes.

13 Put aside the wall-plate elbow and pipe end, and drill and plug the wall.

14 Join the pipe to the projecting elbow and fix the plate to the wall.

FITTING THE TAP

1 Bind PTFE tape one turn anti-clockwise round the tail thread.

2 Screw the tap fully into the outlet of the wall-plate elbow.

3 If the tap is not upright when screwed home, take it off again, put one or two washers over the inlet and refit. Adjust in this way until it is tight and upright.

4 Open up the new stopcock inside, and check all the pipe joints for leaks. Tighten if necessary.

5 Turn on the newly fitted outside tap and check that it is working properly.

6 Use mastic or polyurethane foam filler to seal round the pipe holes in the wall.

Renovating and repairing a bath

Bath renovation is best done by professional firms – listed in *Yellow Pages* under Bath Equipment. They renovate a suite in about one day – cleaning, repairing cracks or chips, and applying a thin coat of hard-wearing plastic, available in a range of colours. Remove lime scale caused by hard water with a proprietary bath cleaner.

REPAIRING BATH ENAMEL

1 Fill small surface chips with an epoxy resin filler, then thoroughly degrease the surface.

2 Rub the surface smooth with fine abrasive paper, then coat the repaired area with two coats of matching bath enamel, following the instructions on the pack.

REPAIRING A PLASTIC BATH

Acrylic is easily damaged by heat, such as a lighted cigarette placed even briefly against the surface of the bath.

Such marks cannot be repaired. But you can polish out surface scratches with metal-polish wadding, because the colour goes right through the material.

Such a repair is not possible with glass-reinforced polyester – it can be damaged by abrasive cleaners and is usually coloured in the top layer of material only.

CHANGING BATH TAPS

Because of the cramped space at the end of a bath, fitting new taps to an existing bath can be difficult. It is often easier to disconnect and pull out the bath (see below) so that you have room to apply enough force to undo the back nuts of the old taps, also to hold each tap body steady and exert counterpressure (page 60) to avoid cracking the bath.

You may have to disconnect and move the washbasin in order to pull out the bath.

The alternative to disrupting the bathroom is to fit new tap headgear only, using a tap conversion kit (page 61).

CHOOSING A BATH

Most modern baths are made from plastic in various colours, and are light and easy to install compared with the traditional, durable porcelain-enamelled cast-iron bath. Vitreous-enamelled pressed-steel baths are lighter and cheaper than cast-iron baths. Some makes are, like plastic, cradled in a support frame to avoid distortion.

Plastic baths may be made of acrylic, which tends to sag and creak when filled, or more rigid, dearer, glass-reinforced polyester. The water in a plastic bath will keep warm longer than in an enamelled bath.

Bath designs include corner-fitting and two-person types. Whirlpool types (with water recirculated through nozzles for underwater massage) are also available.

Removing an old cast-iron bath

A cast-iron bath may weigh around 15 stone (100kg). Unless you want to keep the bath intact and have strong helpers to assist you, it is easier to break it up after disconnecting it than to remove it whole. Be careful when you break it up, as the pieces are often jagged and very sharp.

A pressed-steel bath is lighter. With help, it can usually be moved intact.

You will need
Tools Torch; adjustable spanner; safety spectacles (page 98); club hammer; large blanket; protective gloves. Possibly also: padded pipe wrench; screwdriver; hacksaw.

1 Cut off the water supply to the bath taps (page 58).

2 Remove any bath panelling. It is often secured with dome-head screws, which have caps that are removed to reveal the screw slot.

3 With a torch, look into the space at the end of the bath to locate the supply pipes connected to the tap tails, and the overflow pipe. In older baths, the overflow pipe is rigid and leads straight out through the wall. In more modern types the overflow is flexible and connected to the waste trap.

4 Check the position of the hot supply pipe – it is normally on the left as you face the taps.

5 Use an adjustable spanner to unscrew the tap connectors from the supply pipes and pull the pipes to one side. If unscrewing is difficult, saw through the pipes near the ends of the tap tails.

6 Saw through a rigid overflow pipe flush with the wall.

7 Disconnect the waste trap from the waste outlet. For an old-style U-bend, use an adjustable spanner. A plastic trap can normally be unscrewed by hand, but use a padded pipe wrench if it proves difficult. Pull the trap to one side.

8 Disconnect a flexible overflow pipe from the overflow outlet.

9 If the bath has adjustable legs – normally brackets with adjustable screws and locking nuts – lower it to lessen the risk of damaging wall tiles when you pull it out. But if the adjusters on the far side are difficult to reach, lowering may not be worth the effort.

10 Pull the bath into the middle of the room ready for removal or break-up.

11 To break it up, put on safety spectacles and protective gloves, drape a blanket over the bath to cut down the number of flying enamel fragments, and strike the sides with a club hammer.

CONNECTIONS TO AN OLD BATH

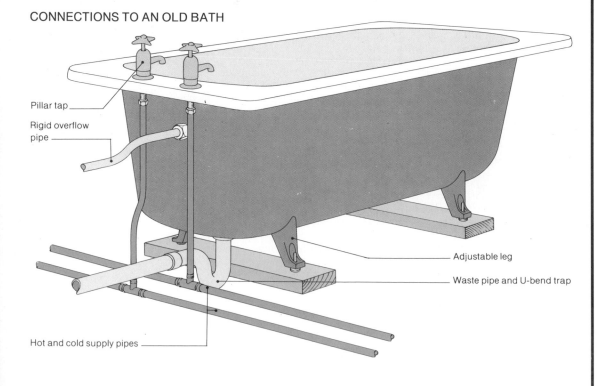

Pillar tap

Rigid overflow pipe

Adjustable leg

Waste pipe and U-bend trap

Hot and cold supply pipes

Installing a new bath

Assemble as many fittings as possible on the new bath before you remove the old one. Not only will fitting be easier before the bath is in position, but the water will not be cut off for so long.

You can fit the new bath in a slightly different position from the old one with the aid of flexible tap connectors and a flexible waste connector. But if you want to put it in a different position altogether, you will have to work out how to re-route the waste pipe and link it to the drain, as well as adapt the supply pipes.

You will need

Tools Two adjustable spanners; spirit level; damp cloth. Possibly also: long-nosed pliers; small spanner; hacksaw; screwdriver.
Materials Bath; two 1in (25mm) thick boards to support feet; two ¾in pillar taps or mixer (with washers); two 22mm flexible tap connectors; 1½in (40mm) waste outlet (unslotted) with plug and two flat plastic washers; bath trap (deep-seal if the waste pipe links to a single stack) with flexible overflow assembly; non-setting mastic filler (silicone type for a plastic bath); PTFE thread-sealing tape; bath sealant (silicone rubber type for plastic).

HELPFUL TIPS

If, on a mixer, the hot and cold indicators are on different sides from the appropriate supply pipes, change over the top plates on the tops of the tap handles, if possible. Otherwise, cross the flexible tap connectors over to reach the correct pipes.

The neatest way to seal the joint between an enamelled bath and the wall is with quadrant tiles laid flat.

---

1 Fit the supporting frame following the maker's instructions. It is usually done with the bath placed upside down. Some glass-reinforced polyester and pressed-steel baths do not need support frames.

2 Fit the taps or mixer unit, and the tap connectors, in the same way as for a kitchen sink. Some deck mix-

ers are supplied with a large plastic washer to fit between the deck and the bath surface.

3 Fit the waste outlet. This may be a tailed grid fitted in the same way as for a sink (use a silicone mastic filler to bed the flange to a plastic bath). Or it may be a flanged grid only, fitted over the outlet hole (with washers on each side of the bath surface) and fixed with a screw to a tail formed at one end of the flexible overflow pipe.

4 Fit the top end of the overflow pipe into the back of the overflow hole and screw the overflow outlet, backed by a washer, in position.

5 Slot the banjo of the flexible overflow onto the waste outlet tail (if applicable). Then fit the bath trap to the waste outlet.

6 Fit the bath in position with a flat board under each pair of feet to spread the load.

7 Place a spirit level on each of the four sides of the bath to check that it is horizontal. If necessary, level it using the adjustable legs. If the legs are not adjustable, use slivers of wood or strips of plastic tile under the feet to level the bath.

8 With the bath level, tighten the locking nuts on adjustable legs.

9 Fit the tap connector on the farthest tap to its supply pipe, making a compression joint (page 63). If the supply pipe is too high, cut it back to a convenient length, leaving it too long rather than too short, as the connector can be bent slightly to fit.

10 Connect the second tap in the same way as the first.

11 Connect the trap outlet to the waste pipe (normally a locking ring-seal joint).

12 Restore the water supply and check the joints for leaks. Tighten if necessary, but not too much.

13 Fix the bath panels according to the maker's instructions. They may screw or clip to a wooden frame, or be fixed to a plywood strip held to the floor with brackets.

14 Wait until the bath has settled in position before sealing the joints between the bath sides and walls to prevent leakage over the sides. This usually means waiting until after the bath has been filled and used at least once.

15 Before sealing the joints of a plastic bath, fill the bath with warm water so that the sealer will be applied while the bath is midway between any movement occurring when in use and when empty, and the flexible sealant will have the minimum stretch each way. Use a silicone rubber sealant if the bath is plastic.

CONNECTIONS TO A NEW BATH

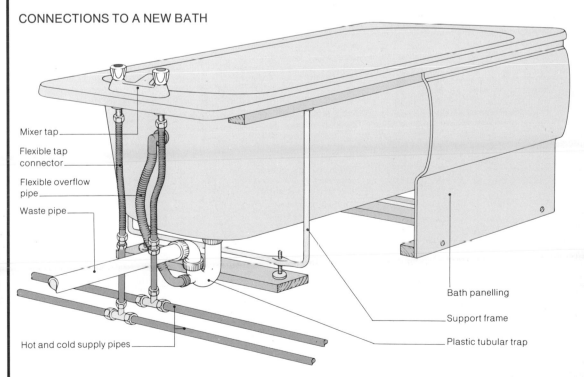

Mixer tap
Flexible tap connector
Flexible overflow pipe
Waste pipe
Hot and cold supply pipes

Bath panelling
Support frame
Plastic tubular trap

CHOOSING A SHOWER

The type of shower that can be installed depends to some extent on the household water system.

Where hot and cold water are both supplied from the household storage system at equal pressure (indirect system, page 55), a mixer is the most economical type of shower.

Where the cold water supply is direct from the mains, an instantaneous type of shower is necessary because it is illegal to mix low-pressure hot water from a hot-water cylinder and high-pressure water from the mains together in one fitting (*see Bath or basin mixer, page 59*).

If the hot water supply is from a multipoint instantaneous gas heater fed from the rising main, it may be possible to have a mixer-type shower installed.

Check the installation requirements with the gas-heater manufacturer, and get the shower connections carried out by a plumber registered with CORGI.

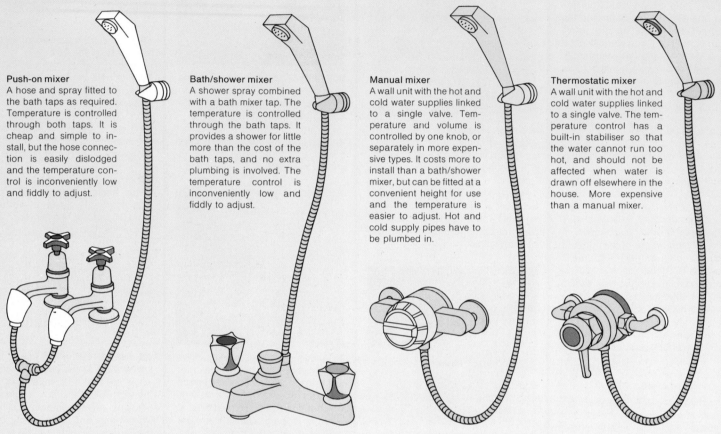

Push-on mixer
A hose and spray fitted to the bath taps as required. Temperature is controlled through both taps. It is cheap and simple to install, but the hose connection is easily dislodged and the temperature control is inconveniently low and fiddly to adjust.

Bath/shower mixer
A shower spray combined with a bath mixer tap. The temperature is controlled through the bath taps. It provides a shower for little more than the cost of the bath taps, and no extra plumbing is involved. The temperature control is inconveniently low and fiddly to adjust.

Manual mixer
A wall unit with the hot and cold water supplies linked to a single valve. Temperature and volume is controlled by one knob, or separately in more expensive types. It costs more to install than a bath/shower mixer, but can be fitted at a convenient height for use and the temperature is easier to adjust. Hot and cold supply pipes have to be plumbed in.

Thermostatic mixer
A wall unit with the hot and cold water supplies linked to a single valve. The temperature control has a built-in stabiliser so that the water cannot run too hot, and should not be affected when water is drawn off elsewhere in the house. More expensive than a manual mixer.

Instantaneous heat exchanger
A wall unit that allows a shower where a mixer would be illegal. It is fed from separate bath taps where the cold tap water is direct from the mains, and can be fitted onto the taps or plumbed-in. The hot supply feeds only the heat exchanger; this heats cold water for the shower. Cooled waste water from the heat exchanger gives a low-level warm spray. No electric power is needed.

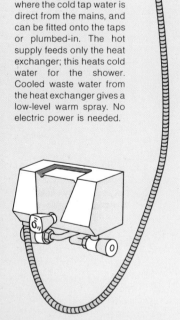

Instantaneous gas shower
A wall unit plumbed-in to indirect hot and cold water supplies, which are heated by a small gas heater, to supply a shower spray only, at an average temperature of 40°C (104°F) without being affected by other taps in use. It incorporates a dual booster pump that gives enough constant pressure to supply two showers simultaneously. The unit is not suitable for DIY installation. It must be installed by a gas fitter, and must have a flue outlet to an outside wall.

Instantaneous electric shower
A wall unit plumbed-in to a mains cold water supply, which is heated by an electric element to feed the shower. It allows a shower where a mixer would be illegal, but mains pressure needs to be at a normal level – at least 10lb/sq in (0.7kg/sq cm). The control knob allows either less water at a higher temperature or more at a lower temperature, so the spray is weaker in winter when mains water is colder. Dearer models have a winter/summer setting. Some models have a temperature stabiliser and cannot run too hot or be affected by other taps in use. The unit must be wired to an electric power supply according to Electricity Board requirements.

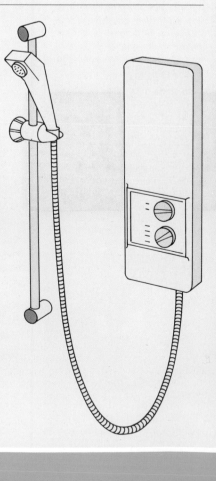

Planning a shower

Unless the water pressure at the shower head is adequate, there will be only a dribble of water from the shower spray.

For a mixer supplied from the household's stored hot and cold supplies, the bottom of the cold-water cistern needs to be at least 3ft (910mm) – and preferably 5ft (1.5m) – above the shower head for the pressure to be adequate.

For an instantaneous shower supplied direct from the mains, the pressure requirement varies according to the model, but in most homes is unlikely to be too low, except, perhaps, at the top of a tower block, for instance. Contact the local water authority if you are in doubt.

ENSURING ADEQUATE WATER PRESSURE

If you do not have sufficient water pressure to supply a shower at the required position, there are two ways by which the pressure can be increased – you can either raise the height of the cistern or have a booster pump installed.

The cold-water cistern can be raised by fitting a strong wooden platform beneath it, constructed from timber struts and blockboard. You will also have to lengthen the rising main to reach the cistern, as well as the distribution pipes from the cistern.

A booster pump incorporates a small electric motor and must be wired into the power supply. There are two main types: a single pump, which is fitted between the mixer control and the spray and boosts the mixed supply to the spray. Or a dual or twin pump that is fitted to the supply pipes and boosts the hot and cold water supplies separately before they reach the mixer.

Depending on the model, a booster pump will provide sufficient pressure with as little as 6in (150mm) height difference between the water level in the cistern and the spray head.

Some dual pumps will provide sufficient pressure to a shower head sited higher than the cold-water storage cistern. This allows a shower to be installed in an attic, for example.

WORKING OUT THE PIPING AND DRAINAGE LINKS

Little or no pipework is involved in installing a shower over a bath, but both piping and drainage routes must be worked out for a shower in a separate cubicle.

The drainage is often more difficult to arrange than the water supply to the shower, and you may need to get approval from the local government authority.

Use 15mm diameter copper supply pipes. For heating economy and to limit loss of pressure, pipe runs to the shower should be as short and straight as possible. Avoid using elbows on corners – bend pipes if possible so that there is less resistance to flow. When routing a pipe, make sure that fixings will not interfere with electric cables or gas pipes.

The two types of shower that will involve additions to the pipework over a bath are a mixer type or an instantaneous electric shower. For a mixer shower you need both hot and cold water supply pipes. For an instantaneous shower you need only a cold supply pipe direct from the rising main.

If you are installing a manual mixer, whether over a bath or in a separate cubicle, you must take the cold water supply direct from the cold-water cistern – not from a branch pipe supplying other taps or cisterns.

Taking the supply from a branch pipe is unsafe because when the other fitting is in use, the cold supply to the shower could be so reduced that the shower becomes scalding hot.

Hot water for the mixer can be taken from a branch pipe, because there is no danger if the hot supply to the shower is reduced, although it can be unpleasant. If you take the hot supply from the cylinder distribution pipe, make the connection at a point above the height of the cylinder top.

With a thermostatic shower mixer, however, both hot and cold water can be taken from the branch pipes, as the water temperature is automatically controlled.

PIPEWORK FOR A SHOWER MIXER

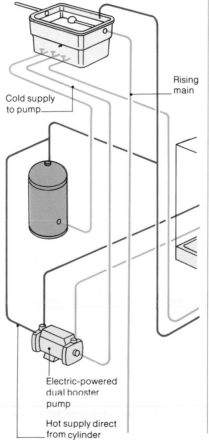

Cold-water cistern

Shower unit

Manual mixer

Hot supply pipe to manual mixer

Hot-water cylinder

Hot-water cylinder supply pipe

Cold supply pipe to manual mixer

Rising main

Bathroom supply pipes

Waste pipes

Hopper head

Down pipe

INCREASING WATER PRESSURE WITH A DUAL BOOSTER PUMP

Rising main

Cold supply to pump

Electric-powered dual booster pump

Hot supply direct from cylinder

PIPEWORK FOR AN INSTANTANEOUS SHOWER

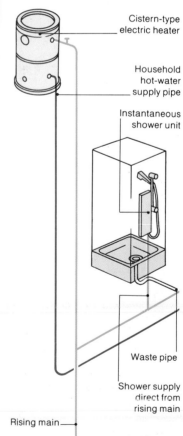

Cistern-type electric heater

Household hot-water supply pipe

Instantaneous shower unit

Waste pipe

Shower supply direct from rising main

Rising main

For a manual mixer, take the cold supply pipe direct from the cold-water cistern so that the flow cannot be reduced by water drawn off from other taps. If that happened, someone taking a shower could be scalded. Take the hot supply from the hot-water cylinder distribution pipe – tee in above cylinder height.

For a thermostatic mixer, which has a temperature stabiliser, you can tee into bathroom supply pipes.

A dual pump boosts the hot and cold water supplies separately. Some types of pump have a hot supply pipe direct from the cylinder casing, some from the vent pipe. Get the dual booster pump fitted by a plumber, as installation can be quite complex.

With an instantaneous electric shower, only a cold supply is needed, direct from the rising main. This is useful where there is no cold-water storage cistern, as mains cold water and stored hot water must not be mixed in one fitting.

Installing a shower

Most types of shower can be fitted either over a bath or in a cubicle. The fixings and pipe routes vary according to the shower type, the bathroom layout and the shower location, but the method of installation is basically the same.

The shower head must either be fitted so as to prevent it coming into contact with water in the bath or base tray, or it must have a check valve (non-return valve) where the hose is attached to the shower control.

1 Decide on the type of shower according to the water system and water pressure available.

2 Mark the required positions of the spray head and shower control.

3 Plan the pipework to the shower control (page 71).

4 If fitting an instantaneous electric shower, work out the positions of the cable route and the switch.

5 If fitting a separate shower cubicle, work out how the waste water will be routed to the drainage system.

6 Fit the shower control. Most units are available as either surface mounted or recessed fittings and come with fixings and instructions.

When fitting a recessed mixer, if possible mount it on a removable panel flush with the wall so that you have easy access to the controls.

7 Cut off the water supply and fit the water supply pipes (*Different ways of joining pipes*, page 63 and page 64).

You can recess the pipes into the

wall and then re-plaster or re-tile. Or you can box them in with surface-mounted casing or wall panelling.

8 Fit the shower head and spray. For a separate cubicle, fit the base tray and waste fittings.

9 Connect the supply pipes to the shower control. An adaptor with a female screw thread (copper to iron) may be needed.

10 Restore the water supply and check piping for leaks. Tighten any joints as necessary.

11 For an electric shower, turn off the electric supply at the consumer unit. Make electrical connections following any maker's instructions. Restore the supply.

12 Fit screening panels and seal the joints between the wall and screening and a cubicle tray.

A TYPICAL CUBICLE INSTALLATION

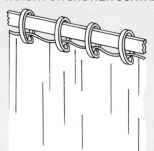

Shower head on sliding bar

Surface-mounted mixer

Recessed 15mm hot and cold supply pipes

Tubular waste trap

1½in (40mm) waste pipe

Base tray

Height-adjusting tray support

Screens are typically about 6ft (1.8m) high. Panel widths can usually be adjusted by 1in-2in (25mm-50mm) to allow for walls that are out of true. Doors may be hinged, folded (with panels shaped to keep water in), sliding with corner entry, or pivoted to give a wide entry without taking a lot of opening space. Some base trays have an adjustable support by which the height can be altered so that the waste pipe and trap can be positioned either above or below the floorboards.

SHOWER FITTINGS

With an over-bath shower, only a shower head, tap or mixer and curtain or screen are needed.

With a separate cubicle, a base tray, trap and waste pipe are also necessary.

SPRAY ROSES

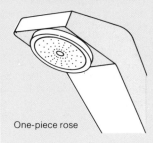

One-piece rose

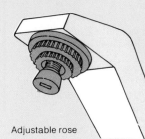

Adjustable rose

Shower heads may be fixed or adjustable, or on a flexible hose. The spray rose may be in one

piece or in a series of rings that allow adjustment of the density of the spray.

TRACK FOR SHOWER CURTAINS

Track for shower curtains is sold in kits with instructions and all necessary fittings. Where there are ceiling brackets, they should be fixed to ceiling joists (*Locating joists*, page 21). Track is in sections and can enclose one

side 6ft (1.8m) long, or two sides of an area 3ft (910mm) square. Extra straight or curved pieces allow variations such as three 3ft sides. In place of curtains there are fold-back over-bath screens that can be opened as needed.

BASE TRAYS

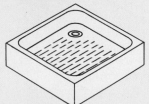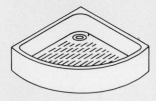

A glass-reinforced polyester base tray is one of the most suitable types for DIY installation because it is light to handle, not easily damaged, and has a non-slip surface. Shower trays are typically 30in (760mm)

square and 8in-12in (200mm-300mm) high. The waste outlet is normally 1½in (40mm) in diameter. The tray does not usually have an overflow fitting.

Curved-front trays, which save floor space, are available.

Repairing a faulty lavatory cistern

Common faults with a lavatory cistern are an overflow or failure to flush properly. A faulty ball-valve can cause either because it affects the water level. Failure to flush properly is caused by either a low water level or a worn or damaged flap valve. To determine the cause, check the water level (see below).

The plastic lever arm linking the spindle of the flush control to the siphon lift rod may eventually wear out and break. A replacement can be bought and is easily fitted.

CHECKING THE WATER LEVEL

1 Remove the cistern lid (it may lift off or be held by one or more screws). When the cistern is full, the water level should be about 1in (25mm) below the overflow outlet. Or there may be a water level marked on the inside wall of the cistern.

2 If the level is low, repair or adjust the ball-valve (page 76).

If the level is too high and the cistern is overflowing or in danger of doing so, flush it, then repair or adjust the ball-valve (page 76).

If the level is correct, renew the flap valve (see below).

RENEWING THE FLAP VALVE ON A STANDARD SUITE

A standard low-level suite has a full-sized cistern separate from the pan. The flap valve may be sold under the names siphon washer or cistern diaphragm. If you do not know the size you want, buy the largest available and cut it down.

A slimline cistern is repaired in the same way as a standard cistern, but some types are linked to the flush pipe with locking ring-seal joint rather than with two nuts.

You will need

Tools Screwdriver; wooden batten slightly longer than the cistern width; string; footprint pipe wrench with a jaw opening of about 2½in (65mm); bowl or bucket. Possibly also: sharp coloured pencil; scissors; container for bailing, or tube for siphoning.

Materials Plastic flap valve. Possibly also: O-ring for ring-seal joint.

1 With the cistern lid removed, lay a batten across the cistern and tie the float arm to it to stop the inflow of water.

2 Empty the cistern. If it cannot be flushed at all, bail or siphon the water out.

3 Use a large pipe wrench to undo the lower of the two large nuts underneath the cistern, then disconnect the flush pipe and push it to one side.

4 Put a bowl or bucket underneath the cistern and undo the large nut immediately under the cistern (this is the siphon-retaining nut). A pint or two of water will flow out as you loosen the nut.

5 Unhook the lift rod from the flushing lever.

6 Lift the inverted U-pipe (the siphon) out from the cistern and lay it on its side.

7 Pull out the lift rod and plate and remove the worn flap valve. If the new valve is too big, cut it down with scissors using the old valve as a pattern. It should touch, but not drag on, the dome sides.

8 Fit the new valve over the lift rod and onto the plate, then reassemble the flushing mechanism.

RENEWING THE FLAP VALVE ON A CLOSE-COUPLED SUITE

On some close-coupled suites, the siphon is held by two or more bolts inside the cistern rather than by a large nut underneath. Except for this difference, the flap valve is renewed in the same way as on a standard suite.

On others, the cistern must be lifted off in order to disconnect the siphon. The flap valve can then be renewed in the same way as on a standard suite. Lift off the cistern as follows:

1 Cut off the water supply to the lavatory cistern in the same way as for a tap (page 58). Empty the cistern by flushing, bailing or siphoning out the water.

2 Disconnect the overflow pipe and water supply pipe from the cistern. They generally have screw fittings with a back nut.

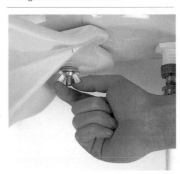

3 Undo the wall screws holding the cistern, and any bolts securing it to the rear platform of the pan.

4 Lift off the cistern from the pan and unhook the lift rod. Turn the cistern over, unscrew the retaining nut, remove the siphon and plate and renew the valve as above.

RENEWING THE FLAP VALVE ON A TWO-PART SIPHON

If a cistern is fitted with a two-part plastic siphon such as a Turbo 88, there is no need to stop the inflow or, with a close-coupled suite, to remove the cistern.

A two-part siphon can be fitted to most types of lavatory cistern. The initial fitting does involve cutting off the water supply and, if necessary, lifting off the cistern (see above). After that, maintenance is as below.

You will need
Tools Screwdriver.
Materials Spares pack for size of siphon (containing flap valve; washers; possibly O-ring seal).

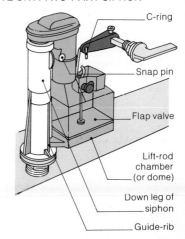

C-ring

Snap pin

Flap valve

Lift-rod chamber (or dome)

Down leg of siphon

Guide-rib

1 With the cistern lid removed, unhook the flush lever from the lift-rod C-ring. Remove a lever-type flush handle, as it may be in the way later.

2 Withdraw the yellow snap pin about 1¼in (32mm) to disconnect the lift-rod chamber from the down leg of the siphon.

3 Slide the chamber upwards to disengage it from the guide rib on the down leg.

4 Remove the C-ring and washer from the top of the lift rod and slide the lift rod from the bottom of the chamber.

5 Take off the lift-rod washers and weight so that you can remove the old flap valve and fit a new one.

6 Before reassembling, check if the O-ring seal at the top of the chamber section is worn. Renew it if necessary.

Dealing with a faulty lavatory pan

The usual faults with a lavatory pan are blockages or leaks. A leak from the pan outlet is not difficult to repair, but a cracked pan will have to be replaced (see below).

CLEARING A WASHDOWN PAN

When a washdown bowl is flushed, the two streams of water, one from each side of the rim, should flow equally to meet at the front. The water should leave the pan smoothly, not eddying like a whirlpool. If the cistern is working properly but the bowl fails to clear, something is obstructing either the flush inlet or the pan outlet.

If the flush water rises almost to the pan rim then ebbs away very slowly, there is most likely a blockage in the pan outlet or possibly in the drain it discharges into.

You will need
Tools Plunger with long handle. Possibly also: flexible drain auger; bucket; mirror; a pair of rubber gloves.

> **HELPFUL TIP**
> If you have no plunger, you may be able to use a mop or broom tied round with rags. Or stand on a stool and tip in a bucket of water in one go.

1 To clear the pan, take the plunger and push it sharply onto the bottom of the pan to cover the outlet. Then pump the handle up and down two or three times.

2 If this does not clear the pan, use a flexible drain auger to probe the outlet and trap.

3 If the blockage persists, clear the underground drain.

4 Flush the cistern to check that water is entering the pan properly, with streams from each side of the rim flowing equally to meet at the front.

5 If the flow into the pan is poor or uneven, use a mirror to examine the flushing rim. Probe the rim with your fingers for flakes of rust or debris from the cistern that may be obstructing the flush water.

CLEARING A SIPHONIC PAN

Blockages rarely occur in double-trap siphonic pans, unless something such as a plastic toy is accidentally flushed through.

Deal with a blockage in the same way as for a washdown pan, but if plunging does not work, get professional help.

The commonest fault is for the water in the pan to rise instead of emptying before the flush water enters. This is because the pressure-reducing air pipe has become blocked with scale or debris from the cistern.

You will need
Tools Screwdriver; an adjustable spanner; container for bailing or tube for siphoning; old toothbrush.

Possibly also: string; wooden batten to fit across cistern.

1 To reach the air pipe, remove the cistern in the same way as for replacing a flap valve on a close-coupled suite.

2 Clean the end of the air pipe with an old toothbrush. There is no need to lift the pipe out. Most of the debris is usually in the top end.

REPAIRING A LEAK IN THE PAN OUTLET

A putty joint sometimes leaks because the putty is old and has become hard, so cracks when a wooden floor vibrates.

To replace an old putty joint with a modern push-fit connector, the pan has to be moved forward, then refitted. An effective repair can be made without moving the pan by using a waterproof building tape or cord (glazing tape) and non-setting mastic filler.

Chip and rake out the old putty with an old chisel, and bind two or three turns of tape round the lavatory pan outlet. Poke more building tape firmly into the rim of the soil-pipe inlet, then fill the space between the rim and pan outlet with mastic filler.

Bind two more turns of tape round the joint.

Replacing a lavatory pan

At one time lavatory pans were always cemented to a solid floor, but the setting of the cement often put a strain on the pan and caused the china to crack. Now they are usually screwed down to a wooden or a solid floor.

An old or cracked lavatory pan with a down-pointing outlet cemented to a floor-exit pipe is the most difficult type to remove.

You will need
Tools Screwdriver; spirit level. Possibly drill and wood or masonry bits; safety spectacles; club hammer; cold chisel; rags; old chisel; thin pen or nail; trimming knife.
Materials Lavatory pan and seat; No. 12 roundhead brass screws (usually 4) with rubber washers; rubber cone connector; suitable push-fit pan connector. Possibly also: wall plugs (for solid floor); packing such as wood slivers or vinyl tile strips.

REMOVING A PAN WITH A HORIZONTAL OUTLET

1 Disconnect the flush pipe by peeling back the cone connector. ALTERNATIVELY, chip away a rag-and-putty joint with an old chisel.

2 Undo the screws holding the pan to the floor.

3 Pull the pan slowly forward, moving it from side to side, to free it from the soil-pipe inlet. It should

come away easily. If you have any difficulty, break the pan outlet in the same way as for a down-pointing outlet (below).

4 If the outlet joint was cemented with putty or mastic filler, chip it off the metal soil-pipe inlet.

REMOVING A PAN WITH A DOWN-POINTING OUTLET

1 Disconnect the flush pipe in the same way as for a horizontal pan.

2 Undo the floor screws, or break cement with a hammer and cold chisel.

3 To free the pan outlet, put on safety spectacles and use a club

hammer to break the outlet pipe just above its joint with the drain socket in the floor. Then pull the pan forward, away from the jagged remains protruding from the drain socket.

4 Stuff rags into the drain socket to stop debris falling in, then chip away the rest of the pan outlet with a hammer and cold chisel. Work with the chisel blade pointing inwards, and break the china right down to the socket at one point. The rest of the china should then come out easily.

5 Chip away any cement from round the collar of the drain socket with a hammer and cold chisel. It does not matter if you accidentally break the collar.

6 Clear away any cement left where the pan was cemented to the floor, leaving a flat base for the new lavatory pan.

FITTING A SEPARATE PAN

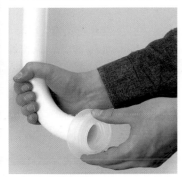

1 Fit a rubber cone connector to the flush-pipe outlet, unless one is already fitted.

2 Fit a plastic push-on connector to the pan outlet.

If the drain socket for the pan is in the floor, use an angled 90 degree connector to link a horizontal pan outlet to the vertical inlet to the soil pipe.

3 If screw holes have to be made in the floor, place the pan in position and mark firmly through the holes in the pan base.

Use a narrow marker such as a thin ballpoint pen or pencil, or a nail tapped with a hammer.

4 With the pan still in position, draw a line round its base so that it can be put back in place. Then move it out of the way.

5 Drill screw holes in the floor at the marked points.

On a solid floor such as concrete,

use a masonry bit and insert wall plugs for the screws.

6 If the soil-pipe inlet is a floor socket, remove the rags, taking care not to spill any of the debris in the inlet.

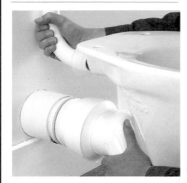

7 Lift the pan into position on the marked outline, and at the same time push the flexible connector into the soil-pipe inlet.

8 Fold back the rubber cone connector and slip it over the flushing horn of the pan.

9 Screw the pan to the floor, with rubber washers inserted between each screwhead and the pan. The washers take the strain off the pan. Do not overtighten the screws; you could crack the pan.

10 Use a spirit level placed across the top of the pan to check that it is level from side to side and from front to back.

11 If the pan is not level, loosen the floor screws and pack under the pedestal with wood slivers or strips of vinyl tile to level it all round.

Once the pan is level, screw it down firmly, but do not overtighten the screws.

FITTINGS FOR A SEPARATE LOW-LEVEL SUITE

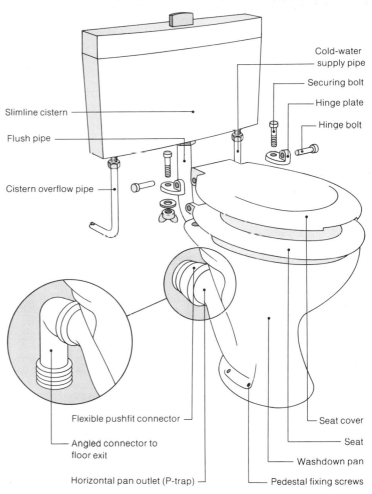

Slimline cistern

Flush pipe

Cistern overflow pipe

Cold-water supply pipe

Securing bolt

Hinge plate

Hinge bolt

Flexible pushfit connector

Angled connector to floor exit

Horizontal pan outlet (P-trap)

Seat cover

Seat

Washdown pan

Pedestal fixing screws

Most modern lavatory pans have a near-horizontal (P-trap) outlet. If the replacement pan has to be fitted to a floor-exit soil pipe in a drain socket on a ground floor, connect the P-trap outlet of the pan to the soil-pipe inlet using an angled pushfit connector.

After fitting a lavatory suite, you may find that condensation – particulary apparent on a ceramic cistern – is a nuisance and leads to damp walls and floors. Make sure the lavatory or bathroom is properly ventilated.

In a bathroom, avoid drip-drying washing over the bath, as this contributes to condensation.

FITTING A NEW SEAT

A lavatory pan seat and cover are usually hinged onto hinge bolts or a rod at the back. These fit into hinge plates or covers at each side of the pan.

Hinge plates or covers are each held in place by a securing bolt that fits through a fixing hole in the back of the pan and is secured by a wing nut.

Make sure you insert washers to shield the pan from the head of the securing bolt and the wing nut. Washers shaped to the pattern of hinge covers are often supplied. Screw the wing nuts firmly finger tight.

A lavatory seat breaks easily if misused – such as by standing on it to close a window.

CHECKING THE FITTING

When fitting a new lavatory pan, make sure that it is level and that the connections to the flush pipe and soil pipe are true. Otherwise slow pan clearance or a blockage could result.

On an existing lavatory pan with old-style joints rather than flexible connectors, blockages can occur because the openings are out of true or partially obstructed by the jointing material. Putty from an old

rag-and-putty joint between the flush pipe and horn may have squeezed into the flush inlet and be impeding the inflow of water.

Putty or other jointing material could be obstructing the joint between the pan outlet and the soil-pipe inlet. This is evident if the water rises slowly in the pan before it flows away.

Make sure the lavatory pan is firmly fixed and that the fixing screws have not worked loose. Check that the pan is horizontal when fixing it in place.

How a ball-valve works

In a cold-water storage cistern or lavatory cistern, the water level is regulated by a ball-valve (or ball-cock) – that is opened and closed by a lever arm attached to a float.

When the cistern is at normal level, the float holds the arm horizontal and the valve is closed. When the water level drops, the float lowers the arm and the valve opens to let more water in. The name ball-valve is from the early type of copper ball float. Modern floats are not always balls, and valves are often called float valves.

Ball-valves may be made from brass, gunmetal or plastic, or may be metal with some plastic parts. The size is measured by the inlet shank diameter; $\frac{1}{2}$in or $\frac{3}{4}$in (15mm or 22mm) sizes are usually needed for domestic cisterns.

A cold-water storage cistern or lavatory cistern where the supply is direct from the mains needs a high-pressure valve. A lavatory cistern supplied from the cold-water storage cistern needs a low-pressure valve. If the pressure is very low because the lavatory cistern is only slightly lower than the storage cistern, a full-way valve is needed.

Low-pressure valves have wider inlet nozzles than high-pressure valves. If a high-pressure valve is fitted where a low-pressure valve is needed, the cistern will fill much too slowly. If a low-pressure valve is fitted in a cistern supplied from the mains, water will leak past the valve.

Most modern valves can be changed from high-pressure to low-pressure operation either by inserting a different fitting into the inlet nozzle or by changing a detachable inlet nozzle. Some types are suitable for high or low water pressure without any alteration.

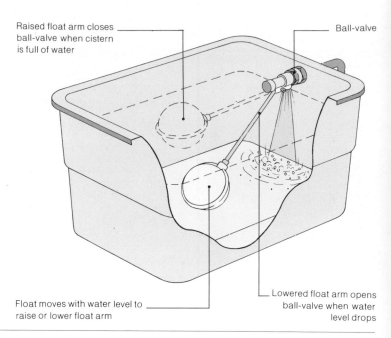

Raised float arm closes ball-valve when cistern is full of water

Ball-valve

Float moves with water level to raise or lower float arm

Lowered float arm opens ball-valve when water level drops

Repairing a faulty ball-valve

If a ball-valve does not open fully, the cistern (lavatory or cold-water storage) will be slow to fill. With a cold-water storage cistern this results in airlocks in the supply pipes and a poor flow from taps.

If the ball-valve does not close fully, the water level in the cistern will become too high and there will be a constant outflow from the overflow pipe.

PORTSMOUTH VALVES

The valve will not work efficiently if the washer is worn or moving parts are clogged by scale or corrosion.

You will need
Tools Combination pliers; small screwdriver; fine abrasive paper; pencil. Possibly also: penknife.
Materials Split pin (cotter-pin); washer; petroleum jelly. Possibly also: penetrating oil.

1 Turn off the main stopcock if you are working on the cold-water cistern, or the gate valve to the lavatory cistern.

2 Use a pipe wrench to loosen the ball-valve end cap, if there is one, then unscrew and remove it.

3 Use pliers to close the end of the split pin securing the float arm, then withdraw the pin.

4 Remove the float arm and put it to one side.

5 Insert a small screwdriver blade into the slot where the float arm was seated. Use it to push the plug from the end of the casing. Catch the plug with your other hand as it comes out.

6 Clean the outside of a metal plug (not a plastic plug) with fine abrasive paper.

7 Wrap fine abrasive paper round a pencil shaft and clean the inside of the metal valve casing.

8 To renew the washer, hold the plug with a screwdriver thrust into the slot and use pliers to unscrew its washer-retaining cap. Do not force it or you may damage the plug. If a metal plug is difficult to undo, smear penetrating oil round the cap edge and try again after about ten minutes.

9 With the cap removed, use a screwdriver to prise out the washer from the inside. (If you were unable to remove the cap, try to pick out the old washer with a penknife through the cap's open centre.)

10 Fit the new washer and screw the plug cap back on. Tighten with pliers. (If the cap is still on, try to force the new washer through the centre hole and push it flat with your finger.)

11 Before refitting the plug, turn on the water supply briefly to flush out dirt from the valve casing still attached to the cistern.

12 Lightly smear the plug with petroleum jelly before reassembling the valve and float arm. Use a new split pin to secure the arm.

13 Restore the water supply.

DIAPHRAGM-TYPE VALVES

The cistern will be slow to refill if the inlet gets clogged or the diaphragm gets jammed against it.

You will need
Tools Screwdriver. Possibly also: pipe wrench; cloth for padding wrench jaws.
Materials Lint-free rag; warm soapy water in container; clear water for rinsing. Possibly also: rubber or synthetic diaphragm.

1 Turn off the main stopcock if you are working on the cold-water cistern, or the gate valve to the lavatory cistern (page 58).

2 Unscrew the large knurled retaining nut by hand. If it is stiff, use a padded pipe wrench.

3 With the nut removed, the end of the float arm and plunger will come away. Put them to one side.

4 Use a screwdriver blade to free the diaphragm from the inlet pipe, taking care not to damage it.

5 Use a piece of clean, lint-free rag to clean out any dirt and debris from the inlet pipe.

6 Wash the diaphragm in warm soapy water, then rinse it. If it is pitted or damaged, replace it. Fit with the rim inwards.
ALTERNATIVELY, if the valve is a servo type with a filter fitted, remove the filter and wash it in warm soapy water, then rinse it. If the servo valve has no filter, flush the part attached to the float arm under the tap.

7 Before reassembling the valve, turn on the water supply briefly to flush dirt or debris out of the casing. Then refit the parts and restore the water supply.

BALL-VALVES IN COMMON USE

TYPE OF VALVE	DESCRIPTION	ADVANTAGES AND DISADVANTAGES
Portsmouth Washered plug Screw-on cap Inlet pipe Water outlet Split pin Float arm 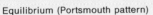	The commonest type in British homes. The water inlet is opened and closed by a washered plug (or piston) that moves horizontally. The plug is slotted onto a float arm and secured with a split pin. Some types have a screw-on cap at the end of the plug. The water outlet is on the bottom of the valve in front of the float arm. The detachable inlet pipe can be changed to suit the water pressure.	Sturdy and long-lasting. Water hammer – vibration of the rising main – can result from the valve bouncing in its seating. The bouncing is caused by ripples on the water surface when the cistern is almost full making the float arm shake; sometimes also by the pressure of incoming water against the valve. Scale or corrosion can prevent the valve from operating properly.
Equilibrium (Portsmouth pattern) Washered plug Inlet pipe Water outlet Watering chamber 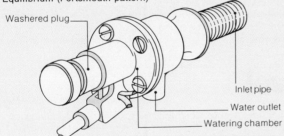	Similar in appearance and operation to a Portsmouth valve, but there is a horizontal channel through the centre of the plug leading to a washered, watertight chamber at the rear of the valve. The inlet water fills the channel and chamber so that water pressure is the same at both ends of the plug. The large inlet pipe is suitable for all pressures.	Designed for use where mains pressure tends to fluctuate. The equal pressures on the valve make water hammer less likely than in standard Portsmouth types, and there is also less wear on the washer, so it rarely needs changing. Scale or corrosion can affect valve operation.
Diaphragm (also known as BRE, BRS or Garston) Outlet nozzle Plunger Float arm Inlet pipe Retaining nut Split pin 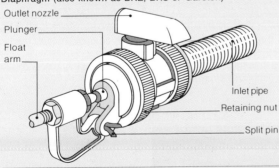	The water inlet is closed by a large rubber or synthetic diaphragm pushed against it by a plunger attached to the float arm. A detachable nylon overhead outlet nozzle discharges water in a gentle shower. The inlet pipe can be changed to suit the water pressure.	The discharge spray cuts down filling noise and rippling, and the diaphragm keeps the plunger and float arm from contact with water, so they are not affected by scale and corrosion. The diaphragm can become jammed, and grit can block the inlet chamber. The valve can be dismantled by hand by undoing a large knurled retaining nut.
Servo-diaphragm (also known as diaphragm/equilibrium or Torbeck) Outlet nozzle Retaining nut enclosing servo chamber Float arm Inlet pipe Collapsible plastic tube fits here 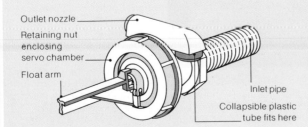	A plastic valve with a small float and short float arm. Behind the large rubber or synthetic diaphragm covering the inlet there is a water (or servo) chamber which is fed via a metering pin. Equal water pressure on each side of the diaphragm keeps it closed. When the float arm drops, it opens a pilot hole in the back of the chamber, covered by a sealing washer. The tiny outflow through the pilot hole reduces pressure in the servo chamber, and the diaphragm opens the inlet. The outlet is overhead, but water flows to below the cistern level through a collapsible plastic tube.	The design allows very rapid and silent delivery. Because the plastic tube is collapsible, it cuts down the noise of filling without the risk of water being drawn back into the main – a risk that makes rigid silencer tubes illegal. The valve can be fitted with an optional filter, which needs regular cleaning but collects grit that might otherwise obstruct the metering pin and pilot hole. Flow restrictors are fitted into the inlet pipe to adapt it for high or low pressures.

Fitting a new ball valve

Fit a new ball-valve if the old one gets damaged or broken, or if you decide to change the type of valve, to get rid of noise and vibration.

You will need
Tools Two adjustable spanners.
Materials Ball-valve with float (of same size as existing valve); two flat plastic washers to fit valve inlet shank ($\frac{1}{2}$in or $\frac{3}{4}$in); mini-stopcock (page 58) with compression fitting inlet and tap connector outlet.

1 Turn off the main stopcock to cut off the cistern water supply.

2 Use a spanner to undo the tap connector securing the supply pipe to the valve tail. You may need to hold the valve body or any securing nut inside the cistern steady with a second spanner.

3 Disconnect the supply pipe.

4 Undo the back nut securing the ball-valve to the cistern. Remove the valve.

5 Take off the back nut from the new ball-valve and put it aside.

6 Slip a flat plastic washer (and an inner securing nut, if supplied) over the new valve tail and push the tail

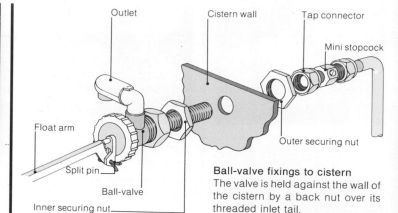

through the hole in the cistern from the inside.

Ball-valve fixings to cistern
The valve is held against the wall of the cistern by a back nut over its threaded inlet tail.

7 Slip another plastic washer over the protruding tail and screw on the back nut by hand. Tighten it half a turn with a spanner.

8 Remove existing tap connector and fit mini-stopcock. Screw connector nut to new valve tail.

9 Restore water supply, making sure mini-stopcock is fully open. Adjust cistern level (see below).

Adjusting the cistern water level

The normal level of a full cistern is about 1in (25mm) below the overflow outlet. The level can be raised by raising the float, or lowered by lowering the float. If the cistern overflows, the level is too high because the float either needs adjusting or is leaking and failing to rise to close the valve (or the valve may be faulty, page 76).

ADJUSTING A BALL-VALVE

You will need
Tools Possibly small spanner; vice.

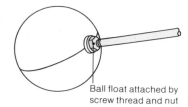

Ball float attached by screw thread and nut

On a Portsmouth-pattern valve with a ball float, unscrew and remove the float from the arm. To lower the level, hold the arm firmly in both hands and bend it slightly downwards. Then refit the float. If the arm is too stiff to bend in position, remove it from the cistern and grip it in a vice.

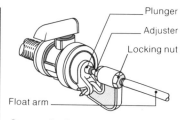

On a diaphragm valve with an adjuster at the top of the float arm, adjust the level by loosening the locking nut and screwing the adjuster forward, nearer to the plunger. ALTERNATIVELY, use an adjuster nut or clip near the float to move the float farther away from the valve along a horizontal arm, or to a lower position if it is linked to the arm by a vertical rod.

REPAIRING A LEAKING FLOAT

For a permanent repair, a new ball float must be fitted. But to get the valve back in action again until a new float is obtained, the old one can be temporarily repaired.

You will need
Tools Small spanner; sharp knife or old-fashioned tin opener; piece of wood to go across cistern.
Materials Plastic bag; string.

1 Raise the float arm to close the valve and cut off the flow of the water. Then tie the arm to a length of wood laid across the top of the cistern.

2 Unscrew and remove the ball float from the float arm.

3 Find the hole through which the water is leaking and enlarge it with either a sharp knife or tin opener.

4 Drain the water from the float, then screw it back in position on the float arm.

5 Slip the plastic bag over the float and tie it securely to the float arm.

6 Release the arm and lower it into position.

GETTING RID OF WATER HAMMER

Banging or humming from the rising main occurs when the pipe vibrates because the cistern ball-valve is bouncing on its seating. Bouncing occurs because the float is shaken by ripples on the water while the cistern is refilling.

To steady the float and cut down the bouncing, fit it with a stabiliser made from a small plastic pot or carton. Pierce the rim of the pot on each side and fit a loop of galvanised wire across, twisting it tightly round the float arm near the float before securing the second side. The pot should trail underwater a few inches below the bottom of the float.

Make sure the rising main is securely clipped to the roof timbers near its entry to the cistern.

The surest way to get rid of water hammer is to replace a Portsmouth valve with a type less affected by high water pressure.

Plumbing-in a washing machine or dish washer

A washing machine (or a dish-washer) is easy to install beside a kitchen sink if the existing water pipes and waste pipe are conveniently positioned for fitting a drain kit and branch pipes for the machine stopcocks. When a washing machine or dishwasher is newly plumbed in, a single check valve (non-return valve) must be fitted to the hot and cold pipes supplying the hoses. The drain kit incorporates a cutting device for fitting it to a 42mm or 1½in plastic waste pipe. The device slices away a circular piece of the waste pipe.

You will need

Tools Hacksaw; half-round file; two adjustable spanners; medium-sized screwdriver; measuring tape; soft pencil; two spring-clip clothes pegs; spirit level. Possibly also: shallow pan.

Materials About 24in (610mm) of 15mm copper piping; two 15mm stopcocks with compression ends; two 15mm single check valves; two 15mm equal tee compression connectors with slip ends; one drain kit; one hose clip of the diameter of the drain hose.

CONNECTING UP THE WATER

1 Check the rising main; turn off water and drain pipe (*Fitting the branch pipe inside*, page 66).

2 Mark the sink cold water supply pipe at a point convenient for connection to the machine. Make a second mark ¾in (19mm) higher.

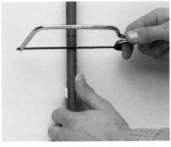

3 Cut through the cold water pipe squarely with a hacksaw at the lowest point marked. If there was not a drain cock above the main stopcock, a small amount of water will run out as you saw through. Cut through the second mark on the cold water pipe and remove the segment of pipe.

4 File the pipe ends smooth and square.

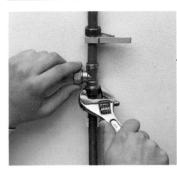

5 Using spring-clip clothes pegs to stop the caps and olives slipping down the pipe, fit a tee connector to the pipe with the branch outlet pointing towards the machine.

6 Cut a 3in (75mm) length of piping, fit it into the tee outlet and connect to a check valve, making sure that the valve's arrow mark points towards the machine.

7 Cut another 3in (75mm) length of piping (or a longer piece if necessary) and fit it to the check valve outlet.

8 Fit the other end of the pipe to compression joint inlet of a machine stopcock. Connect the machine's cold water hose to the stopcock.

9 Turn off the water supply to the hot tap over the kitchen sink (*Taps fed from the cistern*, page 58). Cut the hot water supply pipe, and fit a tee connector, piping, check valve and stopcock as above. Connect the machine's hot water hose to the stopcock and restore the hot and cold water supplies.

FITTING THE WASTE PIPE

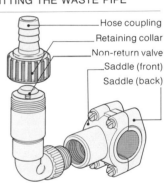

Hose coupling
Retaining collar
Non-return valve
Saddle (front)
Saddle (back)

1 Unscrew the saddle from the rest of the drain kit.

2 Fit the saddle round the plastic waste pipe leading from the sink. Choose a convenient place away from joints, and well beyond the trap.

3 Screw the cutting tool into the saddle until a hole has been cut in the waste pipe.

4 Remove the cutting tool and screw on the rest of the drain kit. It includes a non-return valve to prevent water from the sink flowing into the machine.

5 Push the drain hose from the machine over the coupling and fix it in position with a hose clip. The machine is now ready to use.

6 Every two or three months, unscrew the retaining collar and remove any fluff clogging up the non-return valve. Do this even if subsidence makes it awkward.

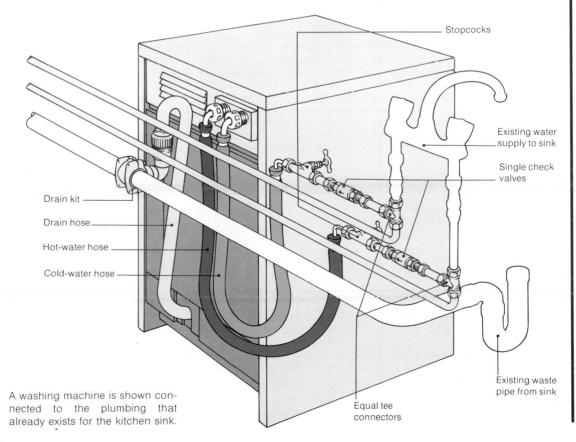

Stopcocks
Existing water supply to sink
Single check valves
Drain kit
Drain hose
Hot-water hose
Cold-water hose
Equal tee connectors
Existing waste pipe from sink

A washing machine is shown connected to the plumbing that already exists for the kitchen sink.

Radiators that do not heat up

A RADIATOR THAT IS COOL AT THE TOP

If a radiator is hot at the bottom and cool at the top, it probably contains air or gas. Turn off the central heating at the programmer.

Put an old rag on the floor under the air vent on the radiator.

Insert a radiator key in the air vent and turn it slowly anticlockwise until air starts to hiss.

Let the air out until no more is left and water starts to flow, then quickly close the vent.

Turn the heating on again.

In a fully pumped system there should be at least one more venting point near the hot-water cylinder. It may have to be undone with a screwdriver or it may be automatic, with a cap that is left loose for the air to escape. If the cap on an automatic vent is tight, loosen it to release the air.

If the radiators are served by pipes from the loft, there may be venting points in the loft which should be bled.

It should not be necessary to bleed radiators once the system is fully operating. If air problems occur frequently there may be a serious fault that requires an expert to repair it.

TOP-FLOOR RADIATORS ARE COLD

If radiators are cold on the top floor only, check that the feed-and-expansion cistern has water in it and that its ball-valve is operating.

Jiggle the ball-valve arm. If no water comes through, it will have to be repaired (page 76).

The water level should be just enough to float the ball when the water in the system is cold. The rest of the cistern is needed to contain expansion of water as it heats up.

COOL RADIATORS THROUGHOUT THE HOUSE

Deposits of sludge caused by internal corrosion can result in poor water circulation and radiators being cooler than they should be. The system needs to be chemically cleaned out (facing page).

COOL RADIATORS FARTHEST FROM THE BOILER

Most heating systems have to be balanced to ensure that each radiator gets the right flow of water. Water will flow most readily round the radiators nearest the pump.

To counter this effect, a lockshield valve is fitted to radiators as well as the hand control valve. It is set by the installer to restrict the water flow through radiators at the beginning of the circuit. Valves are opened wider on subsequent radiators and fully open on the last.

If this balancing has not been properly done, some radiators will get too hot, and some will be cool.

Only attempt to rebalance the system yourself if the problem is minor, otherwise get expert help.

BOILER PROBLEMS

Any faults in the boiler should be dealt with by an expert – especially if it is a gas-fired boiler. Only members of CORGI (Confederation for the Registration of Gas Installers) should carry out work on gas pipework and equipment.

Domestic boilers of all types are very reliable, and failures are usually due to problems created by the rest of the system – for example, internal corrosion, air in the system, poor flue arrangements or lack of air to the burner.

Faults in the boiler itself are usually caused by electrical control failures. They can also result from poor maintenance. It is essential to have gas and oil-fired boilers serviced regularly. Solid-fuel boilers must have the flueways and chimneys kept clean always.

A leak from the boiler should be investigated without delay. In the meantime do not use the system, and drain it down if the leak is bad.

Leaks in a central heating system

A leak of any sort must be prevented because fresh water is drawn into the system to compensate for the loss, and causes internal corrosion.

A LEAKING PIPE JOINT

Leaks from joints can usually only be dealt with by remaking the joint. Compression fittings on copper pipe may only need to be tightened to stop minor leaks, but take great care not to overtighten, or the leak could get worse. If you need to remake a compression fitting, drain the system to below the leak (facing page) and put in a new olive or a completely new fitting.

A leaking soldered capillary fitting needs to be completely remade.

A LEAKING RADIATOR

A small jet of water coming out of the radiator is called a pinhole leak. It is caused by internal corrosion and can happen within a few weeks of a new radiator being fitted if the system has poor air removal arrangements and has not had installation debris properly cleaned out. Radiators can also leak from welded seams, but this is rare.

Turn off the valves on the radiator, and remove it (page 82).

Notify the installer, or replace the radiator yourself with a new one of the same size.

A LEAKING RADIATOR VALVE

If the leak is coming from the compression joint below the valve, drain down the system to below the joint (facing page). Then call in a plumber or try repairing it yourself (page 63).

If the leak is from the union nut connecting the valve to the radiator it can be cured with PTFE tape.

1 Turn off the valves at both ends of the radiator, counting the number of turns on the lockshield valve. Write the number down.

2 Put a towel and a bowl under the valve to catch water, and have a bucket and a second bowl ready.

3 Using an adjustable spanner, turn the union nut anticlockwise

(when looking from the radiator to the valve). Some water may run out.

4 Open the air vent to let the rest of the water flow out.

5 Wind PTFE tape tightly around the male thread on the valve tail. Start at the end and make a 50 per cent overlap on each turn.

6 Screw the nut back on, and open the valves and air vent. Open the lockshield valve by the number of turns that were necessary to close it. Check for leaks and close the air vent when water flows from it.

A leaking valve tail

The leak may be from the valve tail screwed into the radiator. To remove it a plumber uses a special tool, but an Allen key or a large screwdriver will usually do the job. Cover the male thread on the valve tail with PTFE tape as explained in step 5.

A LEAKING RADIATOR AIR VENT

If the radiator air vent leaks, drain down the system to below the vent (facing page). Remove the air-vent fitting using either a spanner or an Allen key.

Bind the screw joint with PTFE tape (see left, step 5), and replace the fitting.

HOW TO AVOID DISTORTING A PIPE

The union nut on a radiator may need force to undo it. There is then a danger of bending the pipe, causing a leak at the compression joint.

To avoid this, apply penetrating oil, and hold the nut just below the valve with a wrench to counteract the pressure as you undo the union nut.

Draining down the system

Central-heating systems sometimes have to be drained down – to repair a leak, for example. The following method is for an open-vented system, the most common type.

1 Switch off the boiler at the programmer or time switch, and pull out the plug that provides electricity to the system, or remove the fuse.

2 Turn off the gas, either at the isolating cock near the boiler or by the meter. Or make sure that the fire in a solid-fuel boiler is out and the boiler cold. There is no need to turn off the oil in an oil-fired system.

3 Shut off the water supply to the feed-and-expansion cistern. There should be a separate stopcock for this on the branch pipe from the rising main connected to the cistern's ball-valve.

If there is no separate stopcock, stop the water flow into the cistern by tying up the ball-valve to a piece of wood laid across the top of the cistern.

4 Locate the drain cock, which may be near the bottom of the boiler. There may be more than one drainage point. Clip on a garden hose and run it to a drain outside, or into buckets.

5 Locate all the points at which air is vented from the system. These will be radiator vents, a vent on the primary flow near the hot-water cylinder in fully pumped systems, and vents in the loft if circulating pipes run there. There could be vents at other points as well.

6 Open the drain cock with a spanner or pliers, turning it anti-

clockwise. Water will start to flow out of the hose at a fairly slow rate.

7 Start opening the venting points at the top of the system. This will greatly speed up the flow from the drain cock. As the water level drops further, open the lower venting points until they are all open.

8 When the water stops flowing, close all vents in case the water is accidentally turned on.

REFILLING THE SYSTEM

1 Close all the drain cocks and all the vents in the system. Check that all work on the system is finished.

2 Turn on the stopcock to the feed-and-expansion cistern, or untie the ball-valve, to let water in.

3 Open one of the lowest air vents until water starts to flow out, then close it. Repeat the process with the lower air vents until the bottom of the system is full of water. Then do the upper vents, and check the system for leaks.

4 Make sure that the ball-valve to the feed-and-expansion cistern has closed itself off. Check that the water level in the cistern is just enough to float the ball. The rest of the cistern space is for expansion of the water as it heats up.

5 If the level is too high, close off the mains water to the cistern, open the drain cock and let some water out. Adjust the arm on the ball-valve so that it closes the valve at the correct water level (page 78). Ensure that the cistern's lid and insulating jacket are in place.

6 Switch on the electricity and turn on the gas. Re-light the pilot light in a gas boiler. Turn on the system at the programmer or timeswitch. Turn up the room thermostat.

7 Re-light the boiler, following the manufacturer's instructions.

8 As the system heats up more venting will be necessary to get rid of air driven off from the water. Minor venting will be required for a few days.

9 Check for leaks again.

10 Remove the hose from the drain cock, and make sure the cock is watertight. If it is leaking you will have to drain the system again, then replace the drain cock yourself or call in a plumber. If the drain cock is fitted to the boiler, it can be unscrewed. But it may be fitted to a pipe with compression or capillary joints.

Preventing a freeze-up during a winter holiday

If you turn off your central heating while you go on a winter holiday, there is a danger that the system will freeze and burst a pipe. Lagging only reduces the speed of heat loss, so eventually the temperature of an unused system will drop to the level of the surrounding air.

On a gas-fired or oil-fired system you could turn the room thermostat down to its minimum setting if you will only be away for a few days.

For a long holiday, you could have a frost thermostat installed (it

is also called a low-limit thermostat). It overrides the other controls and turns on the system when the air temperature approaches freezing point. Rising air temperature makes it turn the system off again.

Alternatively, treat the system with a central-heating antifreeze. Tie up the ball-valve arm in the feed-and-expansion cistern and pour in antifreeze according to the maker's instructions. Then drain off

enough water for the antifreeze to be drawn into the system.

After restoring the cistern to the correct level, turn on the system for a few minutes to thoroughly mix the antifreeze with the water.

Solid-fuel systems can also be protected with antifreeze, but remember that if you boil the system by overrunning it and water is discharged from the vent pipe, the antifreeze will become diluted.

Protecting a system with corrosion proofer

Heating systems consisting of a mixture of metals such as copper, steel and cast-iron corrode internally. Most systems have copper pipes connected to steel radiators and a cast-iron boiler. In many cases corrosion gradually stops and causes little trouble. But sometimes it builds up to the point where circulation is restricted or the equipment is severely damaged.

Chemical products can be added to an indirect central-heating system to counteract corrosion. One chemical cleans out deposits, another inhibits more corrosion.

Unless the system is brand new it must be cleaned out before the corrosion proofing is put in.

In systems up to eight or nine years old, a fairly strong descaling chemical can be used to remove

deposits from pipes and radiators.

In older systems, removing too much solid matter might leave weak areas that could leak, so use a flushing agent which helps to remove loose deposits only.

Follow exactly the instructions given on the product container.

Black sludge in the system indicates fairly slow-acting corrosion. Red sludge indicates prob-

lems that need expert attention before the entire system is ruined.

Getting solid matter out of a system is difficult, but is easier if a large drain-off tap is fitted. A 22mm diameter gate valve on the return pipe low down in the system allows a much greater flow than a 15mm drain cock. It could be fitted by a plumber the next time work is done on the system.

Replacing a radiator

Replacing a radiator is not difficult if the new one is the same size as the old one and the existing valves are working properly.

You will need
Tools Towels or dust sheets; rags; two bowls; pliers; large adjustable spanner; cork; hammer; PTFE tape. Perhaps an Allen key.
Materials Radiator the same size as the old one; radiator air vent, and perhaps a new radiator plug.

1 Lay towels or dust sheets around the radiator and, if possible, to the nearest outside door.

2 Close off the control valve by hand. Use pliers or a small spanner to close the lockshield valve. Count the number of turns needed and write it down.

3 Put a bowl under the control valve, and disconnect the union nut, taking care not to distort the

pipe (page 80). Water will start to flow, and there may be a lot, so have two bowls ready.

4 Open the air vent to increase the flow of water.

5 When it has stopped, undo the union nut on the lockshield valve. Some more water may come out.

6 Remove the valve tail pieces and union nuts from the radiator with the adjustable spanner or Allen key. To do so, turn the valve tail anticlockwise (when looking at the end of the radiator). If it is stiff put some penetrating oil around the thread and wait for half an hour.

7 Hammer a cork into one of the valve openings on the radiator.

8 Lift it off its brackets and carry it out with the corked end lowest. Wipe up any drips immediately.

9 Hold the new radiator in position to check if the wall brackets need replacing (manufacturers sometimes change their design).

10 Wind PTFE tape around the thread of the valve tail pieces. Start from the end and make a 50 per cent overlap on each turn. Screw the tail pieces in place.

11 Fit a new air vent at the same end of the radiator as before, using PTFE tape as for the valve tail. The vent may be made to screw in with either a spanner or an Allen key.
Fit a new plug if there is a spare tapping in the other top end.

12 Fix the radiator on the brackets and reconnect the union nuts.

13 Open the valves to fill the radiator with water. Let air out through the air vent, and check for leaks. Reset the lockshield valve to its original position.

SWINGING DOWN A RADIATOR

A panel radiator can be swung down from the wall if you want to decorate, or retrieve something from behind it, provided that both pipes are fitted to the bottom.

1 Turn off the heating and wait for the radiator to cool.

2 Turn off the control valve. Turn off the lockshield valve, counting how many turns are needed.

3 Put towels or rags beneath the valves and around the pipes.

4 Loosen the union nut on each valve. Turn it anticlockwise (looking along the radiator towards the valve). Take care not to distort the pipe (page 80). Water will dribble out.

5 When both nuts have been loosened, lift the radiator about half an inch to free it from its wall brackets and swing it down to the ground. Rest the edge on a rag.
If the radiator will not lift easily, do not pull. To remove it you will have to drain down the system.

6 Retighten the nuts to stop the dribble of water.

7 To replace the radiator, just reverse the process.

Changing a central heating pump

It is possible to change a central-heating pump fairly easily if gate valves have been fitted on each side to cut off the water. You will also need an identical new pump, or one with identical connections.
Measure the length that the pump takes up along the pipe run, and the diameter and type of connections. Most domestic pumps have 1½in BSP threaded connections. Take these details to a plumbers' merchant, together with the type of pump and the setting of its output regulator.

HELPFUL TIPS
The pump is designed to run full of clean water. Air or sludge in the water can damage it. So keeping the system full of water and limiting corrosion are essential.

If your pump is out of use in summer, as is normally the case with a combined gravity/pumped system, run it for a minute once a month to keep its impeller free.

You will need
Tools Electrician's screwdriver; bowl; towels; pipe wrench/adjustable spanner; pencil and paper.
Materials New pump.

1 Switch off the electricity to the central heating and pull out the plug.

2 Make a note of how the electrical wiring on the pump is fitted. Then disconnect it with a screwdriver.

3 Close down the gate valves on each side of the pump using the valve handle or an adjustable spanner. If there are no gate valves,

you will have to drain the system (page 81).

4 Put a bowl and towels under the pump to catch any water that escapes when you remove it.

5 Unscrew the union nuts holding the pump in place. Turn them anticlockwise (facing along the pipe towards the pump).

6 Remove the old pump.

7 Fit the new pump in place.

8 Open the gate valves (or refill the system) and check that the unions are watertight.

9 Dry the pump to remove any traces of moisture; reconnect the wiring.

10 Test the pump by switching on the electrical supply and turning on the system at the programmer or time switch. You may need to turn up the room thermostat.

11 Check that the open safety vent pipe over the feed-and-expansion cistern does not discharge water when the pump starts or stops. If it does get expert advice.

12 Bleed air out of the system if you have had to add much fresh water to the cistern.

Electrical emergencies: What to do

ELECTRIC SHOCK

WARNING Quick action is essential but do not touch directly a casualty who is still in contact with the faulty electrical equipment. If you do, the current will pass through you as well, giving you an electric shock.

1 Immediately turn off the electricity at the main switch on the consumer unit if you know where it is and have access to it.

2 If you cannot get to the main switch immediately, stand on a dry floor or carpet indoors, or a dry mat or wooden box out of doors. Push or pull the casualty out of contact with the source of the shock, using a wooden chair or stick, or a loop of dry rope, fabric, or even tights.

3 Dial 999 for an ambulance or call a doctor if the casualty is or has been unconscious, or is burnt or unwell. If you have no telephone, send or shout for help.

4 If the casualty is not breathing, give the kiss of life. Tilt the head back, check the airway is clear and pinch the nose shut. Blow four breaths into the mouth then let the chest fall. Continue breathing into the mouth at normal speed.

5 If the casualty has burns, cover the burns with a clean, dry cotton sheet until medical help arrives.

FIRE IN AN ELECTRICAL APPLIANCE OR FITTING

1 Do not touch any part of the burning appliance or fitting.

2 If a plug-in appliance is on fire, switch off at the socket and pull out the plug.

3 If a socket or fixed appliance with no plug is on fire, turn off at the wall switch, if you can, or at the main switch on the fuse board.

4 Do not use water. Smother the fire with a rug or blanket, or use a dry-powder fire extinguisher.

5 Have the appliance or socket checked by a qualified electrical contractor before you use it again.

SPARKS OR SMELL OF BURNING

1 If sparks or a burning smell come from an appliance, first turn off the socket switch and pull out the plug. If it is a fixed appliance with no plug, turn off the main switch at the consumer unit on the fuse-board. It is then safe to turn off the appliance switch. Check the flex connections in the appliance and renew if necessary; if they are sound, have the appliance checked by a qualified electrical contractor.

2 If the sparks or smell come from a socket or a plug, turn off the main switch at the consumer unit on the fuse board before you touch the socket or plug. If the plug is hot, check its connections including the fuse contacts, and examine the flex for damage. Renew them if necessary. If the socket is hot, check it for damage and faulty connections and renew if necessary. Check the cable for damage at the point where it enters the socket mounting box.

NO ELECTRICITY

1 If power throughout your house fails and neighbouring houses are also without power, there is a mains supply failure. Report it, using the emergency number under 'Electricity' in your telephone directory.

2 If the neighbours have power when you have none, the fuse in the sealed unit on your fuseboard may have blown. Do not touch it. Report the power failure as described above.

MINOR EMERGENCIES

1 If one appliance fails, check its plug, fuse and flex and renew them if necessary. If the appliance still fails, try it in a different socket before taking it for repair. If the fault was in the socket, check the socket connections.

2 If several appliances on one circuit stop working at once, switch off at the consumer unit and check the circuit fuse. If it is sound, there may be a fault in the circuit cable. Call in a qualified electrical contractor to test it.

Home electrics: Tools for the job

Much of the work in modernising or extending wiring is non-electrical – cutting chases for cables, raising floorboards, drilling holes and the like. For working with the actual wiring and electrical accessories a few special tools are essential.

Pliers
A pair of 6in (150mm) electrician's pliers with cutting blades is sturdy enough for cutting conductor wires in cables. Make sure the handles are insulated – plastic-covered, for example.

Torch
A powerful torch squat enough to stand on its own will light up work under floors and in lofts. Make sure that it has a plastic or rubber case.

Metal-cased torch
Keep it near the consumer unit for testing cartridges.

Wire cutters
A pair of 5in (125mm) or 6in (150mm) side cutters with insulated handles cuts wires in flexes and the thinner cables.

Wire strippers
These should have insulated handles and may be combined with cutters. The adjustable blades strip the insulation from different-sized flexes and cables without damaging the wire strands inside.

Tester screwdriver
An ⅛in (3mm) blade, insulated screwdriver is used for screwing wires to terminals in plugs and light fittings. It has a neon lamp in the handle which lights up if the tip touches a live screw or conductor.

Insulated screwdriver
Use a 3/16in (5mm) blade screwdriver with an insulating sleeve on the shaft for screws on fuse carriers, plug covers and sockets.

Knife
A sharp knife will cut through thick cable sheath and flex sheath.

Circuit continuity tester
With a simple battery-powered tester you can check the continuity of circuits and whether a socket is on a ring circuit or on a spur.

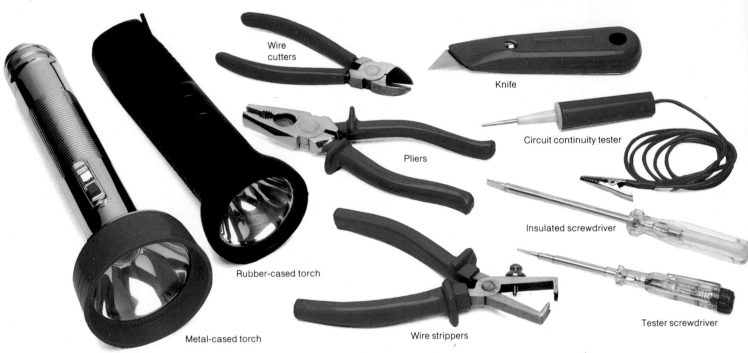

Wire cutters

Knife

Circuit continuity tester

Pliers

Insulated screwdriver

Rubber-cased torch

Metal-cased torch

Wire strippers

Tester screwdriver

CHOOSING CABLES FOR INDOOR CIRCUITS

Cable carries electricity round the household circuits to ceiling roses, light switches, socket outlets and fused connection units. It is the permanently fixed wiring – which is not moved about as flex is.

Modern cable – known as twin-core-and-earth cable – has a grey or white oval PVC sheath with three conductors inside. The red-insulated conductor is now called the line (formerly live or phase); the black-insulated conductor is the neutral; the bare wire is the earth conductor.

The greater the current, the thicker the cable carrying it has to be. Cable size is given in square millimetres. In thermal insulation or for a very long run, cable of a larger size than usual may be needed; ask an electrician.

Sleeving for earth conductors

When you strip off the outer sheath of a cable, cover the bare wire of the earth conductor with a sleeve of green-and-yellow PVC.

KEY TO COLOUR AND CODING

L – Line, live or phase (red)

E – Earth (bare wire)

N – Neutral (black)

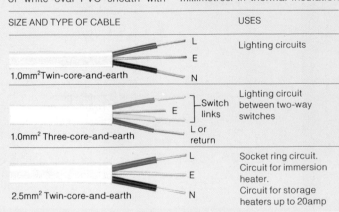
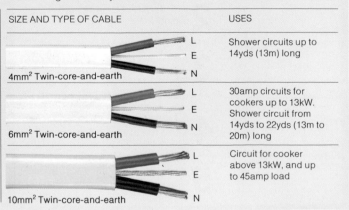

SIZE AND TYPE OF CABLE	USES
1.0mm² Twin-core-and-earth	Lighting circuits
1.0mm² Three-core-and-earth	Lighting circuit between two-way switches
2.5mm² Twin-core-and-earth	Socket ring circuit. Circuit for immersion heater. Circuit for storage heaters up to 20amp

SIZE AND TYPE OF CABLE	USES
4mm² Twin-core-and-earth	Shower circuits up to 14yds (13m) long
6mm² Twin-core-and-earth	30amp circuits for cookers up to 13kW. Shower circuit from 14yds to 22yds (13m to 20m) long
10mm² Twin-core-and-earth	Circuit for cooker above 13kW, and up to 45amp load

Reconnecting a flex to a lampholder

An accidental knock may dislodge a lampholder and stop the light working, but it is a simple matter to reconnect it. You will also need to reconnect if you are shortening the flex, perhaps to fit a new lampshade which needs to be higher.

If the lampholder is a metal one without an earth terminal, replace it with an earthed one – or with a plastic lampholder if the flex has no earth conductor. You must have three-core flex with a metal lampholder or metal lampshade.

If the flex is discoloured or cracked, fit a new one.

You will need
Tools Insulated screwdrivers, one with a small, fine tip; wire cutters and strippers; pliers.
Materials Heat-resisting flex. Perhaps petroleum jelly and a new ring or lampholder.

1 Turn off the switch at the consumer unit and remove the fuse for the circuit you will be working on.

2 Remove the light bulb and unscrew the ring that holds up the shade. If it sticks, rub petroleum jelly round it and leave it for half an hour. With a very old lampholder, you may have to break the ring; some shops sell the new rings separately. Remove the shade.

3 Unscrew the upper cover of the lampholder and push it up the flex to reveal the flex connections. Prise the flex conductors out of the clamping grooves which are part of the central pillar.

4 With the fine-tipped screwdriver, unscrew the terminals enough for you to draw out the flex conductors.

5 Push each terminal plunger inside the body of the holder to see if the tension is still firm. If not, or if the moulding is damaged or scorched, fit a new lampholder.

6 Prepare the ends of the flex afresh for connection.

7 If you are fitting a new lampholder, thread the cover onto the flex.

8 Screw the brown and blue conductors tightly into the terminals; it does not matter which each goes to. In a metal lampholder you must connect the green-and-yellow earth conductor to the earth terminal; it is usually on the cover.

9 Fit the flex conductors into the grooves on the central pillar.

10 Screw down the upper cover, making sure that the conductors are not disturbed. If they are, the tension will be affected on the plungers which contact the bulb.

11 Insert the lampholder into the lampshade and screw the retaining ring in place to secure the shade.

12 Fit the light bulb and shade.

13 Replace the circuit fuse and switch on at the consumer unit.

THE PARTS OF A LAMPHOLDER

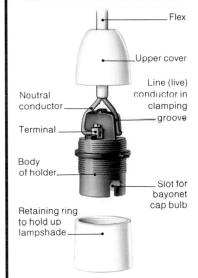

Connecting a light flex to a ceiling rose

If a light flex has discoloured or become brittle, it is easy to connect a new one between the ceiling rose and the lampholder.

Inside a modern ceiling rose on a loop-in wiring system is a row of terminals in groups which are not always marked. A separate terminal is marked E or ⊥ for the earth conductors.

Use the right flex for the installation (page 87). If it connects with a metal lampholder or light fitting, it must have an earth conductor.

You will need
Tools Insulated screwdrivers, one with a small, fine tip; sharp knife; wire cutters and strippers.
Materials Heat-resisting flex.

JUNCTION BOX SYSTEM

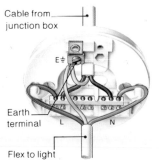
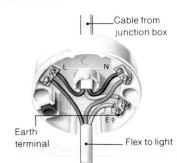

A ceiling rose for a loop-in system might have been used on a junction box system (above). There will be one cable entering the base of the rose. The flex connection is the same as for a loop-in system (instructions 5–7, facing page, top).

Another type of ceiling rose used on a junction box system (above right) has three or four sets of terminals, not in line.

1 Connect the blue flex conductor to the same set of terminals as the black cable conductor.

2 Connect the brown conductor from the flex to the same set of terminals as the red conductor from the cable.

3 Connect the green-and-yellow earth conductor from the flex to the same set of terminals as the earth conductor from the cable.

If the earth from the cable has not already been sleeved with green-and-yellow insulation, disconnect it and sleeve it before connecting it – with the flex earth – to the terminal.

DISCONNECTING THE OLD FLEX

1 At the consumer unit, turn off the main switch and remove the fuse for the circuit you will be working on. It is not enough simply to turn off the light switch.

2 Remove the light bulb and shade to avoid the risk of dropping them.

3 Unscrew the cover of the ceiling rose and slide it down the flex.

4 Using the small screwdriver, loosen the terminal at each end of the row. Withdraw the conductors.

5 If the flex has an earth conductor, unscrew the earth terminal enough to withdraw it. Do not dislodge the other earth conductors.

CONNECTING THE NEW FLEX

1 Connect the new flex first to the lampholder (above).

2 Thread the new flex through the cover of the ceiling rose.

3 Prepare the new flex for connection. Take care not to strip off too much of the outer sheathing. The conductors have to reach the terminals without strain, but they must not show below the ceiling-rose cover; the outer sheathing of the flex must enter the hole in the cover.

4 Slip the tip of the green-and-yellow-insulated earth conductor of the flex under the metal cover of the separate earth terminal in the ceiling rose. Make sure before you screw it down that the other earth conductors, from the cables and the switch, have not been dislodged from under the terminal. Drive the screw down tightly.

5 Connect the blue conductor at the outer hole of the outer trio.

6 Connect the brown conductor at the outer hole of the pair.

7 Press the blue and brown conductors into the notches above the knobs at the ends of the row of terminals. Slide the cover up the flex but it must stay on the outer sheath.

8 Screw on the ceiling-rose cover and replace the shade and bulb.

9 Replace the circuit fuse and switch the electricity back on.

Rewiring a table lamp or standard lamp

If a lamp flex is fraying or cracking, fit a new one. Heat-resisting flex is not necessary. For a table or standard lamp with no exposed metal parts, or for a double insulated lamp (marked ▣), use a flex with no earth conductor (page 87). For a lamp with metal parts which is not double insulated, use twin-core-and-earth flex.

If the lamp is a treasured old one with a brass lampholder without an earth terminal, you must fit a new brass lampholder with an earth terminal, or a plastic lampholder. If it is not possible to fit a new lampholder, do not use the lamp.

Do not run the flex up the outside of the lamp. It must be threaded up inside the lamp base. The hole to thread it through is often on the side of the lamp near the bottom. If the hole is underneath, the lamp base should have small feet to raise it and keep its weight off the flex.

Some lamps have a push-through switch in the lampholder. Others need to have a switch fitted in the flex; otherwise they can be switched on and off at the socket, but this may be inconvenient.

You will need
Tools Insulated screwdrivers; sharp knife; wire cutters and strippers; pliers.
Materials Lamp; suitable flex. Perhaps also a flex switch.

1 Unplug the lamp and remove the light bulb.

2 Screw off the first narrow ring and lift off the lampshade.
ALTERNATIVELY, screw off the upper half of the plastic cover and remove the lampshade.

3 Unscrew and remove the second narrow ring so that you can lift out the outer lampholder section and then raise the inner section which has the flex connected beneath it. ALTERNATIVELY, unscrew the rest of the plastic lampholder from the base, then screw down the lower cover to reveal the terminals.

4 Release the flex conductors from the terminals. Wind the wire tips securely round the end of the new flex and tape the two together.

5 Gently pull out the old flex from below, using it to pull the new flex through the lamp base.

6 Prepare the flex for connection and then finish drawing it through the lamp base until only about 1½in (38mm) is protruding.

7 Screw the brown conductor tip into one terminal and the blue conductor tip into the other.
If the terminals are marked L and N, the brown conductor goes to L and the blue to N. If you are using twin-core-and-earth flex, connect the green-and-yellow conductor to the terminal marked E or ⏚.

8 Lower the inner section of the lampholder back into place. Fit the outer section on top and secure it with the screw-on ring.
ALTERNATIVELY, screw the plastic cover over the terminals and screw the lampholder to the lamp base. As you do so, turn the flex or it will become twisted.

9 Replace the lampshade support and secure it with the upper narrow ring or plastic cover.

10 Fit the light bulb and shade.

FITTING A SWITCH IN THE FLEX

If you are using twin-core-and-earth flex, use a switch with an earth terminal. For a two-core flex on a double-insulated lamp, no earth terminal is necessary.
If you are adding a switch to a lamp already in use, switch off and unplug the lamp.

1 Cut the flex where the switch is to go and prepare the ends for connection.

2 Unscrew and remove the cover of the switch.

3 Take out a screw from the flex clamp at each end so that you can swivel the clamps aside.

4 Feed the flex ends under the clamps and screw the clamps down on the outer sheath.

5 Release the terminal screws and wind each conductor tip clockwise round the screws – brown to the terminals marked L, blue to the terminals marked N, and green-and-yellow to the terminals marked E or ⏚. Tighten the screws.

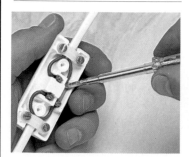

ALTERNATIVELY, in a switch with no earth terminal, connect the two brown conductors to the terminals behind the switch mechanism and the two blue conductors to each end of the through terminal block.

6 Screw the switch cover back in place.

TWO TYPES OF LAMPHOLDER

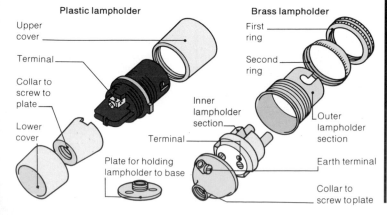

Plastic lampholder
Upper cover
Terminal
Collar to screw to plate
Lower cover
Terminal
Plate for holding lampholder to base

Brass lampholder
First ring
Second ring
Inner lampholder section
Outer lampholder section
Earth terminal
Collar to screw to plate

CHOOSING FLEXES FOR APPLIANCES AND LIGHTS

Flexible cord, usually called flex, connects an appliance or light to a circuit supplying power. The connection may be made with a plug and socket or with a fused connection unit.

On fixed lights, the flex connects with a lighting circuit at a ceiling rose and with the light bulb at a lampholder.

Most appliances – irons, toasters, table lamps, hairdryers, for example – have the flex permanently wired into them. Others, including sewing machines, kettles and tape recorders, have flexes that connect to them by a push-in connector.

Most flex is round in cross-section. Non-sheathed figure 8 and twin-twisted flex are not now permitted and should be replaced. The sheathing depends on the temperature it must withstand. Ordinary rubber and PVC withstand temperatures up to 60°C. Heat-resistant rubber or PVC withstand up to 85°C. Rubber-sheathed flexes have an outer cover of braided fabric. Flexes that may be used out of doors should be orange-sheathed to make them easy to see.

Flex with two conductors is for double-insulated appliances (marked ▣), or non-metal light-fittings; flex already wired into a double-insulated appliance may be oval instead of round in cross-section. Metal light fittings and most appliances need three-core flex, which has an earth conductor. A conductor in flex consists of many fine strands of wire twisted together – which is what makes it flexible. The thicker the conductor, the more strands it has; the thickness determines how much current it can carry.

Never join lengths of flex with insulating tape. Use a cable connector or fit a flex of the right length. Do not run flex under a carpet; it could fray and cause a fire. Do not trail flex across a room; somebody could trip over it and damage its connections.

Curly flex

Two and three-core curly flexes are sold in several lengths and colours. Some have connectors and plugs already fitted; others have the ends free for connecting. The flex extends when you move the appliance – a lamp, perhaps – out from the socket and contracts neatly when you put the appliance near the socket again.

KEY TO FLEX CODING

L – Line, live or phase (brown)

E – Earth (green and yellow)

N – Neutral (blue)

APPEARANCE OF FLEX	FLEX SIZE IN MM²	FOR AMPS UP TO	FOR WATTS UP TO	NUMBER OF CORES	SHEATH	EXAMPLES OF USE
L N	0.5	3	720	Two; colour coded	Heat-resisting PVC (85°C)	Non-metal lamps and pendant light fittings up to 4½lb (2kg) in weight
L N	0.75	6	1440	Two; colour coded	Ordinary PVC (60°C)	Non-metal lamps with flex more than 7ft (2m) long. Some hair dryers, food mixers and other double-insulated appliances up to 1.4kW
L N	0.75	6	1440	Two; colour coded	Heat-resisting PVC (85°C)	Pendant light fittings up to 6½lb (3kg) in weight
L E N	0.75	6	1440	Three; colour coded	Ordinary PVC (60°C)	Metal table and standard lamps. Some vacuum cleaners, hair dryers, food mixers, refrigerators, television sets
L E N	0.75	6	1440	Three; colour coded	Heat-resisting braided rubber or PVC (85°C)	Room heaters up to 1kW. Irons, toasters, and other appliances that become hot and could damage ordinary PVC
L N	1.0	10	2400	Two; colour coded	Heat-resisting PVC (85°C)	Pendant light fittings up to 11lb (5kg) in weight
L E N	1.0	10	2400	Three; colour coded	Ordinary PVC (60°C)	Kettles or jugs up to 2kW. Slow cookers. Frying pans
L E N	1.0	10	2400	Three; colour coded	Heat-resisting braided rubber or PVC (85°C)	Room heaters up to 2kW
L E N	1.25	13	3120	Three; colour coded	Ordinary PVC (60°C)	Kettles or jugs from 2kW to 3kW
L E N	1.25	13	3120	Three; colour coded	Heat-resisting braided rubber or PVC (85°C)	Room heaters up to 3kW
L E N	1.5	15	3600	Three; colour coded	Ordinary PVC (60°C)	Some extension leads
L E N	1.5	15	3600	Three; colour coded	Heat-resisting rubber (85°C)	Immersion heaters up to 3kW. Storage heaters up to 3kW

Ten easy ways to avoid a burglary

Most break-ins are carried out by casual thieves looking for easy pickings. A thief is unlikely to persist if he encounters locked doors and windows. Rapid entry and exit are vital for him, and he will not climb in and out of the house through broken glass.

The tips on this page will all help to keep your home secure.

If you want specific advice on how to protect your home, telephone the Crime Prevention Officer at your local police station. He will visit the house if necessary, point out weak spots in your defences and suggest the most appropriate security devices for your circumstances.

GETTING HELP FROM THE POLICE

If you see anyone loitering in your street or acting suspiciously, do not disturb them. Call the police, then continue to watch unseen until they arrive.

Neighbourhood Watch groups, run in collaboration with the local police, are intended to encourage neighbours to work together by watching for anything suspicious in the area. They also stress the importance of protecting property, and marking valuables. If you are interested in getting involved in a group, contact your local Crime Prevention Officer.

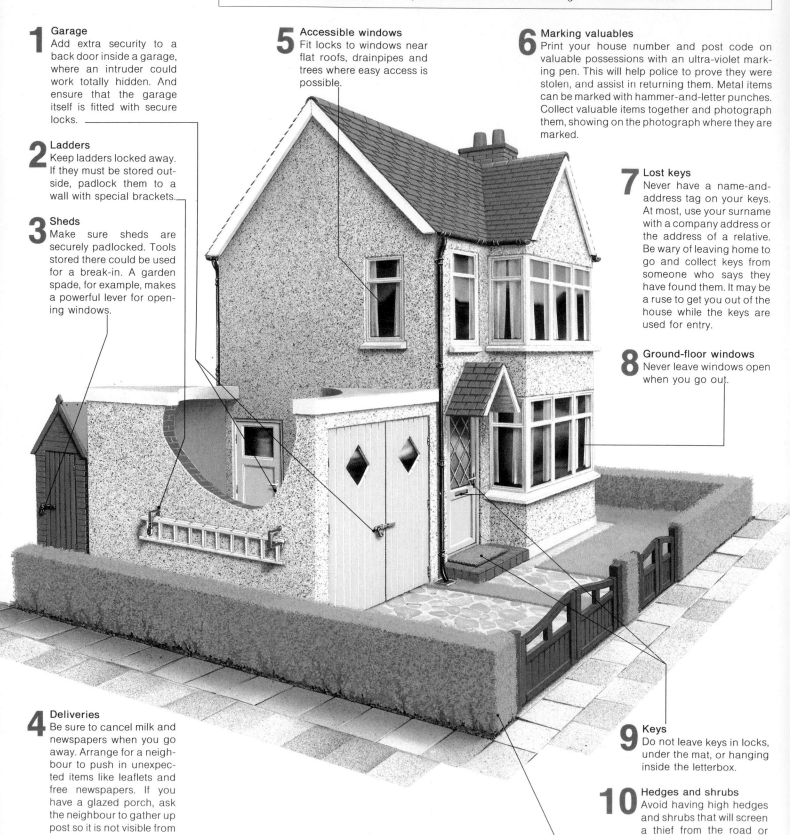

1 Garage
Add extra security to a back door inside a garage, where an intruder could work totally hidden. And ensure that the garage itself is fitted with secure locks.

2 Ladders
Keep ladders locked away. If they must be stored outside, padlock them to a wall with special brackets.

3 Sheds
Make sure sheds are securely padlocked. Tools stored there could be used for a break-in. A garden spade, for example, makes a powerful lever for opening windows.

4 Deliveries
Be sure to cancel milk and newspapers when you go away. Arrange for a neighbour to push in unexpected items like leaflets and free newspapers. If you have a glazed porch, ask the neighbour to gather up post so it is not visible from outside.

5 Accessible windows
Fit locks to windows near flat roofs, drainpipes and trees where easy access is possible.

6 Marking valuables
Print your house number and post code on valuable possessions with an ultra-violet marking pen. This will help police to prove they were stolen, and assist in returning them. Metal items can be marked with hammer-and-letter punches. Collect valuable items together and photograph them, showing on the photograph where they are marked.

7 Lost keys
Never have a name-and-address tag on your keys. At most, use your surname with a company address or the address of a relative. Be wary of leaving home to go and collect keys from someone who says they have found them. It may be a ruse to get you out of the house while the keys are used for entry.

8 Ground-floor windows
Never leave windows open when you go out.

9 Keys
Do not leave keys in locks, under the mat, or hanging inside the letterbox.

10 Hedges and shrubs
Avoid having high hedges and shrubs that will screen a thief from the road or from neighbours.

CHECKING THE SECURITY OF YOUR HOUSE DOORS

Any lock or bolt, however thief-proof, is only as strong as the door and frame to which it is fitted. A heavy boot applied to a door will often splinter the frame or even rip the lock from the door, allowing easy entry with no sign of damage on the outside. So ensure that exterior doors are tough; if necessary, have a new door frame installed. Or a metal reinforcement, called a London bar, can be fitted to the frame beside a mortise lock. It has to be ordered to size.

All surface-mounted locks and bolts are only as strong as the screws anchoring them in place. Be sure to use the length and gauge recommended for the fitting; never use anything smaller.

SECURITY LOCKS FOR FRONT DOORS

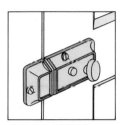

Cylinder nightlatch

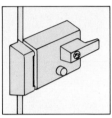

Deadlocking
cylinder nightlatch

Cylinder nightlatch
Many front doors are fitted with a cheap cylinder nightlatch, which is easy for a burglar to open. If you want no more than one lock on the door, it can be replaced with a more secure model. Often this will fit in place of the old one with little or no alteration to the door or frame. When choosing the lock, look for the British Standards Institution kitemark and the number BS 3621, which ensures that the lock is made to a reasonable standard.

A problem with the standard nightlatch is that if a burglar breaks the glass in the door, he can reach in and turn the knob of the latch. This can be prevented by fitting a deadlocking cylinder nightlatch, also called a deadlatch. When you turn the key as you leave the house, the lock becomes immovable.

To keep the door locked when you are indoors as well, choose a model with knob locking, so that it can be locked from the inside as well as the outside. But make sure that a key is kept near the door in case of fire.

Mortise deadlock
Rather than replacing an existing nightlatch, you can add additional security by fitting a mortise deadlock lower down the door. The lock, which has a single bolt, is inserted into a hole, called a mortise, cut in the edge of the door. If the door already has a cheap, two-lever mortise deadlock, it can be removed and replaced with a new five-lever model of the same size, with a box-type striking plate.

Latchbolt
If the nightlatch is to be removed, choose a latchbolt (also called a locking latch) which has both a bolt and a latch. The latch is operated by a handle on the inside while the bolt is key-operated. Do not put both a nightlatch and a latchbolt on one door or you will have to turn two knobs every time the door is opened.

Cutting a mortise in a door weakens it to some extent, so if you have a front door less than 1¾in (44mm) wide ask for a thin-pattern mortise lock.

BOLTS FOR FRENCH WINDOWS

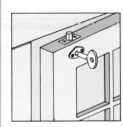

In timber frames, fit rack bolts in the doors, shooting up into the frame at the top and down into the sill or floor at the bottom. Fit the bolts on the overlapping door. Hinge bolts also give added security (see overleaf).

On metal doors, fit surface-mounted self-locking bolts in the same way (see overleaf).

SECURITY LOCKS FOR BACK AND SIDE DOORS

Sashlock
A sashlock – combining latch and bolt and with a handle on both sides of the door – is usually fitted to a back or side door. An existing sashlock often has only two or three levers, giving poor security. It can be removed and replaced with an 'up-grader' unit which has five levers and a dead-locking action. Take the exact dimensions of the old lock when buying a new one, as sizes vary according to make.

Deadlocking is even more important on side and back doors, as they are often glazed and in secluded positions. Burglars often break the glass and turn the latch from the inside.

SECURITY LOCKS FOR PATIO DOORS

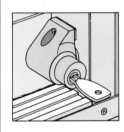

Small security locks are mounted on the inside door. A bolt engages in a hole in the other door.

The locks can be fitted to either wood or metal-framed doors, provided they come with the correct screws – either wood screws or self-tapping screws.

For maximum security, fit locks at both top and bottom of the door. This is particularly advisable for old aluminium-framed patio doors which can sometimes be jemmied out of the sliding track and lifted out of the frame.

A MULTI-LOCKING SYSTEM FOR FLATS

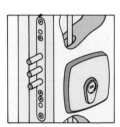

External doors in flats above ground level are often in secluded positions where an intruder is unlikely to be seen. To counter this, a multi-locking system is available. Turning the key engages a lock on the opening face of the door, and also moves bars to engage in the top, bottom and hinge-side frames. Once locked, the door becomes part of the wall and is almost impossible to break down. The system may either be surface-mounted or installed within the door itself.

With a multi-locked door it is important to have a spare set of keys kept with a trusted person. You would have to call a locksmith to drill out the cylinder if you locked your keys inside.

INTERNAL DOORS: TO LOCK OR NOT?

Unless a house is shared, and security between rooms is needed, internal doors are best not locked when the house is empty. Once a thief is inside he will usually not be deterred by locked doors unless they are particularly strong. He will kick or jemmy them open, causing extra damage to the house. The same applies to wardrobe doors and to drawers. Put valuables in a hidden safe (page 94), then leave all the doors and drawers unlocked.

When the house is occupied, ground floor doors could be locked at night. A burglar trying to get from, say, the living room to the rest of the house will probably make so much noise that he will wake the occupants.

For this purpose, fit a sashlock, as you would for a back or side door. Handles on both sides of the door will be necessary for normal use in the daytime.

ADDITIONAL DEVICES FOR DOOR SECURITY

Rack bolts

With every external door it is advisable to fit rack bolts to prevent forcing. The bolts are mortised into the edge of the door (see facing page). Fit two to each door – one in the closing edge and one at the top or bottom.

Rack bolts are an alternative method of locking a front door at night when the house is occupied.

If the glass is broken it is hard to see where the bolts are fitted. Even if the holes are found, a fluted key is needed to undo them.

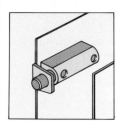

Hinge bolts

It is possible to unhinge a door by using a jemmy on the hinge side. To prevent this, fit hinge bolts – two per door – about 3in (75mm) away from the hinges (see facing page).

Self-locking bolts

Where a door is too thin to house a rack bolt without being weakened, fit a surface mounted, self-locking bolt. It is merely screwed in place; when fitted, all screws are concealed. Pushing the bolt end slides it into the locked position, where it deadlocks and cannot be moved without the use of a key.

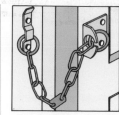

Door chains

To prevent an intruder forcing his way in after ringing the doorbell, fit a chain to the front door. It allows the door to be opened just far enough to speak to a caller, but the door has to be shut again before the chain can be released to allow entry.

The strength of the device depends entirely on how well the chain is anchored to door and frame, so the longest and heaviest-gauge screws possible should be used.

Various patterns are available, including a simple chain, a chain combined with a sliding bolt, a chain which can be unlocked from the outside with a key, and a chain with an alarm built in which is triggered by an attempt to enter.

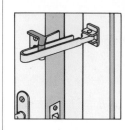

Door limiter

A more substantial version of the door chain is called a door limiter, with a sliding bar replacing the chain. When in place the bar engages with the retaining part of the unit, restricting the door's opening. The door has to be closed and the bar swung away before it can be fully opened.

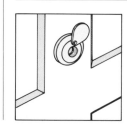

Peephole viewer

A simple lens system offers a wide-angle view of the area immediately outside the door. The occupant can look out, but a person outside cannot see in. A peephole viewer is best used in conjunction with a porch light.

Fitting a new mechanism to a lock

If the keys are lost, or if you want to be sure of security when taking over a new house, it is cheaper to replace the working part of a lock than to buy a completely new unit.

CYLINDER NIGHTLATCH

Buy a new cylinder and keys, as long as it is a straightforward lock. You cannot replace the cylinder on the type which has a locking interior handle.

You will need
Tools Screwdriver; pliers; self-grip wrench or vice. Perhaps a mini hacksaw.
Materials New cylinder and keys.

1 Unscrew the lock cover from inside the door to expose the con-

necting screws which hold the cylinder in place.

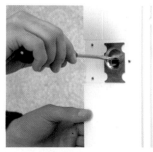

2 Unscrew the connecting screws until the cylinder can be removed. The connecting bar will come too.

3 Hold the new connecting bar in a self-grip wrench or vice and use

pliers to snap it to the same length as the old one, so it is correctly housed in the interior handle when the cylinder is in place.

The bar is divided into breakable segments along its length.

4 Make sure that the connecting screws are also the right length. They can be cut to length with a mini hacksaw.

5 Insert the new cylinder into the hole. Tighten the screws and replace the cover, making sure that the handle of the lock connects with the bar.

MORTISE LOCK

Buy a complete set of levers and keys for the right model of lock. If possible take the lock with you to the locksmith when you buy the new set.

You will need
Tools Screwdriver; hammer; small piece of wood, such as a pencil or dowel.
Materials Lever set and keys.

1 Remove the lock (see facing page).

2 Carefully unscrew the cover plate and lift out the existing set of levers.

3 Put the new ones in place. It is vital to keep the levers in the order in which they are supplied.

4 Replace the cover plate, and fix the lock back into the door.

Replacing a mortise lock

When buying a new mortise lock make sure that it is the same dimensions as the old one and that the holes for the key and the handle spindle are in the same place. If possible, take the old lock with you to the locksmith when buying the replacement.

The following technique for replacing a lock applies to any mortise lock, whether it has a bolt and latch or just a bolt.

You will need
Tools Screwdriver; hammer; small piece of thin wood (or a pencil would do).
Materials New five-lever mortise lock.

1 Unscrew the handles or knobs.

2 Unscrew the lock face on the edge of the door.

3 Tap the spindle with a hammer towards the door edge to loosen the lock. Remove the spindle.

4 Lever out the lock at the top and bottom with the screwdriver, using a small piece of wood under the screwdriver to protect the edge of the door. You can use a pencil instead of a piece of wood.

5 Insert the new lock in the slot, making sure it is the right way round. Screw it in place.

6 Replace the spindle and the handles or knobs.

Adding security bolts to doors

FITTING A RACK BOLT

You will need
Tools Pencil; drill and bits (sizes according to the manufacturer's instructions); pliers; ¾in (19mm) chisel; screwdriver; try square.
Materials Rack bolt.

1 Mark a central point on the edge of the door where you want to fit the bolt.

2 Use a try square and pencil to continue the mark onto the inner face of the door.

3 Drill a hole into the edge of the door to the width and depth of the body of the bolt.

4 Wind out the bolt and push it into the hole. Mark round the faceplate, withdraw the bolt with pliers and cut a shallow recess for the faceplate with the chisel.

5 Hold the bolt flush with the face of the door, and mark the spot for the key. Drill a hole (see the manufacturer's instructions for the size) through the inside face of the door only.

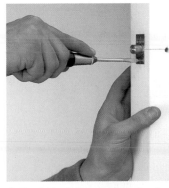

6 Push the bolt back into the door and screw the faceplate to the edge of the door. Check with the key that the bolt operates correctly. If necessary, enlarge the keyhole.

7 Screw the keyhole plate to the inside of the door.

8 Close the door and wind out the bolt to mark the door jamb. One way to make the mark is to push a piece of carbon paper between the bolt and the jamb.

9 Open the door and drill an engagement hole at the mark. Check that the bolt will go smoothly into this hole.

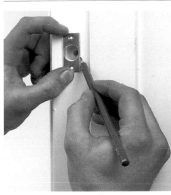

10 Hold the cover plate over the hole, draw around it, cut out a shallow recess, and screw the cover plate in place. Check the operation of the bolt, and make any necessary adjustments.

FITTING HINGE BOLTS

You will need
Tools Pencil; drill and bits (sizes according to the manufacturer's instructions); adhesive tape; mallet; chisel; screwdriver.
Materials A pair of hinge bolts.

1 Open the door fully and mark the centre of the door edge quite close to the two hinges at the top and the bottom.

2 Drill a hole into the door edge to the width and depth given on the maker's instructions.

Wrap a piece of coloured ad-
hesive tape around the bit as a guide to the depth.

3 Fit the bolt into the hole. Partially close the door so that the bolt marks the frame.

4 At this spot, drill a hole into the frame to the depth of the protruding bolt, plus a little more for clearance. Close the door to test that it shuts easily. If necessary, enlarge the width or depth of the hole.

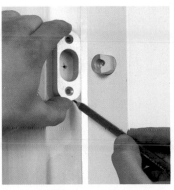

5 Open the door and hold a cover plate over the hole. Mark the edge of the plate with a pencil, and chisel out a recess so the plate lies flush with the frame.

Fix the plate in place with the screws provided.

Protecting outbuildings

SHEDS AND WORKSHOPS

The hasp and staple fitted to many prefabricated buildings have little security value, and need to be replaced with a strong locking bar.

Where possible, choose a locking bar which leaves no screw or bolt heads visible when it is closed. The hinged section should have a totally enclosed pin.

Buy a five-lever padlock to give a large number of key combinations. Raised shoulders on the padlock will protect it from attack by hacksaw, bolt cutters or crowbar.

Ideally the locking bar and staple should bolt right through the frame of the building.

If screws are used, buy clutch-head ones which can be tightened with a screwdriver but cannot be undone.

GARAGES

Securing hinged doors

Garages with hinged doors can be padlocked in the same way as sheds and workshops.

If a garage with hinged doors is attached to the house and there is a door leading inside, extra security is needed; once in the garage a thief can work unseen. A beam can be dropped into brackets fixed to the garage door and frame, ensuring that the doors can only be opened from the inside while you are away from the house.

You can make your own brackets by bending one arm of a large angle bracket into a U-shape.

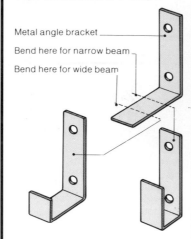

Metal angle bracket
Bend here for narrow beam
Bend here for wide beam

Securing up-and-over doors

Up-and-over doors are normally fitted with a cylinder lock which forms part of the door handle. If the keys are lost, a replacement handle unit should be available from the door manufacturers.

If a garage with up-and-over doors is attached to the house and there is access from the garage into the house, put a locking bar on the inside of the door about 4in (100mm) down from the top, so that the door can be locked to the vertical frame member with a padlock. This ensures that the door could only be opened from inside. Fit the hasp to the frame and the staple to the door.

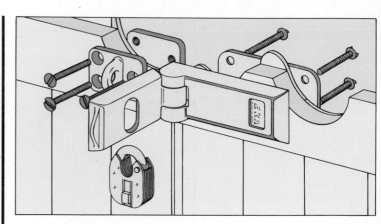

Locking bar and padlock To provide maximum security for a shed or garage, a heavy-duty locking bar, bolted through the frame, is locked with a high-shouldered, five-lever padlock.

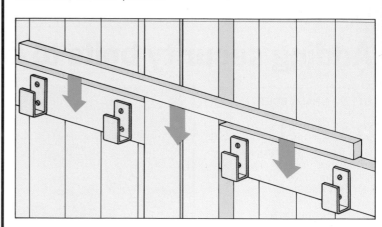

Garage-door beam A strong beam, made of either wood or metal, can be dropped into brackets fixed with stout screws to the inside of the garage door and the frame around the door.

Fitting a lock to a casement window

Surface-mounted locks are easy to fit to casement windows, provided that the fixed frame and the opening frame are at right angles to each other. If the fixed frame is tapered, wood may have to be chiselled away so that the lock fits against the opening frame. Some locks are supplied with a wedge to get over this problem.

For large windows, or for extra security, fit two locks on each frame, at top and bottom. They will withstand a jemmy attack better than a single lock.

The technique shown here is for a particular model of surface-mounted lock, but other models are installed in a similar way.

You will need
Tools Pencil; drill and twist bits; bradawl; screwdriver. Perhaps a small chisel.
Materials One or two window locks, depending on size of window.

1 Close the window firmly, and hold the body and lockplate on the opening edge. The lockplate goes against the opening frame and the body against the fixed frame.

2 Mark the shape of the lockplate with a pencil, and the screw positions for the body with a bradawl.

3 Remove the lockplate from the body. Put it in position, mark the

screw positions, drill pilot holes and screw it in place.

4 Drill the pilot holes for the body into the edge of the fixed frame.

5 Lock the body to the plate and screw it to the frame.

LAMINATED GLASS TO THWART BURGLARS

Particular windows in a house may be at risk from burglars. They may be ground-floor windows hidden from the neighbours, or they may be upstairs windows which are accessible from an extension roof, a tree or a drainpipe.

Fitting laminated glass would greatly add to the security. It consists of a sandwich of glass with a clear plastic film between. Although the glass may be cracked by a blow, the plastic will resist efforts to break through.

Do not use wired glass; it has little security value.

SECURITY FOR PLASTIC WINDOWS

An increasing number of plastic windows are being used in houses, and they can pose a security problem. Most manufacturers of security devices do not recommend them for plastic windows because a thin plastic section offers no grip for screws.

If a plastic window frame is known to have a timber inner frame, security devices suitable for wooden frames could be used.

If there are steel inserts within the plastic section, self-tapping screws could be used, as for metal frames.

But locks cannot be fitted to hollow sections of windows filled with rigid foam.

The ideal solution is to consult the installer of your windows at the time they are being made.

CHOOSING SECURITY LOCKS FOR YOUR WINDOWS

Windows are main points of entry for burglars. The most common method of breaking in is to smash the glass and release the catch.

Most window locks will either lock the frames together, make the handle immovable, or lock the stay arm. Locking the frames together gives the best result.

Before buying window locks, make sure they are suitable for your windows. A lock for timber frames will come with woodscrews. Locks for metal windows will have self-tapping screws. Make sure the frames are thick enough to accommodate the device.

When choosing security devices, consider how often the window is used. Some locks, such as a dual-screw, can be a nuisance if the window is in constant use. On the other hand, windows that are rarely opened can be screwed together.

WOODEN SLIDING SASH WINDOWS

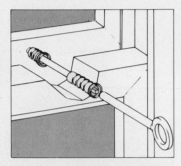

DUAL SCREW A bolt goes through a barrel in the inner frame into the outer frame. Fit two dual screws if the window is large.

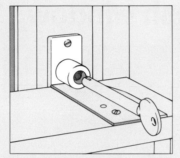

SURFACE-FITTED BOLT A bolt on the upper sash allows the window to be opened a little for ventilation. Fit two to large windows.

METAL WINDOWS

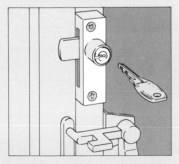

SURFACE-FITTED LOCK Fitted with self-tapping screws near the centre of the opening edge of the window. The bolt locks against the fixed frame.

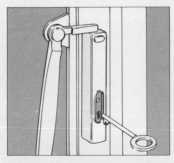

COCKSPUR BOLT When the cockspur handle is closed, the case of the bolt is moved up on the fixed frame and locked, preventing the cockspur from opening.

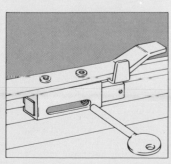

STAY BOLT Fits underneath the stay arm. A bolt slides under the stay retainer, preventing the arm from being lifted.

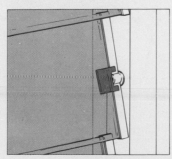

LOUVRE LOCK Metal inserts for Beta Naco windows lock the glass in the bladeholders. A blocking bolt can lock the handle.

WOODEN CASEMENT WINDOWS

For locking frames together

MORTISE BOLT The lock is mortised into the opening frame, and the bolt slides into a hole in the fixed frame. May be too large for narrow frames. More difficult to install than a surface-fitting lock, but gives excellent security. Fit close to the centre of the opening edge. On large windows, fit a mortise bolt at each end of the opening edge.

SURFACE-FITTED LOCK The catch is screwed to the fixed frame and the lock plate to the frame that opens. It is locked by a push-button action, and unlocked with a key. Suitable for narrow frames that may not accommodate a mortise bolt. Fit it close to the centre of the opening edge. On large windows, fit one at each end of the opening edge.

For locking the handle

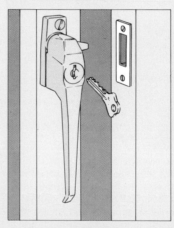

LOCKING HANDLE A new handle with a lock replaces the existing cockspur handle. Once locked, it cannot be opened without the key. Make sure you buy the correct right-hand or left-hand type for your window.

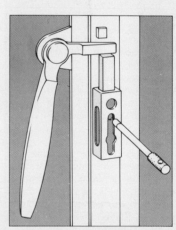

BLOCKING BOLT The lock is fitted to the fixed frame and prevents the cockspur handle from being moved. The bolt is retracted with the key. Only suitable when the cockspur is on the surface of the frame.

For locking the window stay

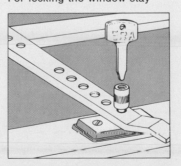

THREADED STAY PEG The lock replaces the stay peg nearer the hinge. It can secure the window in the closed position or in an open position. The device is only suitable for window stays that are pierced by holes. Locked and unlocked with a key.

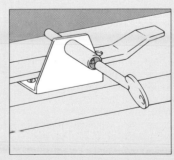

STAYBOLT A plate is screwed to the fixed frame, and a bolt passes through it to hold the stay in the closed position. The bolt can be used for stays without (or with) holes. It is fitted in place of the original stay peg which is first removed and discarded.

Fitting a lock to a metal frame

Locks are fitted to a steel or aluminium window frame with self-tapping screws, which should be supplied with the lock.

To drill a pilot hole in the frame, use a high-speed-steel (HSS) twist bit. Most locks come with instructions giving the drill size.

If in doubt, make the hole the same diameter as the 'core' of the screw, not the shank. Use a bit that is too small rather than too big.

You will need

Tools Bradawl or ball-point refill; electric drill; HSS twist bits; screwdriver.
Materials Window lock with self-tapping screws.

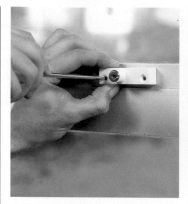

1 Hold the lock in position and mark the screw hole with a bradawl or ball-point refill.

2 Drill a pilot hole just through the metal. Provided the bit is sharp, it should not skid on the metal.

3 Screw the lock to the frame. If the screw hole is too tight, re-drill the hole one size bigger.

Fitting a dual screw to a sash window

A dual screw is a highly secure device for locking a sash window, but it is not convenient if the window is frequently opened. In that case, use a surface-fitted bolt (see chart, page 93).

For large windows, fit two locks, one at each end of the centre meeting rail.

Dual screws vary in design. Some have barrels for both inner and outer frames; others have a lockplate for the outer frame.

You will need

Tools Drill and flat bit the width of the lock barrel; hammer and piece of wood, or a large screwdriver (depending on the model). Perhaps a small screwdriver, small twist bit and chisel (depending on model).
Materials One or two dual screws.

1 Ensure that the window is fully closed.

2 Use the flat bit to drill through the inner meeting rail and into the outer meeting rail to a depth of ⅝in (16mm). Wind some coloured insulating tape around the bit as a guide to the depth of the hole.

3 Tap the longer barrel into the inner meeting rail, using a hammer and a piece of wood to protect it from being damaged.
ALTERNATIVELY, if the barrel has a slot, use a large screwdriver to screw it into the rail until it is flush with the wood.

4 Reverse the sashes. Tap the shorter barrel into the outer meeting rail.
ALTERNATIVELY, fit the locking plate to the outer meeting rail. If the sashes clash as they pass, recess the plate with a chisel.

5 Close the window and screw the bolt into the barrel with the key.

Installing a small home safe

Locked drawers and cupboards offer no protection against a thief who has entered an empty house. The best protection you can provide for small objects inside your house is to install a domestic model safe.

Some models are designed to be installed in the floor, others in a wall, others inside a cupboard. Some are key operated, others have combination locks.

With any type of safe, it is vital that the fitting instructions are followed exactly so that it cannot be jemmied out. Each model comes with its own instructions, and can be obtained from a locksmith or from a shop specialising in home security.

The alternative to a safe is to deposit valuables with your bank when you are away from home. Small objects, such as jewellery, can be left at the bank whenever you are not using them.

THREE MODELS OF HOME SAFE

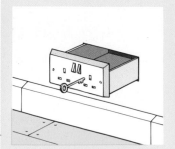

POWER-POINT SAFE The steel box has a front designed like a power socket. The drawer is opened with a key inserted into one of the pin holes. There is no electrical wiring.
The safe is big enough to hold cash and jewellery.

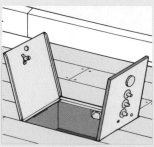

UNDER-FLOOR SAFE Designed to fit between the joists of a suspended wooden floor, and then be covered with carpet. It is screwed to the joists from inside. The combination lock is operated by three dials, each with the letters of the alphabet.

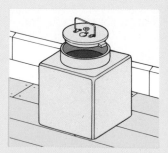

ABOVE-FLOOR SAFE A strong steel safe can be fixed on top of a suspended timber floor inside a cupboard, loft or other inconspicuous place. It is bolted to the joists from the inside on a steel frame. It can be fitted with a seven-lever or combination lock.

CHOOSING A BURGLAR ALARM TO PROTECT YOUR HOUSE

Most thieves are likely to be deterred by locks on windows and doors, but you may decide to install an alarm system as a defence against a burglar who tries to force his way in. A noisy alarm may deter him from entering the house, or greatly reduce the time he stays there.

Before buying a system, check that the alarm is loud enough. Anything below 95 decibels has little effect and cannot be heard over any distance. If possible, fit the type which resets after about a minute or two to avoid nuisance to neighbours. Notify neighbours that an alarm has been fitted.

A valuable addition to a system is a panic button which can be used to trigger off the alarm at any time. It can be comforting to older people.

Some burglar-alarm systems are designed for DIY installation; others need to be professionally fitted.

AVOIDING FALSE ALARMS

Ninety-eight per cent of all burglar alarms that go off are false. So if you have one installed by a security firm, make sure that it is regularly checked.

If you install your own system, there are a couple of checks that you can do yourself. Arm the system, then rattle windows and doors to discover if the alarm is triggered by any looseness. Any movement in doors and windows can set off magnetic switches.

With the system armed, run your hand over pressure mats to see if the alarm is triggered. Mats fail with age.

WHOLE-HOUSE SYSTEMS THAT WARN OF A BREAK-IN

The most common alarm systems are designed to set off a bell or siren if a burglar tries to break in. Before buying one, ensure that the alarm has a 'closed' electrical circuit. This means that when the system is turned on the circuit is completed. If there is any interference – such as the wires being cut – the alarm will go off. Each system has three main components – the switches, the control and the alarm.

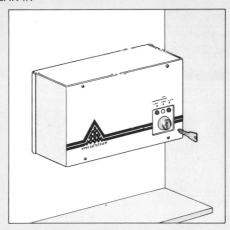

Automatic light switches
A magnet and switch are fitted to a door or window. If the magnet is moved, the switch is activated. They can be fitted top or bottom of a door. A passive infra-red detector turns on lights when it detects movement in a room.

The alarm
The alarm itself can be a bell, siren or buzzer. Some alarms will be set off if an intruder tries to remove the cover.

A circuit may also be included to switch on lights, both inside and outside. This can frighten off a potential intruder, as well as alerting the neighbours.

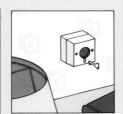

Panic button
A manually operated switch can be fitted as a panic button – at the bedside or by the front door. It is usually wired so that it will trigger the alarm whether or not the rest of the system is switched on. Panic buttons can be very sensitive; the slightest pressure will set off the alarm.

The control unit
The 'brain' of the system is the control unit which receives signals from the switches and sends an electric current to activate the alarm. The system is turned on or off with a key or a push-button panel to which a code number is first keyed in.

Connected with the control unit will be some form of power supply, either mains or batteries. In some models mains power will feed the system under normal conditions, but if the power is cut off for any reason, a battery will take over. The battery is later recharged automatically from the mains.

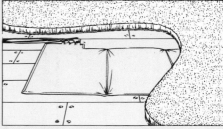

Pressure pad
The pad is placed under a mat or carpet. When it is trodden on, the alarm is triggered. Ideally, it should be wired to a separate circuit from the main alarm.

ONE-BOX UNITS THAT WARN OF A BREAK-IN

Small, inexpensive devices can be fixed to a door or placed in a particular room to give warning of an attempted break-in at that point. They could be particularly useful in a flat where there is only one main point of entry, or in a room which contains valuable possessions.

The alarms may be set off by movement of the door or by noise made by the burglar as he tries to break in.

Acoustic alarm
The noise of a break-in will set off an acoustic alarm. It listens for unusual noises such as the breaking of glass or the splintering of wood, and will then react. It is not triggered by normal traffic noise.

Units may be fixed or movable, working off both mains and rechargeable batteries. And they may be used to turn on lights, inside and out.

Door alarm
The unit can be fitted to an external door, and will set off an alarm if the door is opened. It operates on batteries, so no wiring is needed. The alarm is turned off with a push-button code that you decide yourself, or with a key. A delay switch allows several seconds for the householder to enter or leave the house without triggering the alarm.

ALARMS THAT DETECT AN INTRUDER ONCE HE IS INSIDE

Internal alarms are designed to detect an intruder once he has entered a house. They are self-contained units powered by either batteries or mains electricity. No special wiring is needed.

Many models can be moved about the house to protect different areas at different times of the day and night. The unit can be set up in a room where valuables are kept, or at a part of the house where you feel a burglar may enter, or on the stairs.

Before installing one of these alarms study the instructions carefully. Curtains wafting in the breeze, the heat waves from a radiator warming up, or even a ringing telephone may set one off.

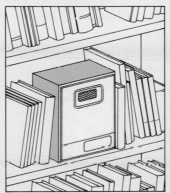

Infra-red alarm
A unit, no larger than a speaker, detects the body heat of an intruder. It is armoured against attempts to switch off the alarm, and once the siren is operating, only the correct key will disconnect it.

Ultrasonic alarm
The unit sends out a sound-wave signal which bounces back to it. A door opening or a person moving will set off the alarm. An area of 600sq ft (56sq m) is protected. To extend the range, 'bugs' can be added.

CHOOSING TIME CONTROLS FOR SECURITY AND CONVENIENCE

A dark, silent house can arouse the interest of burglars. If you make the house appear occupied, by day or night, a prowler is likely to move on to an easier target.

Voices, music and lights after dark can suggest you are in – but only if used with discretion; a single light in the hall left on all evening, or a radio playing all day are more likely to betray that you are out. The illusion that you are there is given by a change in the house – music stopping, or a light going off in one room and on in another.

Sockets and switches operated by timers help to create the illusion. Some sophisticated controls will memorise your schedule of switching lights on and off and reproduce it.

LIGHT-SWITCH TIMERS

Time-controlled light switches are connected to the lighting circuit in place of normal switches and are wired in exactly the same way. Some will switch on and off many times. Others switch on only once – at dusk – so there is no danger of the light shining in the daytime because a power cut has interfered with the setting.

Sunset switch

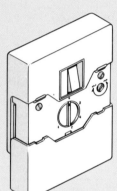

Switching on is controlled by a light-sensitive eye that activates the switch when daylight fades. The lower part of the switch has a cover that slides down to reveal a knob for setting the switch-off time between 2 and 8 hours after the light comes on.

Programmable switch (tungsten lighting)

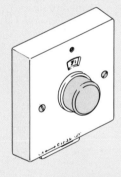

The timing is set by turning the knob until the switch-on time shows in the window and then pressing the knob. The switch is set in the same way to turn off. It will switch on and off up to 48 times a day and operate manually at any time. It can also memorise times when you switch the light on and off, and repeat the pattern.

AUTOMATIC OUTDOOR LIGHT

An infra-red sensor or photoelectric switch is activated when anyone – visitor or burglar – comes within its field of vision. They are either combined with the light, or switch lights on remotely. The lamps go off automatically after a few minutes.

IMMERSION HEATER TIMESWITCH

A timeswitch can be fitted to an immersion heater to heat water at particular times of the day, or to use cheap-rate electricity. A seven-day timeswitch will give hot water at different times on each day of the week.

The timeswitch must be wired to a fused connection unit and to the immersion heater.

SOCKET TIMERS

A plug-in timer will control any appliance that plugs into a 13amp socket – a radio or lamp for security; a heater, electric blanket or tape recorder for convenience; a washing machine for night-time electricity.

Set the required programme on the timer, plug it into a switched-on socket, plug the appliance into the timer and switch on the appliance. It will not actually come on until the programmed time. You can override the set programme manually.

Timers vary in the number of times they will switch on and off, and in the shortest possible 'on' period. There are one-day and seven-day timers.

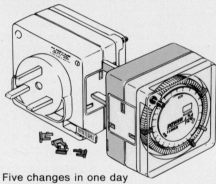

Five changes in one day

On this one-day timer a marker at the top points to the time of day on the dial. The dial is marked every 15 minutes, and coloured clips snap on at the required times. The shortest period for which it can be switched on is half an hour. It will switch on and off up to five times in 24 hours.

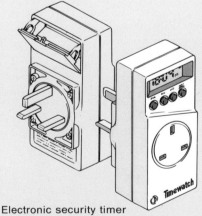

Electronic security timer

This electronic device is intended for security only. Four lighting periods can be set over 24 hours. The power is switched on and off several times at random during each programmed on period, giving the impression of people entering and leaving a room. The on-off programme is repeated daily but you can cancel or override it. The battery lasts for at least 12 months.

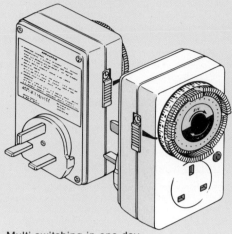

Multi-switching in one day

A one-day timer with multiple on-off times. A marker at the left points to the time of day on the side of the coloured outer ring. Pegs round the dial slide inward to activate the mechanism that turns the socket on and off. The socket is below the dial.

Each of the pegs round the dial represents 15 minutes – the shortest period for which the socket can be switched on. The control mechanism can switch on and off up to 48 times a day and the pattern will be repeated every day until it is switched off or changed.

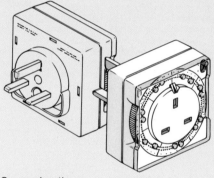

Seven-day timer

On a seven-day timer the dials are divided into seven sections, and the devices that activate the switches are usually set at two-hour intervals; so two hours is the shortest time the power can be on.

The control mechanism can switch the socket on and off up to six times a day on some models. The timer can be set to switch on and off at different times for each day of the week. The on-off pattern will repeat itself each week.

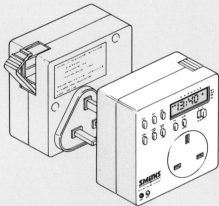

Seven-day electronic timer

The settings for the socket to be switched on and off can be adjusted to the minute. A small light over the digital time display indicates the day of the week. You can set the control to switch on and off up to 14 times a day. The controller can work on either a 24-hour cycle or a seven-day cycle.